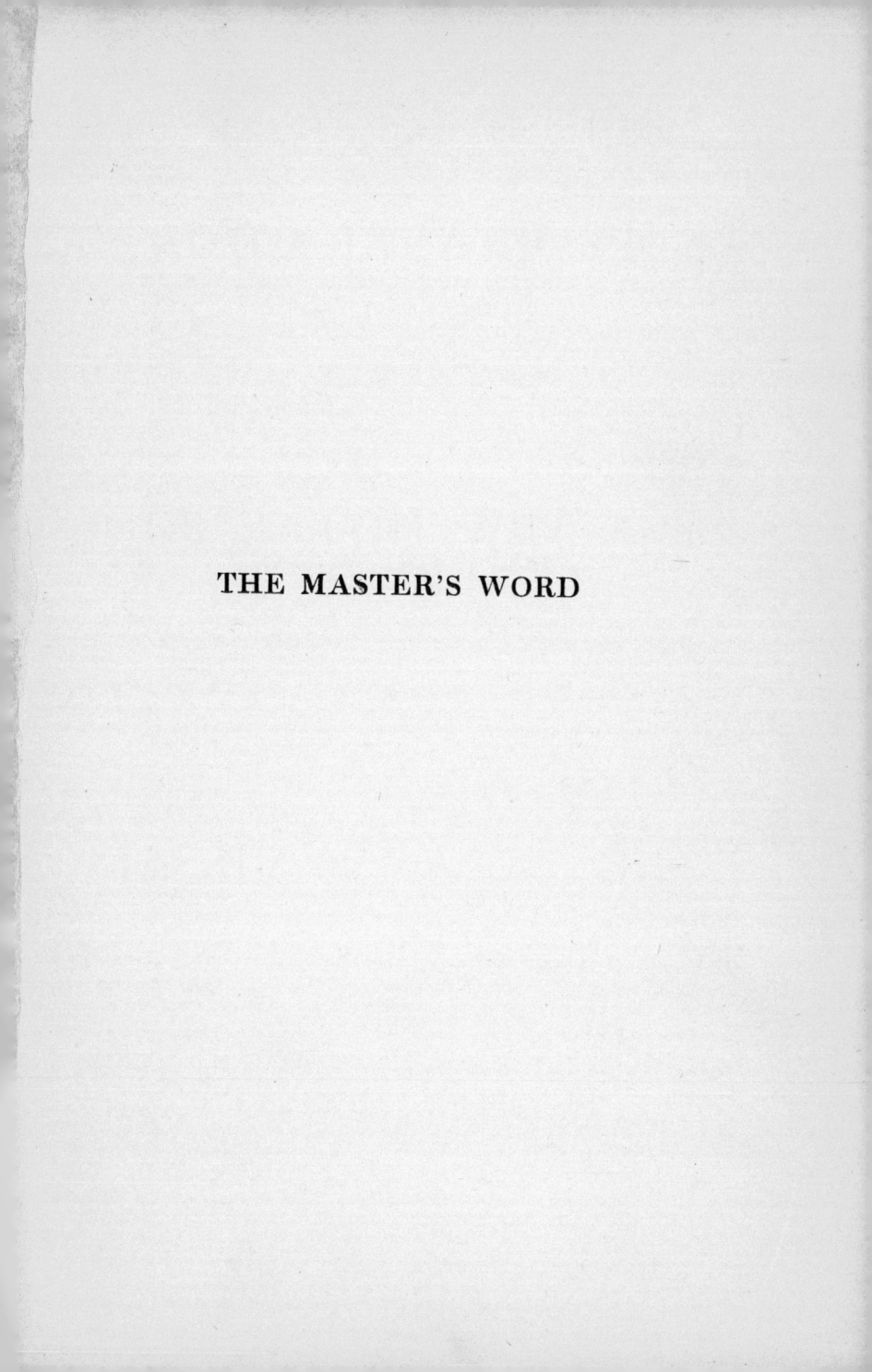

THE MASTER'S WORD

THE MASTER'S WORD

IN

THE EPISTLES AND GOSPELS

*Sermons for all the Sundays and
the Principal Feasts of the Year*

BY

REV. THOMAS FLYNN, C.C.

"Master, What must I do to possess eternal life?"
(St. Luke x. 25.)

VOLUME II

NEW YORK, CINCINNATI, CHICAGO

BENZIGER BROTHERS

PRINTERS TO THE | PUBLISHERS OF
HOLY APOSTOLIC SEE | BENZIGER'S MAGAZINE

1917

Nihil Obstat.

REMIGIUS LAFORT, S.T.D.,
Censor Librorum.

Imprimatur.

✠ JOHN CARDINAL FARLEY,
Archbishop of New York.

NEW YORK, May 17, 1916.

COPYRIGHT, 1917, BY BENZIGER BROTHERS.

CONTENTS

Part IV
THE MASTER

	PAGE
Ascension Day—His Proof	9
Sunday After Ascension—His Test	18
Pentecost Sunday—His Power	28
Trinity Sunday—His Glory	38
First Sunday After Pentecost—His Love	48
Feast of Corpus Christi—His Banquet	58
Second Sunday After Pentecost—His Guest	68
Third Sunday After Pentecost—His Care	77
Feast of the Sacred Heart—His Sympathy	86
Fourth Sunday After Pentecost—His Word	95

Part V
THE RESULTS

Fifth Sunday After Pentecost—Enemies	107
Sixth Sunday After Pentecost—Life	116
Seventh Sunday After Pentecost—Fruits	125
Eighth Sunday After Pentecost—Friends	134
Ninth Sunday After Pentecost—Failure	143
Tenth Sunday After Pentecost—Success	152

Eleventh Sunday After Pentecost—Miracles 162
Twelfth Sunday After Pentecost—Privileges 171
Thirteenth Sunday After Pentecost—Gratitude 180
Fourteenth Sunday After Pentecost—Loyalty 189

Part VI
THE DUTIES

Fifteenth Sunday After Pentecost—Of Energy 201
Sixteenth Sunday After Pentecost—Of Humility 210
Seventeenth Sunday After Pentecost—Of Charity 219
Eighteenth Sunday After Pentecost—Of Penance 228
Nineteenth Sunday After Pentecost—Of Good Will 237
Twentieth Sunday After Pentecost—Of Zeal 246
Twenty-first Sunday After Pentecost—Of Defense 255
Twenty-second Sunday After Pentecost—Of Perfection 264
Twenty-third Sunday After Pentecost—Of Perseverance 274
Twenty-fourth Sunday After Pentecost—Of Judgment 283

PART IV

THE MASTER

*"Is it not lawful for me to do what I will?
Is thy eye evil, because I am good?"*
(Matt. xx. 15.)

XXXI

ASCENSION DAY

HIS PROOF

"You shall be witnesses to Me."
(LESSON: Acts i. 1–11.)
"The Lord Jesus was taken up into heaven." (GOSPEL: Mark xvi. 14–20.)

WE HAVE now followed the history of the life of our divine Master from His birth in the stable at Bethlehem in poverty and sufferings to His glorious resurrection from the dead in joy and triumph. To-day we arrive at the final scene in His bodily existence amongst men, when He entered heaven in all His glory and was enthroned as man at the right hand of His Eternal Father.

From the preparation for His coming during the holy season of Advent to these last few weeks of the spiritual enjoyment of His blessed company in His glorified humanity, our holy mother the Church has placed before us, as St. Paul says in the Epistle of to-day, an account "of all things, which Jesus began to do and to teach, until the day on which, giving commandments by the Holy Ghost to the apostles whom He had chosen, He was taken up," "leaving us an example that we should follow His steps," as St. Peter says. (1 Peter ii. 21.) She has shown us the nature of the work we have to accomplish in order to do the Master's will. She has pointed out the dangers and the difficulties which are inseparable from its due fulfilment and has explained some of the qualities with which the true servants of God must be provided. She has also encouraged us by laying before us the hope of success, the magnitude of the reward and the privilege of being servants of Him whose "yoke is sweet and whose burden is light." (Matt. xi. 30.) Finally, she has explained the nature of the many practical helps toward success with which Almighty God Himself has provided us. And presently she is about to place before us some of the chief characteristics of the Master Himself who is leaving us to ascend to His heavenly Father, so that we shall be strengthened in our knowledge and love of Him and thus be the better prepared to profit by those lessons of divine truth which He promised would be taught to us by the Holy Spirit of truth itself. "The Holy Ghost, whom the Father will send in My name, He will teach you all things, and bring all things to your mind, whatsoever I shall have said to you." (John xiv. 26.)

As the final object of the mission of Our Lord Jesus Christ upon earth was to open heaven for fallen man, it is only when He actually ascended into heaven as man that human nature entered into actual possession and enjoyment of its lost rights and privileges. Hence, though our divine Saviour had already given superabundant proof of the divinity of His mission and of the infallible truth of His promises not only on the occasion of His resurrection but also on the many occasions on which "He showed Himself alive after His passion, by many proofs, for forty days appearing to them, and speaking of the kingdom of God," it was not till the Ascension that He accomplished the fact by actually leading into heaven with Him in glorious triumph the souls of all those holy men and women who had fulfilled the law but who had been detained in the prison of Limbo until the happy day of their release by the Redeemer Himself in person.

The circumstances of this glorious and final scene in the life of our divine Master upon earth are briefly recorded in to-day's Epistle. Although He had frequently told His disciples that His bodily presence amongst them was to be of short duration—"a little while,

and now you shall not see Me" (John xvi. 16.)
—and that He was to ascend into heaven to
His Father, not to be seen by them again until
He should come at the last day to judge the
living and the dead—"and again a little while,
and you shall see Me; because I go to the
Father" (John xvi. 16.)—yet He never definitely informed them as to the exact time of
His departure. He made them acquainted,
however, with the chief objects of their mission; namely, to be witnesses of His divinity,
and to propagate His Gospel throughout the
whole world. He commanded them not to depart from Jerusalem until they had received
the Holy Ghost, whom He promised to send.
He was to teach them all truth, for they had
not yet been completely instructed in the
mysteries of the kingdom of God, as is clear
from the questions they asked Him. "I have
yet many things to say to you," He said, "but
you can not bear them now. But when He,
the Spirit of truth, is come, He will teach you
all truth." (John xvi. 12, 13.) They still
had some idea that the temporal glory of the
chosen people was to be one of the results of
the divine mission, for when they were assembled together for the last time on Mount Olivet
they asked Him, saying: "Lord, wilt Thou
at this time restore the kingdom to Israel?"

Almost immediately our blessed Lord was raised up in their presence, and they watched Him until a cloud hid Him from their view. As the Gospel relates, "He was taken up into heaven, and sitteth on the right hand of God." This happened on the fortieth day after His resurrection.

With what lively sentiments of joy and sorrow must the hearts of the apostles and disciples have been filled on this occasion! They rejoiced at the grand and glorious fulfilment of all the prophecies concerning Himself, and especially of His own; but they were sorrowful at losing sight, even for the time of this short life, of His adorable presence amongst them; and they were fearful for the future without His intimate assistance and direction. As they were lost in astonishment and admiration at the wondrous spectacle, "behold, two men stood by them in white garments. Who also said: Ye men of Galilee, why stand you looking up to heaven? This Jesus who is taken up from you into heaven, shall so come as you have seen Him going into heaven."

From which admonition they received the consolation of knowing that they could with certainty look forward to a similiar appearance of their divine Master at the last day, when they themselves would be present with

Him enjoying once more, without further fear of ever losing Him, the happiness and the glory of His blessed company: and at the same time they were forcibly reminded that their own share in Christ's mission had not yet been ended, or, indeed, properly begun. For they were to give testimony of Him and preach His holy Gospel everywhere, assisted by the power and inspiration of the Holy Ghost. Hence they immediately returned to Jerusalem, as Christ had commanded them, and remained in a large upper room, where they waited in prayer and supplication for the promised coming of the Holy Spirit.

In placing before us for our consideration to-day the circumstances connected with this holy mystery, the Church wishes in a special manner to draw our attention to two important facts. Firstly, that the final proof of our redemption was given and its entire plan was completed by our Lord and Saviour Jesus Christ taking His place as true God and as true man at the right hand of His Eternal Father in the kingdom of heaven. And secondly, that as the apostles and their successors received the official commission to preach and teach and bear witness to the truths of the Gospel by active labors in the service of their divine Master, so we, too, by our influence and example, are bound to bear witness to the true Faith of Jesus Christ, and, if necessary, to sacrifice our lives in defense of it, in order that we may deserve a share in the merits and intercession of our blessed Redeemer.

When Jesus returned in triumph to His Eternal Father in heaven He completed the fulfilment of all the ancient prophecies and of His own promises. The Psalmist had sung long before, for instance: "The Lord said to my Lord: Sit Thou at My right hand." (Ps. cix. 1.): and again: "Lift up your gates, O ye princes, and be ye lifted up, O eternal gates: and the King of Glory shall enter in." (Ps. xxiii. 7.) And St. Paul was able to say afterward with certain knowledge: "Ascending on high, He led captivity captive." (Eph. iv. 8.) "He humbled Himself, becoming obedient unto death, even to the death of the cross. For which cause God also hath exalted Him." (Philipp. ii. 8, 9.) It was in heaven, at the right hand of His Father, that the sacred humanity of Christ was exalted and formally put in full possession of the supreme power which He claimed and exercised on earth. "All power is given to Me in heaven and in earth," He had said to His apostles. (Matt. xxviii. 18.) He had promised to go and prepare a place for them, saying: "I go to prepare a place for you . . . that where I am, you also may be." (John xiv. 2, 3.) St. Paul was afterward to declare: "He is able also to save forever those that come to God by Him; always living to make intercession for us." (Heb. vii. 25.) And St. John: "If any man sin, we have an advocate with the Father, Jesus Christ the just. And He is the propitiation for our sins: and not for ours only, but also for those of the whole world." (1 John ii. 1, 2.)

We have a perfect right, therefore, to expect a place in the kingdom of heaven, through the merits and intercession of Jesus Christ, no matter how sadly we lost our original inheritance by the sin of our first parents, or deserved to be again deprived of it on account of our own sins, for we have an advocate there in the person of our divine Master, who is continually presenting to His Eternal Father the merits of His passion and death and pleading for the grace of repentance and pardon for us.

But lest we remain inactive in the contemplation of the happiness of our delivery from Satan and from sin and of the pleasing prospect of the joys that await us as the disciples stood transfixed on Mount Olivet at the sight of the glory of the Lord, we, too, are reminded that the same Lord is to come at the end of the world to judge us and see if our actions in giving testimony to Him are worthy to make us be considered His true disciples. "My sheep hear My voice: and I know them, and they follow Me," He says. (John x. 27.) Let us, then, be up and doing. "Not every one that saith to Me, Lord, Lord, shall enter into the kingdom of heaven: but He that doth the will of My Father who is in heaven. . . . Many will say to Me in that day: Lord, have we not prophesied in Thy name, and cast out devils in Thy name, and done many miracles in Thy name? And then I will profess unto them, I never knew you." (Matt. vii. 21–23.)

We must, then, imitate our divine Master. We must study His life and practise His virtues and, like the apostles by their preaching, we must by our example lead others also to the possession of His kingdom. They "going forth preached everywhere; the Lord working withal, and confirming the word with signs that followed." God will co-operate with us also by His holy grace and will confirm the good work, if we ask Him in fervent prayer. Therefore, "So let your light shine before men, that they may see your good works, and glorify your Father who is in heaven." (Matt. v. 16.)

XXXII

SUNDAY AFTER ASCENSION

HIS TEST

"Before all things have a constant mutual charity among yourselves."
(EPISTLE: 1 Peter iv. 7–11.)
"These things will they do to you, because they have not known the Father, nor Me."
(GOSPEL: John xv. 26–xvi. 4.)

LAST Sunday we were told that it is our duty to bear witness to the divinity of Christ and His teaching by the bright example of our own Christlike virtues, by which all men should recognize us as faithful followers of our divine Master and true models of His perfection. To-day we are reminded in the Gospel of the very same obligation and the reason for it: "You shall give testimony of Me, because you are with Me from the beginning." We are "predestinated to be made conformable to the image of His Son" (Rom. viii. 29.), says St. Paul. Hence we should be very familiar with the teaching and example of the Saviour.

Whilst we endeavor by fervent and persevering prayer and by constant watchfulness over ourselves, to imitate as far as we can the example of our divine Master and Model, we are reminded in the Epistle that if we are to be recognized as His true disciples, "that in all things God may be honored in Jesus Christ our Lord," we must show in our lives and characters a fair likeness of the divine original. Whenever we wish to form a correct idea of the value of any copy we always select some of the most prominent characteristics of the original for the purpose of comparison, and thereby provide ourselves with a *test*.

On previous occasions some of the general characteristics of our Blessed Saviour's disposition were referred to; such as His love of holy poverty, as shown in the circumstances surrounding His birth at Bethlehem; His love of obscurity, as seen from His hidden life at Nazareth; His love of peace, as shown by His great desire "to direct our feet into the way of peace" (Luke i. 79.); His humility, meekness, patience, kindness, and mercy, as seen from the whole tenor of His life and its object—"I am not come to call the just but sinners." (Matt. ix. 12.) But to-day our attention is drawn to His great prevailing characteristic, that which is the very essence of His nature as God and of His personal character and disposition as the Redeemer of the souls of men—His charity. Hence we are told in the Epistle: "Above all things have a constant mutual charity among yourselves."

The virtue of charity, then, is the great test of the true Christian, the most essential characteristic. If we are without it, we are not of Christ. If we possess it, we surely belong to Him. "He that keepeth His word," says St. John, "in Him in very deed the charity of God is perfected: and by this we know that we are in Him." (1 John ii. 5.) "If I have not charity, I am nothing," says St. Paul (1 Cor. xiii. 2.), who treats of this divine virtue as the necessary prevailing and informing motive of all our meritorious actions. The possession of it brings with it all other gifts and graces by which we are made rich in God, who Himself is Charity, for "God is charity," says St. John (1 John iv. 8.), who argues that if we have not charity we can not even know God, much less be like Him. According to this apostle, who, on account of His great love for Jesus and the special love of Jesus for Him, is known as "the beloved disciple" (John xxi. 20.), we are created for no other purpose than to know, love, and serve our divine Master. The test of our knowledge of Him is the manner in which we obey Him and keep His word—"By this we know that we have known Him, if we keep His commandments." (1 John ii. 3.) The test of our love of Him is the very same—"He that keepeth His word, in him in very deed the charity of God is perfected." (ii. 5.) And the test of our likeness to Him is still the same—"And by this we know that we are in Him. He that saith he abideth in Him, ought himself also to walk, even as He walked" (ii. 5, 6.), for, "he that abideth in charity, abideth in God, and God in him." (iv. 16.) This is what St. Paul means when he says that the sinner who is sincerely converted is dead to sin and lives not only for God but by Him and in Him—"I live, now not I; but Christ liveth in me." (Gal. ii. 20.) No wonder, then, he concludes that "There remain faith, hope, and charity, these three; but the greatest of these is charity." (1 Cor. xiii. 13.)

But how can this divine virtue be a test unless it is an outward proof to others of our conformity, with the image of Christ, since it is a quality of the soul, an inward spiritual condition of the heart, "for man seeth those things that appear, but the Lord beholdeth the heart" (1 Kings xvi. 7.), says Holy Scripture. The answer is given by our divine Lord Himself when He says: "By this shall all men know that you are My disciples, if you have love one for another." (John xiii. 35.) This is the final test given by St. John also, who says: "If God hath so loved us; we also ought to love one another. No man hath seen God at any time. If we love one another, God abideth in us, and His charity is perfected in us. . . . He that loveth not his brother, whom he seeth, how can he love God, whom he seeth not? And this commandment we have from God, that he, who loveth God, love also his brother." (1 John iv. 11–21.)

The early Christians were especially remarked for their true brotherly charity, even by their pagan neighbors, who used to say: "See these Christians, how they love one another." Our Lord called this precept "a new commandment" and in His sermon on the mount He explains clearly what is meant by it. "You have heard that it hath been said, An eye for an eye, and a tooth for a tooth. But I say to you not to resist evil: but if one strike you on thy right cheek, turn to him also the other. . . . You have heard that it hath been said, Thou shalt love thy neighbor, and hate thy enemy. But I say to you, Love your enemies: do good to them that hate you; and pray for them that persecute and calumniate you: that you may be the children of your Father who is in heaven." (Matt. x. 38–45.)

Up to that time men were very ignorant of the perfections of Almighty God. Even the chosen people, to whom He had partly revealed Himself, did not recognize the immensity of His love for man or the depth of His charity, which is His very essence—"for God is charity,"—and "of His fulness we have all received," says St. John (i. 16.). It is of the essence of goodness to diffuse itself and share its happiness with others, and so Almighty God, infinitely good and happy in Himself from all eternity, created man to His own image and likeness and made all things for his use and benefit. We know how ungrateful human nature proved itself. "Man when he was in honor did not understand." (Ps. xlviii. 21.) And we know how God, instead of punishing him forever, forgave him and offered still further proofs of His love and goodness in the sacrifice of His own divine Son, "who when He was reviled, did not revile: when He suffered He threatened not" (1 Peter ii. 2, 3.), but prayed for His persecutors even when He was dying on the cross. No wonder, then, that the first and most essential quality of a true child of God, a faithful follower of Christ and a model of Christian perfection, should be his charity toward God and his neighbor, whether the latter be friend or enemy, for, as our divine Master Himself says: "If you love them that love you, what reward shall you have? Do not even the publicans this? And if you salute your brethren only, what do you more? Do not also the heathens this? Be you therefore perfect, as also your heavenly Father is perfect." (Matt. v. 46–48.)

Our Lord Jesus Christ warned the disciples of the injuries they were to receive at the hands of those who were wanting in the knowledge of God, and so without true charity, lest they might wonder why Divine Providence should allow their enemies to persecute and triumph over them. "These things have I spoken to you that you may not be scandalized." He explained to them that the world would hate them because, though they had to live in it for a time, they were not of it and had not its spirit, which is opposed to God and the things of God, through ignorance of the divine perfections. "These things will they do to you, because they have not known the Father, nor Me." But His disciples were to be different, and the difference was to be clearly shown by the great test of charity, as proved in their holy love toward all, both friends and enemies, for the sake of God. By this shall all men know that you are My disciples, if you have love one for another." (John xiii. 35.)

Charity toward our neighbor is always, therefore, not only the test of the true Christian, but the want of it is also the test of the real enemies of Christ. "He that is not with Me, is against me" (Matt. xii. 30.), He says Himself. It is important, therefore, for us to apply this test to ourselves, lest our apparent virtues may be in reality only mere natural likes or instinctive repugnances toward what may be good or evil, as the case may be, according to the law of God. In the first place, let us ask ourselves if we are amongst those who are a source of pain, inconvenience, or suffering to any one, especially to the good and virtuous. Many apparently holy people are often guilty of grave injury to their neighbor. Under the cloak of zeal and virtue they are forever disturbers of peace and good will, never at rest except when injuring the characters of others by calumny or detraction, or both. Surely they are enemies of Christ and "they have not known the Father nor Him." As St. Paul says, "They profess that they know God: but in their works they deny Him." (Titus i. 16.) Secondly, let us ask ourselves how we deal with our enemies, and what is our spirit toward them. Some wrongly imagine that because they feel an injury or an insult and are conscious of a natural resentment or opposition to such that they have not the proper spirit. St. Paul says: "You suffer if a man strike you on the face." (2 Cor. xi. 20.) We feel a blow and it may leave a mark. That is purely a physical consequence, entirely beyond our control. The mind, the spirit, the heart can likewise be injured, and may sustain a deeper wound and leave a bigger mark. But if we submit to the injury and bear the suffering for the love of God we will show no resentment, seek no revenge and return good for evil, even as Jesus Himself, who has said to us: "Blessed are ye when they shall revile you, and persecute you, and speak all that is evil against you untruly for My sake." (Matt. v. 11.) Let us be sure that no evil can be spoken *truly* of us and we can rest content with Jesus.

Be faithful imitators, then, of the meekness, humility, and patience of our divine Master, and above all of His spirit of divine charity. Let us be merciful and forgiving to all for the sake of the good God. Let us bear with resignation all our trials and sufferings, for "if any man will come after Me, let him take up his cross." (Matt. xvi. 24.) At the same time, "Let not your heart be troubled, nor let it be afraid" (John xiv. 27.), for, "If God be for us, who is against us?" (Rom. viii. 31.) And He will be surely for us if we stand the test of charity.

XXXIII

PENTECOST SUNDAY

HIS POWER

"They were all filled with the Holy Ghost."
(LESSON: Acts ii. 1–11.)
"If any one love Me, he will keep My word."
(GOSPEL: John xiv. 23–31.)

WHEN our divine Master ascended into heaven His personal share of the work of establishing the Church was finished. But the work itself was not yet complete. The Holy Ghost, whom He had promised to send, was still to come, and by His influence on the apostles and on the hearts of all men, was to change the whole face of the earth and establish on a permanent spiritual basis the kingdom of God's love. For forty days after His Resurrection Our Saviour had conversed with His disciples and had given them various directions and precepts with regard to their future conduct and course of action. Just before He left them to return to His Heavenly Father he had "commanded them that they should not depart from Jerusalem, but should wait for the promise of the Father" (Acts i. 4.), saying: "I have yet many things to say to you: but you can not bear them now: but when He, the Spirit of truth, is come, He will teach you all truth." (John xvi. 12, 13.)

Although the apostles had been with Him all through His public life—"you are with Me from the beginning" (John xv. 27.)—and had therefore witnessed a most astonishing series of the most wonderful miracles, they were still ignorant of many things concerning the Master's ultimate aims and objects—"It is not for you to know the times or the moments, which the Father had put in His own power." (Acts i. 7.) They still had an idea that the temporal kingdom of His power was to be established in worldly glory, and they were anxious as to their own share in the authority and dignity appertaining thereto, for they asked Him: "Who thinkest thou is the greater in the kingdom of heaven?" (Matt. xviii. 2.) This was on the occasion when He cured the boy possessed by an unclean spirit, as related by St. Luke, who records that "All were astonished at the mighty power of God. But while all wondered at the things He did, He said to His disciples: the Son of man shall be delivered into the hands of men. But they understood not this word, and it was hid from them, so that they perceived it not. And they were afraid to ask Him concerning this word. And there entered a thought into them, which of them should be the greater" (Luke ix. 44–46.) Indeed, they sometimes warmly disputed this matter among themselves—"There was also a strife among them, which of them should seem to be the greater." (Luke xvii. 24.) Whilst on another occasion there "came to Him the mother of the sons of Zebedee with her sons, adoring and asking . . . that these my two sons may sit, the one on Thy right hand, and the other on Thy left, in Thy kingdom." (Matt. xx. 21.) And even on the occasion of His very last discourse to them on Mount Olivet, just before His Ascension, they asked Him: "Lord, wilt Thou at this time restore again the kingdom to Israel?" (Acts i. 6.)

When they had seen Christ surrounded by His enemies in the garden of Gethsemani they had lost hope and courage through the weakness of their faith in Him and had fled precipitately —"His disciples leaving Him, all fled away" (Mark xiv. 50.)—although they had solemnly assured Him on that very same evening that they would never abandon Him. "Although I should die together with Thee, I will not deny Thee," said St. Peter. "And in like manner also said they all," as St. Mark relates. (xiv.) St. Peter no doubt followed Him, but "afar off" and afterward thrice denied Him and swore he knew Him not. They were wanting in the spirit of mortification and prayer, as well as having the spirit of the world —for they fell asleep after Our Lord had told them to "watch and pray." And St. Thomas positively refused to believe the story of the Resurrection until he had personally satisfied himself of the fact by feeling the sacred wounds. And after His crucifixion they were afraid to show themselves for fear of the Jews and remained hidden in an upper room in the Holy City.

Our divine Master, even as man, knew all their faults and was aware of all their weakness and want of lively faith in Him and in His promises, for He often chided them. "Why are you fearful, O ye of little faith?" (Matt. viii. 26.) And again: "Sleepest thou? Couldst thou not watch one hour?" (Matt. xiv. 37.) But though He complained of their weakness He also encouraged them, saying: "You shall receive the power of the Holy Ghost coming upon you, and you shall be witnesses unto Me in Jerusalem, and in all Judea, and Samaria, and even to the uttermost part of the earth." (Acts i. 8.) And He consoled them, as the Gospel of to-day relates, by the promise of the Holy Ghost, the Spirit of truth, the Paraclete, the Comforter, and by His own lovely blessing: "Peace I leave with you, My peace I give unto you; not as the world giveth, do I give unto you. Let not your heart be troubled, nor let it be afraid."

Ten days after the Ascension the promise was fulfilled, and the power of God was made manifest to all by the coming of the Holy Ghost, the Spirit of truth, of holiness and of strength, upon the apostles and disciples who "were persevering with one mind in prayer with the women, and Mary the mother of Jesus, and with His brethren." (Acts i. 14.) "And when the days of Pentecost were accomplished, they were all together in one place: and suddenly there came a sound from heaven, as of a mighty wind coming, and it filled the whole house where they were sitting. And there appeared to them parted tongues as it were of fire, and it sat upon every one of them: and they were all filled with the Holy Ghost, and they began to speak with divers tongues, according as the Holy Ghost gave them to speak. Now there were dwelling at Jerusalem, Jews, devout men, out of every nation under heaven. And they were all amazed and wondered, saying: Behold, are not all these that speak, Galileans? And how have we heard, every man our own tongue wherein we were born?" (ii. 1-8.)

What amazing effects the Holy Spirit caused in the hearts of all! The apostles and disciples were completely transformed and became as new men. Before, they were dull, ignorant, cowardly, and unspiritual; now they saw clearly and fully the sublime truths of the Gospel of Jesus, of which they had previously but a comparatively confused and imperfect idea. Before, they were troubled and anxious about their share of the glories of the temporal kingdom of Israel; now they despised the world with its honors and pleasures, and set a true value on the spiritual kingdom of their divine Master, unselfish in their love for one another. Him they had previously abandoned and denied, but now they had the true courage of their strong convictions and were prepared and even anxious to suffer bravely even death itself for His Name's sake. Before, they were afraid of the Jews who had crucified Him; now they walked openly amongst them and accused them face to face in their public assemblies of the crime they had committed against Him. When St. Peter preached his first sermon to them he fearlessly declared: "Ye men of Israel, hear these words: Jesus of Nazareth, a man approved of God among you by miracles and wonders and signs, which God did by Him, in the midst of you, as you also know: This same being delivered up, by the determinate counsel and foreknowledge of God, you by the hands of wicked men have crucified and slain. Whom God hath raised up, having loosed the sorrows of hell, as it was impossible that He should be holden by it." (Acts ii. 22–24.) And the result of his sermon was that about three thousand souls were converted by it to the true faith of Jesus Christ. The other apostles preached in like manner and with similar results: "But they going forth preached everywhere: the Lord working withal, and confirming the word with signs that followed." (Mark xvi. 20.) Their preaching was miraculously and visibly helped by the marvelous gift of tongues, by which people of different nations heard them speak each in his own language "the wonderful works of God."

We celebrate the feast of Pentecost as we celebrate no other feast in the Church's calendar. On all other occasions we merely commemorate a past event, such as the Nativity, the Crucifixion, the Resurrection, the Ascension, which, having happened once, can never occur again. But when the Holy Ghost descended upon the apostles and made the power of God's grace in the human soul so manifest, it was not to be the only occasion on which that great privilege was to be given to men. The Holy Spirit came to dwell for all time in the hearts of the faithful and to manifest His power over their whole lives by the gift of divine charity which His living presence infuses into their souls. "Behold I am with you all days, even to the consummation of the world." (Matt. xxviii. 19.) Hence, to-day this sacred mystery is not merely commemorated by the Church but is actually renewed in the souls of her children. And as the power of God is no less to-day than it was in the time of the apostles, so the Holy Spirit is capable of producing in our souls all the vivifying and sanctifying effects which it caused on the day of Pentecost. Such outward effects as the gift of tongues, of prophecy, or of miracles, are no longer necessary, but the inward spiritual effects ought to be none the less certain when we receive the formal visitation of the Holy Spirit in the grace of the Sacraments.

We should examine ourselves, therefore, and see what results have been produced in us by the many visits of the Holy Spirit which we have been privileged to receive. Have we that spirit of faith which makes us see in all things the holy will of God and act accordingly? Do we bear with patience and resignation all our contradictions, trials, and crosses, "rejoicing that we are accounted worthy to suffer reproach for the Name of Jesus"? (Acts v. 41.) Do we ever through human respect or unworthy fear practically deny Christ even in small matters? Is our motto that of the apostles: "We ought to obey God rather than man"? (Acts v. 29.) Do we lead carnal and selfish lives, devoted to ease and pleasure, rather than to the service of God? If so, it is our own fault and we place obstacles to the work of the Holy Ghost in us by our own unmortified and unspiritual desires. "You always resist the Holy Ghost" (Acts vii. 51.), said St. Stephen.

But, however weak we may be in the flesh we may become strong in the spirit by the power of God. "I can do all things in Him who strengtheneth me," says St. Paul. (Philipp. iv. 13.) No matter how difficult the task may appear, no matter how strong our temptations or how dangerous our circumstances, the love of God will conquer all, for the Spirit of Love will make our task easy and our labor light. This was the secret of the complete change of heart in those who received the Holy Ghost at Pentecost. "This is the charity of God, that we keep His commandments; and His commandments are not heavy," says St. John. (1 John v. 3.) And our divine Master Himself says in to-day's Gospel: "If any one love Me, he will keep My word . . . and we will make our abode with him."

XXXIV

TRINITY SUNDAY

HIS GLORY

"To Him be glory forever."
(EPISTLE: Rom. xi. 33–36.)
"In the name of the Father, and of the Son, and of the Holy Ghost."
(GOSPEL: Matt. xxviii. 18–20.)

Now that we have learned something of the nature and attributes of Almighty God, and have realized in some way the qualities which are referred to each of the three Divine Persons separately, according to our way of thinking, our holy mother the Church wishes to begin to teach us some of those wonderful truths which, according to the promise of our divine Master, were to be shown to us by the Holy Ghost, who was to "teach us all things and bring all things to our mind whatsoever He Himself should have said to us" (John xiv. 26.)—when "the hour cometh when He will no more speak to us in proverbs, but will show us plainly of the Father." (John xvi.

25.) And she naturally begins with the greatest and most incomprehensible mystery of all—the mystery of the Blessed Trinity, Father, Son, and Holy Ghost, three Persons in one only God, and one only God in three Divine Persons.

During the holy seasons of Advent and Christmas we were made acquainted with the infinite love and kindness of God the Father, who, having created man to His own image and likeness and been offended by him, nevertheless offered him the privilege of forgiveness by sending His own divine Son to pay the price of his redemption. During the weeks commemorating the chief events in the life of our divine Saviour we were shown the love of the Second Person of the Blessed Trinity when "The Word was made flesh and dwelt among us, and we saw His glory, the glory as it were of the only-begotten of the Father, full of grace and truth." (John i. 14.) And during Pentecost we were shown the wonderful love of God in the regenerating, sanctifying, and strengthening influence of the Holy Ghost, the Spirit of Love, the Third Person of the Blessed Trinity.

It is most appropriate, therefore, that we should now consider something of the nature and attributes of the Triune God in this most adorable mystery. Moreover, it is most necessary, for without an explicit knowledge of the Trinity and an explicit belief in its truth as an article of our holy Faith no one can possibly be saved. It is an abridgment of all the mysteries of our holy religion, the foundation of all our belief, and the distinguishing mark of Christianity, because it intimately concerns the very nature of Almighty God Himself. Furthermore, of all other mysteries this is the most incomprehensible to human reason. So the Church bows down to-day in reverent and humble faith, submitting her weak and fallible human understanding to the wisdom of the great God, who has Himself honored her by its revelation. And as she adores with lively faith, with firm hope, and with ardent charity, the Trinity of Persons in the Oneness of the Divine Nature, she exclaims with St. Paul in the Epistle: "O the depths of the riches of the wisdom and of the knowledge of God! How incomprehensible are His judgments and how inscrutable His ways! For who hath known the mind of the Lord? Or who hath been His counsellor?"

Although Almighty God revealed Himself in many ways to His chosen people the Jews, even giving them a knowledge of the Redeemer who was to come, yet He never deigned to re-

TRINITY SUNDAY

veal, except perhaps in a general way to a very few, the mystery of the Blessed Trinity. This was a privilege reserved for the New Law, and the doctrine was taught in no uncertain way by our divine Master Himself, and is clearly laid down in Holy Scripture. Thus, in the account of the Incarnation given by St. Luke, we find distinct mention of the three Divine Persons—"the Lord God," "the Son of the Most High," and "the Holy Ghost." (Luke i. 32–35.) At the Baptism of Christ St. Matthew tells us that "Jesus being baptized, forthwith came out of the water: and lo, the heavens were opened to Him: and He saw the Spirit of God descending as a dove and coming upon Him. And behold a voice from heaven saying: This is My beloved Son, in whom I am well pleased." (Matt. iii. 16, 17.) At the Last Supper our divine Master declared: "I am in the Father, and the Father in Me . . . and I will ask the Father, and He shall give you another Paraclete, that He may abide with you forever." (John xiv. 11–16.) And when He gave the apostles the commission to preach and teach, He said: "Going, therefore, teach ye all nations: baptizing them in the name of the Father, and of the Son, and of the Holy Ghost." (Matt. xxviii. 19.) Whilst, according to St. John, "There are three who give testimony in heaven, the Father, the Word, and the Holy Ghost. And these three are one." (1 John v. 7.)

Seeing the importance of this doctrine our holy mother the Church is anxious that it should be brought under our notice as early and as frequently as possible; for unless we know and believe explicitly that there are three Divine Persons in one God, and yet only one God in three Divine Persons, we cannot be saved. Hence the very first lesson of our holy religion that we are taught as children is the doctrine of the Blessed Trinity. It is a mystery entirely incomprehensible to human reason, and so a firm belief in it on God's authority is the greatest act of faith and the purest act of homage by which we can do honor to the divine revelation. Though we can not understand it, owing to the limitations of our intellect, the Church endeavors to render our poor view of it less obscure by explaining that God the Father, knowing His divine perfections, and that from all eternity, produced an image of Himself in His own divine mind. This image is the Son, or the *Word* (as St. John calls Him) because He is the *expression* of the divinity of His Eternal Father. And the Father, seeing the image of the divine perfections in His Son, the Holy Ghost proceeds from their mutual love. Hence the three Divine Persons are each infinitely good, infinitely perfect, and equally eternal in essence, One God forever, without beginning and without end, "who is, and who was, and who is to come, the Almighty." (Apoc. i. 8.) Although in our weak and imperfect manner of speaking of the operations of the three Divine Persons we refer the works of power and creation to the Father, the works of redemption to the Son and the works of love and sanctification to the Holy Ghost, we must remember that in reality, as the three Divine Persons have the same nature and essence, all works proceed alike from the Father, the Son, and the Holy Ghost, as from one and the same Almighty God.

Some kind of explanation or illustration is also attempted by the holy Fathers of the Church in order to help us to a clearer, though of course still a very imperfect, idea of at least the possibility of such a stupendous mystery. Light and heat, they say, proceed from the same source, the sun. The roots, trunk, and branches all form the tree. Three lamps in a room produce the one light. The powers of memory, understanding, and will are found in the same rational soul. But, as St. Hilary observes, "these comparisons are more useful to man than suitable to God." That they are useful to man is proved by the fact that St. Patrick converted the pagan king of Ireland by showing him the triple leaf of the shamrock as an emblem of the Blessed Trinity. Let us, then, bow down our souls in humble submission to the authority of God, who has been pleased to make this revelation to us as a proof of His love and regard. How many mysteries of nature and of science do we not willingly and firmly believe in on the authority of learned men, though as far as we are concerned they are entirely incomprehensible to us! As St. John says, referring to this holy mystery, "If we receive the testimony of men, the testimony of God is greater." (1 John v. 9.) And our divine Master Himself has said: "Blessed are they that have not seen, and have believed." (John xx. 29.)

Let us, then, with reverence and humility say with Holy Church: "Blessed be the holy and undivided Trinity." "Bless ye the God of heaven, give glory to Him in the sight of all that live, because He hath shown mercy to us." (Tob. xii. 6.)

Let us, then, excite ourselves to lively sentiments of faith in this adorable mystery, praying with the apostles: "Lord, increase our faith" (Luke xvii. 5.); to sentiments of hope in the merits of our Blessed Redeemer, saying with the Psalmist: "Give glory to the Lord, for He is good: for His mercy endureth forever" (Ps. cv. 1.); and to sentiments of charity which the Holy Spirit of Love will infuse into our souls together with a knowledge of His truth, saying: "O praise the Lord, all ye nations: praise Him, all ye people. For His mercy is confirmed upon us: and the truth of the Lord remaineth forever." (Ps. cxvi.)

To preserve us in the practice of these holy affections and to remind us continually of this greatest and holiest of all mysteries, our holy mother the Church keeps constantly before our minds in all her prayers, blessings, and ceremonies the separate invocation of the three Divine Persons. When we are made Christians and children of God and heirs to the kingdom of heaven, we are baptized "in the name of the Father, and of the Son, and of the Holy Ghost." In Confirmation the same words are used to bring down upon us all the graces of the Holy Spirit. In the sacred tribunal of penance our sins are forgiven in the name of the same Holy and Undivided Three. All objects of devotion, the relics of the saints, the materials to be used in her religious ceremonies, the vestments of her sacred ministers, the sacred ministers themselves and our own selves are blessed by the Church in the very same formula. All her actions and prayers are begun and ended with the sign of the cross and the devout invocation of the Holy Trinity. And when we come to die we are delivered by the priest into the hands of God, our bodies are laid to rest in the blessed clay, and we are dismissed for the day of this short life to sleep till the sound of the last trumpet calls us again, "In the name of the Father, and of the Son, and of the Holy Ghost. Amen."

Let us, then, as an act of devotion and gratitude to Almighty God, and as an act of faith in all the truths of our holy religion, frequently and fervently make upon ourselves the sign of the cross with the usual invocation of the Holy Trinity. It will not only be a token of our belief in the Father's power, the Son's mercy and the Holy Spirit's love, but it will be also a source of many spiritual advantages for us, and a reminder of the end for which we were created. It will be at the same time an act of faith, an act of hope, and an act of love. Glory be to the Father, then, who created us, that we might be happy with Him forever. Glory be to the Son, who redeemed us by His own most precious blood. And glory be to the Holy Ghost, whose temples we are and who sanctifies us by His grace and abiding presence. "Blessed be the Holy and Undivided Trinity now and forevermore." Amen.

XXXV

FIRST SUNDAY AFTER PENTECOST

HIS LOVE

"God hath first loved us."
          (EPISTLE: 1 John iv. 8–21.)
"Be ye therefore merciful."
          (GOSPEL: Luke vi. 36–42.)

THE love of Almighty God is so wonderful in itself and in its relations to us that on the same Sunday on which she celebrates the love of the three Divine Persons for one another our holy mother the Church also celebrates the mystery of their love for man, and reminds us on this day how unselfish, noble, generous, and truly divine is the charity of Almighty God. "In this is charity," she says in the Epistle, "not as though we had loved God, but because He hath first loved us, and sent His Son to be a propitiation for our sins." Whilst in the Gospel she quotes the very words of our divine Master Himself in support of the same beautiful principle, beginning: "Be ye therefore merciful, as your Father also is merciful."

AFTER PENTECOST

When Our Lord Jesus Christ sent forth His apostles on their mission, saying to them: "Teach ye all nations, baptizing them in the name of the Father, and of the Son, and of the Holy Ghost," He intended them not only to teach the mystery of the Most Holy Trinity, but also to make known the love of the three Divine Persons for man, so that we might make some return of love to the God who created us, redeemed us, and sanctifies us. "In this is My Father glorified," He said to them: "that you should bring forth very much fruit, and become My disciples. As the Father hath loved Me, I also have loved you. Abide in My love. You have not chosen Me: but I have chosen you: and have appointed you that you should go, and bring forth fruit, and your fruit should remain" (John xv.)—the fruit of divine charity.

When Almighty God created us He did so because He was goodness and love itself. Goodness is in its very essence diffusive of itself; that is, it is desirous of communicating itself to others, to love others, and to make them sharers in its happiness. We know from experience that a really good man is generous, kind, and thoughtful toward others, and wishes to make every one happy by sharing with them whatever he has. It is a natural outcome or expression of his inherent goodness and hence it is usual to refer to such a one as "good-natured," which is synonymous with "generous" or "open-hearted," and always indicates unselfishness. Thus Almighty God is "good-natured" in an infinite degree, for He is in His essence goodness and love itself. "God is charity" (1 John iv. 8.), says St. John. And He is generous accordingly toward us, His creatures. He is indeed our "Father who is in heaven, who maketh His sun to rise upon the good and the bad, and raineth upon the just and the unjust" (Matt. v. 45.), and has equal care of all. When He created man, therefore, as the Catechism says, "to know, love, and serve Him here on earth, and afterwards to see and enjoy Him forever in heaven," He made him the noblest work of His hands, for He "created man to His own image: to the image of God He created him" (Gen. i. 27.); and He blessed him and gave him dominion over the whole earth and "the fishes of the sea, and the fowls of the air, and all living creatures that move upon the earth" (Gen. i. 28.), for He wished man to share in His own infinite happiness. In order that we might know, love, and serve Him He endowed us with the wonderful faculties of intellect, memory, and will. Hence St. Paul, quoting from the Royal Psalmist, says: "What is man that Thou art mindful of him: or the son of man, that Thou visitest him? Thou hast made him a little lower than the angels: Thou hast crowned him with glory and honor, and hast set him over the works of Thy hands: Thou hast subjected all things under his feet." (Heb. ii. 6-8.) And what makes this expression of love so remarkable is the fact that it was quite spontaneous on the part of Almighty God, for, as St. John says in to-day's Epistle: "In this is charity: not as though we had loved God, but because He had first loved us." All praise and glory, then, to the great and good Eternal Father, who created us and who loved us from eternity. "The Lord hath appeared from afar to me," says the prophet Jeremias, "Yea, I have loved thee with an everlasting love, therefore have I drawn thee, taking pity on thee." (Jer. xxxi. 3.)

But the prophet immediately proceeds to foretell the ingratitude of man and the still further proofs of God's love for us in sending His own Divine Son to redeem and save us and make us His children once again in the bosom of His one true Church on the holy mount of Sion. "And I will build thee again, and thou shalt be built, O virgin of Israel: thou shalt again be adorned with thy timbrels. . . .

For there shall be a day, in which the watchmen on Mount Ephraim shall say: Arise, and let us go up to Sion to the Lord our God. . . . For the Lord hath redeemed Jacob, and delivered him out of the hand of one that was mightier than he." (Jer. xxxi. 4–11.)

And so it happened. Ungrateful man proved false to the trust his Creator had placed in him. He disobeyed the divine commands and thereby brought upon himself eternal ruin. By his sin he lost all right to heaven, and was condemned to death with all his posterity. But "the goodness and kindness of God our Saviour appeared" (Titus iii. 15.) in a still stronger light when Jesus Christ, the second Person of the Blessed Trinity, the only-begotten Son of the Eternal Father, became man in order to sacrifice Himself for our salvation, since only a Man-God could offer an act of infinite reparation for the crime of a creature toward his Creator. "By this hath the charity of God appeared toward us," says the Epistle, "because God hath sent His only-begotten Son into the world, that we may live by Him."

But God was not satisfied with merely becoming man to save us. He wished to go further and prove the immensity of His love for us. As St. Augustine says: "Christ

AFTER PENTECOST

came that man might know how much God loves him." He wished to live amongst us, to share our sufferings and even allow Himself to be tempted so that He might be "a high priest who hath compassion on our infirmities, one tempted in all things like as we are, without sin." (Heb. iv. 15.) He "emptied Himself, taking the form of a servant, being made in the likeness of men, and in habit found as a man." (Philipp. ii. 7.) But even this was not enough. "He humbled Himself, becoming obedient unto death, even to the death of the cross" (Philipp. ii. 7, 8.), after having endured a life of poverty, labor, and suffering and been subjected to the most agonizing tortures of mind and body, the most shameful and humiliating insults that the most wicked and cruel minds could conceive, so that the prophet Isaias described Him as "despised, and the most abject of men, a man of sorrows and acquainted with infirmity: and His look was as it were hidden and despised, whereupon we esteemed Him not." And he concludes: "Surely He hath borne our infirmities and carried our sorrows: and we have thought Him as it were a leper and as one struck by God and afflicted. But He was wounded for our iniquities, He was bruised for our sins: the chastisement of our peace was upon Him, and by His bruises we are healed." (Is. liii. 3–5.)

Such an outpouring of the love of God upon His sinful creatures is a mystery which the human mind could never conceive and can not possibly understand. All praise and glory, then, to Our Lord and Saviour Jesus Christ, who redeemed us by His precious blood.

One would surely imagine that God, having done so much in order to show His love for man, could do no more. But as the love of God is infinite, so is His mercy to His fallen creatures. "The mercy of the Lord is from eternity and unto eternity," says the Psalmist. (Ps. cii. 17.) It seems as if each of the three Divine Persons wanted to take a share in proving His love for man, because in spite of man's further ingratitude, the Third Person of the Blessed Trinity came down from heaven on Pentecost Sunday to dwell with us forever, inflaming our cold hearts with the fire of His divine love, and filling our souls with the rich treasures of grace purchased for us by the merits of Our Lord and Saviour Jesus Christ, who sent Him as He had promised. When the Holy Spirit came, He came in the form of tongues of fire—"And there appeared to them parted tongues, as it were of fire." (Acts ii. 3.) He had formerly appeared as a dove, the emblem of peace and purity, as at the baptism of Jesus—"I saw the Spirit coming down, as a dove from heaven, and He remained upon Him." (John i. 32.) As a bright cloud at the Transfiguration: "Behold a bright cloud overshaded them. And lo a voice out of the cloud, saying: This is My beloved Son, in whom I am well pleased." (Matt. xvii. 5.) The cloud was an emblem of divine grace. And the fiery tongues were an emblem of the fire of divine love which the Holy Spirit enkindles in our hearts by His presence when we receive the sacraments, and by the holy thoughts, pious inspirations, and good resolutions which He is constantly suggesting to us. "Likewise," says St. Paul, "the Spirit also helpeth our infirmity. For we know not what we should pray for as we ought; but the Spirit Himself asketh for us with unspeakable groanings." (Rom. viii. 26.) All praise and glory, then, to the Most Holy Spirit, who sanctifies us by His presence and assists us by His grace, "to live, move, and have our being" (Acts xvii. 28.) in the love of the God who created us for no other purpose than to love and be loved by Him.

As the love of God for man, then, is so great and indescribable, it is quite clear that He expects us to love our fellow-men. As St. John says in the Epistle, "if God hath so loved us; we ought to love one another." So our divine Master Himself said on one occasion: "Thou shalt love the Lord thy God with thy whole heart, and with thy whole soul, and with thy whole mind. This is the greatest and the first commandment. And the second is like to this: Thou shalt love thy neighbor as thyself." (Matt. xxii. 37–39.) Hence we are told in the Gospel that the least we can do is to deal with others even as God has dealt with us. Some seem to imagine that when they forgive an enemy or speak well of a neighbor they are to be thanked for their magnanimity, never realizing that it is the strict command of God to do so; and forgetting that they pray in the "Our Father" to be forgiven their trespasses *as* (that is, according to the measure and spirit) *they forgive them that trespass against them*. What right have we to become inflamed with anger, or pretended disgust, or pharisaical indignation under the false appearance of apparent holy zeal, with the sins or failings of others, when God, who is offended Himself, has mercy on them? This is a very dangerous error to fall into and it is not at all an uncommon one. Thus it is that we are warned by our divine Master in to-day's Gospel to be charitable even from the selfish motive which is suggested: "Be ye therefore merciful, as your Father also is merciful. Judge not, and you shall not be judged. Condemn not, and you shall not be condemned. Forgive, and you shall be forgiven. Give, and it shall be given to you: good measure and pressed down and shaken together and running over shall they give into your bosom."

XXXVI

FEAST OF CORPUS CHRISTI

HIS BANQUET

"Take ye and eat."
(Epistle: 1 Cor. xi. 23–29.)
"This is the bread that came down from heaven." (Gospel: John vi. 56–59.)

ALTHOUGH we have already seen many extraordinary proofs of the love of our divine Master for us in becoming man in order to lay down His life for our salvation, and although before His sacred passion and death he knew full well that even still we should prove ungrateful for the many gifts and graces He had purchased for us, He had not even then exhausted all the proofs of His love or all the treasures of His mercy. "Having loved His own who were in the world, He loved them unto the end," says St. John. (xiii. 1.) Knowing that the time for His departure from this life was near at hand, He wished like a loving Father to leave His children the greatest token of all by preparing for us no less than the Heavenly Banquet of His

FEAST OF CORPUS CHRISTI

own most precious body and blood in the Most Holy Sacrament of the Altar. So the Church to-day begins the celebration of a special feast of eight days in honor of this most signal favor, which is known as the "Feast of Corpus Christi," the Feast of the "Body of Christ."

Strange to say, it was just at the very time that Our Lord Jesus Christ was about to be delivered into the hands of sinful men that He left us this greatest token of His love and kindness, for, as the Epistle of to-day says, "the Lord Jesus, the same night in which He was betrayed, took bread, and giving thanks broke, and said: Take ye and eat: this is My body which shall be delivered for you."

Our Divine Saviour had previously promised that He would indeed give us His flesh to eat and His blood to drink, but the people did not realize either the immensity of His love or the extent of His power, and many of them refused to believe Him. He had fed about five thousand people by the miraculous multiplication of the loaves and fishes shortly before the Jewish feast of the Passover. On the following day the same multitude again sought Him, and our divine Master made use of the opportunity to draw their attention clearly and definitely to the nature and effects of the spiritual food He was about to give us in the Banquet of the Most Holy Sacrament. He began by referring to the miracle of the previous day in order to point out the difference between the wonderful bread He had already given them and the Bread of the Blessed Eucharist, which He was about to promise them. "You seek Me," He said, "not because you have seen miracles, but because you did eat of the loaves, and were filled." (John vi. 26.) And He immediately added: "Labor not for the meat which perisheth, but for that which endureth unto life everlasting, which the Son of man will give you." (27.) He then made frequent reference to the miraculous manna which God had sent down from heaven to feed the Israelites during their forty years in the desert; for He wished them to understand clearly that the Bread which He was promising was even still more wonderful. "My Father," He said, "giveth you the true bread from heaven. For the bread of God is that which cometh down from heaven, and giveth life to the world. They said therefore unto Him: Lord, give us always this bread. And Jesus said to them: I am the bread of life." (32–35.) This they could not understand and they began to murmur, saying: "Is not this Jesus, the son of Joseph, whose father and mother we know? How then saith He I came down from heaven?" (42.) But Jesus continued to insist and made still plainer the nature of the Heavenly Banquet He was promising them. "I am the bread of life which came down from heaven. If any man eat of this bread, he shall live for ever; and the bread that I will give, is My flesh for the life of the world." (51, 52.) Which extraordinary statement caused them still more to wonder, and they "strove among themselves, saying: How can this man give us His flesh to eat?" But Jesus literally meant what He had said. He did not attempt to explain away or qualify in any particular His plain statement. He always did this when people took Him up wrongly or misunderstood Him, as, for instance, when He said to Nicodemus, to whom He had been explaining the sacrament of Baptism: "Unless a man be born again, he can not see the kingdom of God." Nicodemus took Him up literally and so asked Him how a man could be born again in his old age. Our Lord then explained that He had been speaking in a figurative sense of spiritual regeneration, saying: "Unless a man be born again of water and the Holy Ghost, he can not enter into the kingdom of God. That which is born of the flesh is flesh; and that which is born of the spirit, is spirit. Wonder not, that I said to thee, you must be born again." (John iii. 1-8.) But when Jesus spoke of giving His own flesh as food, and the people wondered and asked, like Nicodemus, how such a thing could be, He merely repeated with even greater clearness and stronger emphasis the real plain and simple fact: "Except you eat of the flesh of the Son of man, and drink His blood, you shall not have life in you. He that eateth My flesh, and drinketh My blood, hath everlasting life: and I will raise him up in the last day. For My flesh is meat indeed: and My blood is drink indeed. He that eateth My flesh, and drinketh My blood, abideth in Me, and I in him." (54-57.) Nothing could be plainer. And so the people understood it. But they could not understand the manner of it, and even some of His own disciples refused to believe in its possibility and "walked no more with Him," declaring "This saying is hard, and who can hear it?" But the apostles knew their divine Master better. They knew He could do all things, for they knew that He was God. And so St. Peter, on behalf of his brethren and himself, answered His challenge "Will you also go away?" by the beautiful confession of faith, hope, and love: "Lord, to whom shall we go? Thou hast the words of eternal life. And we have believed and have known, that Thou art the Christ, the Son of God." (vi. 67-70.)

Their confidence was not misplaced, for it was not long until Our Lord Jesus Christ literally and truly fulfilled the promise He had made and gave them His body and blood as the Heavenly Food of their souls, as is related by St. Paul in to-day's Epistle. And He gave it not only to them but also to us, for He had promised that it was to "give life to the world." (John vi. 33.) So at the Last Supper He directed them to repeat in His name and by His authority the same Sacred Mystery: "Do this for a commemoration of Me. For as often as you shall eat this bread and drink the chalice, you shall show the death of the Lord, until He come." Until the Last Day, therefore, the renewal of this great Mystery of the body and blood, soul and divinity, of Our Lord and Saviour Jesus Christ will take place upon our altars and provide us with the Heavenly Banquet of the Bread of Life, thus literally fulfilling in the daily offering of the holy sacrifice of the Mass all over the world those words of the prophet Malachias; "From the rising of the sun, even to the going down, My name is great among the Gentiles, and in every place there is sacrifice, and there is offered to My name a clean oblation" (Mal. i. 11.); and in His continual presence amongst us in the Most Holy Sacrament of the Altar in all the tabernacles over the globe the prophetic signification of His name, "Emmanuel," which signifies "God with us." (Isaias vii. 14; Matt. i. 23.)

No wonder, then, that Holy Scripture declares: "Neither is there any other nation so great, that hath gods so nigh them, as our God is present to all our petitions." (Deut. iv. 7.) No wonder our divine Master Himself has said to us: "Many prophets and just men have desired to see the things that you see, and have not seen them." (Matt. xiii. 17.) The disciples were greatly rejoiced indeed when they were able to announce the glad tidings: "We have seen the Lord." (John xx.) But we not only see Him ever present on our altars, but He actually abides in us and we in Him whenever we receive Him worthily in holy communion.

How, then, do we appreciate this most extraordinary privilege? Do we frequently visit Him in the sacrament of His love? Do we often assist at the holy sacrifice of the Mass? Do we receive Him as often as we should in the Divine Banquet of holy communion? He has told us Himself that unless we "eat of the flesh of the Son of man, and drink His blood, we shall not have life in us" (John vi. 54.), that is, we can not remain long in the state of grace. He tells us, too, that unless we receive Him worthily we only render ourselves more guilty in the sight of God. "He that eateth and drinketh unworthily, eateth and drinketh judgment to himself, not discerning the body of the Lord." So He accordingly says: "Let a man prove himself"; that is, let him by a good confession obtain pardon of his sins and partake of the Holy Banquet of Christ's Supper with a clean heart and a good conscience. For, as food will keep up the life of the body, but will not restore the dead to life; so the reception of holy communion by a soul dead in sin only increases its corruption. At the same time, it is not necessary to be perfect in order to receive worthily, for it is a food intended for men, not for angels, and though we can never be really worthy to partake of it, we should do our best to render ourselves by the grace of God at least less unworthy.

If we truly realized the immensity of the love of Jesus for us in the Blessed Sacrament we should never need such warnings or such advice. If we only realized our own wants and how ready and willing our divine Master is to help us by His presence in the Most Holy Sacrament we should, like the early Christians, receive Him as often as we possibly could in holy communion. We should visit Him in the holy tabernacle and lay all our wants before Him. And we should love to assist with devotion and reverence at the holy sacrifice of the Mass on every possible occasion. "With desire I have desired to eat this pasch with you," He said (Luke xxii. 15.); and again: "My delights are to be with the children of men." (Prov. viii. 31.) He is with us for the sole purpose of relieving all our wants, and for giving us all that is necessary for soul and body. Therefore He invites us to His Divine Banquet to assist and comfort and console and strengthen us. "Come to Me, all you that labor, and are burdened, and I will refresh you," He says. (Matt. xi. 28.)

If the shadow of St. Peter falling upon the sick and infirm in the streets of Jerusalem relieved them from their infirmities (Acts v. 15.); if wherever Jesus walked "virtue went out from Him and healed all" (Luke vi. 19.); how much more will not His presence continually amongst us in the Most Holy Sacrament of the Altar send forth power and virtue and grace and strength to all those for whose very love He exists there. How much more will His abiding presence with us, and ours with Him, in the intimate union that exists between Him and us at the Sacred Banquet of holy communion, where we eat and drink His most precious body and blood.

XXXVII

SECOND SUNDAY AFTER PENTECOST

HIS GUEST

"Let us not love in word, nor in tongue, but in deed and in truth."
(Epistle: 1 John iii. 13–18.)

"A certain man made a great supper, and invited many."
(Gospel: Luke xiv. 16–24.)

So important is the frequent and worthy reception of the body and blood of Our Lord and Saviour Jesus Christ in the Most Holy Sacrament of the Altar that to-day our holy mother the Church continues her discourse of last Sunday by drawing our attention to certain necessary dispositions on the part of those privileged guests who have been invited to partake of this heavenly Food at the Divine Banquet of our dear Lord and Master.

In the Gospel we are told under the form of a parable that we have all been invited to approach the Holy Table of the Lord. "A certain man made a great supper, and invited many." We are told that it is our duty to accept the invitation and present ourselves as guests duly prepared. "He sent his servants at the hour of supper to say to them that were invited, that they should come, for now all things were ready." In the Epistle is pointed out the great indispensable condition, or necessary disposition—the state of grace, or freedom from mortal sin; and also the means of knowing if we are truly possessed of it—the usual test of charity, most clearly seen in the love which we show for our neighbor. "We know that we have passed from death to life, because we love the brethren." (1 John iii. 14.)

When Our Lord Jesus Christ instituted the holy sacraments He provided for all the wants of the soul. We are regenerated by Baptism, strengthened by Confirmation, restored to God's favor after the commission of sin by Penance, consoled and comforted, in danger of death, by Extreme Unction, and nourished every day of our lives by the Bread of Life in the Holy Eucharist. Hence there are two main divisions of the sacraments—those which we must receive in the state of grace, and those which restore us to the friendship of God after mortal sin committed. The former are known as "sacraments of the living," and the latter as "sacraments of the dead." Whilst Penance belongs to the latter class it is clear that the Holy Eucharist belongs to the former, and that in order to receive it worthily it is necessary to be in the state of grace. According to the Council of Trent "He who desires to communicate should call to mind the injunction of the Apostle: *'Let a man prove himself.'* Now this necessary proving of one's self, according to the practice of the Church, consists in this, that no one who has been guilty of a grievous sin, approach the Holy Eucharist unless he has first sacramentally confessed." (Sess. xviii. Chap. vii.)

Whilst the state of grace is absolutely necessary for the worthy reception of the Holy Eucharist, it is also sufficient, and a high degree of sanctity is not required, although we are advised by Holy Church to have our souls adorned with all the faith, reverence, and devotion possible. According to the same Holy Council, the Holy Eucharist is "an antidote which delivers us from venial sin, and preserves us from mortal sin." Hence we are advised by authorities on the spiritual life that it is often more advantageous to the soul to get rid of venial faults by acts of love and contrition in Holy Communion rather than in the sacrament of Penance. Holy Communion is not a reward of sanctity, but a means of acquiring it.

Mortal sin kills the soul by depriving it of its true life, which is sanctifying grace. A soul in mortal sin can not, therefore, derive any spiritual nourishment from the Divine Food of the Holy Eucharist any more than a dead body can be nourished by corporal food. According to the Epistle, the true test of spiritual life in the soul is that of charity toward our neighbor. "We know that we have passed from death to life, because we love the brethren. He that loveth not, abideth in death. Whosoever hateth his brother is a murderer. And you know that no murderer hath eternal life abiding in himself. In this we have known the charity of God, because He hath laid down His life for us: and we ought to lay down our lives for the brethren." We must, then, be charitable toward our neighbor at all costs and at any sacrifice, if we are to derive advantage from the Holy Sacrament of Christ's love.

It is to be greatly feared that the evident want of definite spiritual results from even frequent approach to the Holy Table on the part of many Christians is to be traced to this unfortunate and deplorably common want of charity. How many otherwise good and apparently holy people receive Holy Communion regularly and frequently who both before and after their reception of the precious body and blood of Jesus Christ indulge without scruple in uncharitable conversation and even in calumny and detraction. Their whole lives and conversation are not only wanting in the spirit of Christlike charity, but they seem to be permeated by the murderous spirit of the devil. "You are of your father the devil, and the desires of your father you will do. He was a murderer from the beginning" (John viii. 44.), and "no murderer hath eternal life abiding in himself," says St. John. Such people truly "eat and drink judgment to themselves, not discerning the body of the Lord" (1 Cor. xi. 29.), although they frequently approach the divine fountain of life and grace in the holy sacraments. St. Paul warns us of the very same dangerous error of judging of our spiritual condition by the number and the greatness of the favors Almighty God has conferred on us, rather than by the test of charity as shown in the love of our neighbor. "I would not have you ignorant, brethren," he says, "that our fathers were all under the cloud, and all passed through the sea. And all in Moses were baptized, in the cloud and in the sea. And did all eat the same spiritual food. And all drank the same spiritual drink; (and they drank of the spiritual rock that followed them, and the rock was Christ). But with most of them God was not well pleased: for they were overthrown in the desert. . . . Now all these things happened to them in figure: and they are written for our correction, upon whom the ends of the world are come. Wherefore he that thinketh himself to stand, let him take heed lest he fall." (1 Cor. x. 1-12.)

"Therefore are there many infirm and weak among you," says the same Apostle, "and many sleep. But if we would judge ourselves we should not be judged." (1 Cor. xi. 30, 31.) We should, therefore, seriously and carefully examine ourselves on this very important matter of charity toward our neighbor, particularly with regard to our conversation. Some willingly give their services and their goods to a neighbor in want of them, but they have no scruple in robbing him of his character by their uncharitable comments on him. "If I should distribute all my goods to feed the poor, and if I should deliver my body to be burned, and have not charity, it profiteth me nothing" (1 Cor. xiii. 3.), says St. Paul. No wonder, then, St. James says: "If any man offend not in word, the same is a perfect man." (iii. 2.) Let us, then, follow the advice of our divine Master Himself when approaching Holy Communion: "If, therefore, thou offer thy gift at the altar, and there thou remember that thy brother hath anything against thee: leave there thy offering before the altar, and go first to be reconciled to thy brother" (Matt. v. 23.) by restoring to him as far as possible the character you have robbed him of and by guarding your tongue for the future concerning the faults and failings of others.

With regard to the proximate preparation for the worthy reception of the Holy Eucharist, it is enough to say that whilst the efficacy of this Divine Sacrament does not consist in acts of the various virtues but in the inherent sanctifying power of the living body and blood, soul and divinity, of Jesus Christ Himself within us, yet the increase of sanctifying grace and the actual graces necessary for our special needs depend upon the perfection of the dispositions with which we approach the Holy Table. The best disposition of all is a strong desire to receive and be united with our divine Master in the Sacrament of His love." With desire I have desired to eat this pasch with you" (Luke xxii. 15.), He says Himself. If this is also our prevailing sentiment we shall naturally be led to make acts of faith, hope, love, and contrition, and Jesus will do the rest—"All the multitude sought to touch Him, for virtue went out from Him, and healed all." (Luke vi. 19.)

It is within our power, then, by the help of God's grace to be raised from death to life and so be rendered capable of being nourished by the Divine Food at the Heavenly Banquet of the Eucharist. But if we refuse to accept the invitation of our Lord and Master and remain away from His Holy Table, we can not have any hope of eternal life. We are told in the Gospel the various excuses made by such people and the fate that awaits them. Similar reasons of business, or pleasure, or want of time or opportunity are alleged by those who neglect Holy Communion, although in reality it is the want of desire or attachment to sin and to creatures that keeps them away from the source of life and spiritual strength.

The result is that Almighty God is offended and punishes them by abandoning them to spiritual starvation, death and destruction. "The master of the house being angry, said . . . none of these men that were invited shall taste of my supper." It is no use to excuse ourselves from frequent and regular attendance at the Holy Table by saying that we have not time or opportunity. The early Christians were just as busy as we are and yet they found time to receive Holy Communion every time they assisted at the holy sacrifice of the Mass, which was generally every day. In this important matter as in every other "where there is a will there is a way." Neither can we say that we are too weak, or too sinful, or too much tempted, to be worthy guests at the Divine Banquet, for the Gospel relates that the master said to his servant: "Go out quickly into the streets and lanes of the city, and bring in hither the poor, and the feeble, and the blind, and the lame." If we are poor, and feeble, and blind, and lame, we have all the more need of the healing presence and sanctifying power of our merciful and loving Saviour, who says: "They that are in health need not a physician, but they that are ill." (Matt. ix. 12.)

Let us, then, with great faith and devotion frequently accept of the Master's kind invitation to His Heavenly Banquet. There "you shall draw waters with joy out of the Saviour's fountains: Rejoice, and praise, O thou habitation of Sion: for great is He that is in the midst of thee, the Holy One of Israel." (Is. xii. 3–6.)

XXXVIII

THIRD SUNDAY AFTER PENTECOST

HIS CARE

"He hath care of you."
        (EPISTLE: 1 Peter v. 6–11.)
"This man receiveth sinners."
        (GOSPEL: Luke xv. 1–10.)

LEST some might imagine that as our divine Master bestows His favors in the Holy Sacrament of His Love only on those who are in the state of grace, or that He dispenses only spiritual favors to His faithful children, our holy mother the Church to-day draws our attention to the great love of Our Lord Jesus Christ for even the greatest sinners, His ardent desire to seek them and confer upon them not only grace and mercy but even such temporal blessings as are necessary for their welfare and happiness.

In the Epistle we are told that the sorrows and troubles of this life, as well as tribulation of spirit from the assaults of the world, the flesh, and the devil, are permitted by Almighty God for our trial and greater merit, and that "the God of all grace, who hath called us unto eternal glory in Christ Jesus, after you have suffered a little, will Himself perfect you, and confirm you, and establish you." Whilst in the Gospel we are plainly told, in the words of the Master Himself, of the great object He had in view in becoming man—the redemption, forgiveness, and sanctification of the sinner, whom He seems to love even more than the just.

It has been frequently pointed out to us that it is the lot of man to suffer. From the cradle to the grave his life is one long round of trial, disappointment, and sorrow. "Man born of a woman," says holy Job, "is filled with many miseries." (Job xiv. 1.) And yet it is hard to convince the wicked that they deserve all they suffer on account of their sins. If we have ever been guilty of deliberately offending Almighty God, it would be but little to suffer all our lives in order to be restored to His grace and favor. Indeed, God, in His great desire to save the sinner, often sends him chastisements in order to bring him to a sense of his position when words and entreaties fail to move him. "Thou hast given a warning to them that fear Thee" (Ps. lix. 6.), says the Psalmist; and again: "Before I was humbled I offended." (Ps. cxviii. 67.) What an additional misfortune it is, then, for those who disregard such forcible reminders and foolishly say: "Why should God punish me so?" Our loving Father sometimes also sends failure and unhappiness, sickness and death and other misfortunes to the good and virtuous in order not only to try them and prove their virtue, but even to draw them nearer to Himself and preserve them in His grace and love. "For whom the Lord loveth He chastiseth," says St. Paul (Heb. xii. 6.), and prosperity often turns the heart away from God: "When they have eaten, and are full and fat," says Holy Scripture, "they will turn away after strange gods and will serve them: and will despise Me, and make void My covenant." (Deut. xxxi. 20.)

In all our trials and temptations, therefore, whether spiritual or temporal, we should always recognize the hand of Divine Providence mercifully guiding and protecting us, endeavoring to lead us and keep us to Himself, "casting all our care upon Him, for He hath care of us," as the Epistle says. That loving care is nowhere shown more strongly or more clearly than in the incident recorded in the Gospel of to-day and in the two beautiful parables which our divine Master made use of in order to explain His attitude toward sinners.

As His great object in coming down from heaven was the salvation and sanctification of sinners, He made it His chief business to seek them out, converse familiarly with them, and strive to influence them by His word and example as well as by His kindness and consideration toward them. "They that are whole," He used to say, "need not the physician: but they that are sick. I am come not to call the just, but sinners, to penance." (Luke v. 31.) And He commanded His apostles to "go rather to the lost sheep." (Matt. x. 6.)

Such wonderful condescension was not understood by the proud and haughty Pharisees. They looked upon themselves as the favored ones of God, and they were, no doubt, like many of the apparently holy people of the present day—highly respectable citizens in the eyes of their fellow-men on account of their outward performance of various good works, their scrupulous observance of all the exterior details of the law, and their publicly professed hatred of sin. But at the same time their hearts were inwardly corrupt. Their virtues were such as appealed to the public eye: their fasts and prayers and other good works were performed in order to be paraded before the admiration of men. Our divine Master openly and frequently accused them of this shameful hypocrisy and publicly called their attention to their secret sins. He denounced them as hypocrites who attended to small matters but neglected "the weightier things of the law: judgment, and mercy, and faith," who "outwardly indeed appear to men just; but inwardly are full of hypocrisy and iniquity," "like to whited sepulchres, which outwardly appear to men beautiful, but within are full of dead men's bones, and of all filthiness." (Matt. xxiii.) Hence even their best actions were vitiated by the want of a proper motive and the presence of an evil one. Their whole lives failed to respond to the true test of real religion—charity toward the neighbor. Nay, they were even remarkable for the very opposite vice, and hated and despised sinners, whilst they openly boasted of their own virtues. Wanting charity they wanted everything, and so, though they practised a certain kind of exterior virtue, they had no real religion at all. Against which misfortune Our Lord warns us when He says: "I tell you that unless your justice abound more than that of the scribes and Pharisees, you shall not enter into the kingdom of heaven." (Matt. v. 20.)

As the Pharisees hated sinners so much they naturally avoided their company as much as possible. We can well imagine their surprise, therefore, when they saw Jesus conversing familiarly with publicans and sinners, and even enjoying their hospitality. "The publicans and sinners drew near unto Jesus to hear Him. And the Pharisees and scribes murmured, saying: This man receiveth sinners and eateth with them." Thus they unconsciously summed up the chief characteristics of Our Saviour's personality—His love and kindness toward sinners—and at the same time gave Him an opportunity of formally declaring and explaining His attitude toward them, by His beautiful parables of the lost sheep and of the lost coin.

In these two parables the immense love and mercy of Almighty God is made strikingly clear. The goods lost are of little value. The loss of one sheep to a man owning a hundred is comparatively small. The loss of the coin, of little value in itself, is a lot to a poor woman. Our souls are of little value as far as we contribute to the happiness of God. In themselves also they are worthless, but in the eyes of God they are of immense value, having been "bought with a great price" (1 Cor. vi. 20.)—the precious blood of Our Lord and Saviour Jesus Christ. And as the owners of the lost property rejoice over its recovery, so, according to Our Lord "there shall be joy before the angels of God upon one sinner doing penance."

There is nothing so comforting and consoling as the kindness and mercy of our dear Lord to poor sinners, seeing how unmerciful and uncompromising are the judgments of men. The all-holy God Himself alone knows the chastisement the sinner deserves, as He alone knows the awful malice of sin. Yet He is merciful, kind, and forgiving. How many who think themselves holy have no mercy for the wrongdoer! Like the Pharisees, they have an exalted but mistaken idea of their own personal sanctity and they may be correct in their outward conduct as far as it goes. But they are vain, proud, strict, harsh, and intolerant. In their virtuous indignation they are to be feared rather than respected or loved. They are entirely wanting in the spirit of Jesus. See how the Pharisees were shocked at the manner in which her dear Lord treated Mary Magdalen, "the sinner of the city." Through His love and mercy she afterward became a great saint and was privileged to be the first to see Jesus after His resurrection. See how their same spirit prevailed when they brought to our divine Lord in the portico of the temple the woman taken in adultery.

They wanted to stone her to death, according to the Law. But Christ stooping down wrote with His finger in the fine sand that strewed the pavement and said: "He that is without sin among you, let him first cast a stone at her." It is said that He wrote there the secret sins of her accusers, for as they read they all slunk away one by one, until the unfortunate sinner was left alone with Jesus, who said to her kindly, as St. John relates: "Hath no man accused thee? Who said: No man, Lord. And Jesus said: Neither will I condemn thee. Go, and sin no more." (John viii. 1–11.)

How truly holy we should be before we proceed to condemn others even in our own minds! The truly holy never condemn, for such have the spirit and the mind of Jesus. No wonder that our divine Master says to those who think themselves virtuous: "Unless your justice exceed that of the scribes and Pharisees you shall not enter the kingdom of heaven." (Matt. v. 20.)

We should be truly grateful to our dear Lord and Master for His care, kindness, and merciful consideration for us. We are worse than sheep going astray when we forsake the path of virtue, for we know full well the occasions, the dangers, and the dreadful consequences of sin. But still our loving Master is anxious to save us and even seeks us and offers us His love and forgiveness. He is constantly watching over our temporal and eternal welfare, for He is our good Shepherd and "the good shepherd hath care for his sheep." Let us return to Him, then, and, forsaking forever the paths of evil and of danger, take refuge in the one true fold, where we shall be nourished in the pastures of life eternal under the personal care and guidance of our loving Shepherd, who will rejoice over us as if we were the only beings ever created, and as if His happiness depended upon ours alone. And "the God of all grace, who hath called us unto His eternal glory in Christ Jesus, after you have suffered a little, will Himself perfect you, and confirm and establish you" in the kingdom of heaven forever.

XXXIX

FEAST OF THE SACRED HEART

HIS SYMPATHY

"You shall draw waters with joy out of the Saviour's fountains."
(LESSON: Isaias xii. 1-6.)
"There came out blood and water."
(GOSPEL: John xix. 31-35.)

THE SECRET of our divine Master's most amiable human character was His immense love for men, especially for poor sinners, who were the very special objects of His love and affection. In order to win their confidence and love He assumed human nature and appeared amongst them in the most lovable personality He could assume. He was a poor, helpless babe in the stable at Bethlehem. When He grew to manhood He was always a gentle, kind, and loving friend to all, and went about doing good, healing the sick, curing the blind and the lame, comforting the poor and the afflicted, raising the dead to life and restoring them to their weeping loved ones, forgiving and consoling sinners, even those who persecuted and reviled Him, admiring, loving, blessing and protecting little children.

So when He came to die He proved that His great love for man had, as it were, exhausted itself, by appearing as a criminal dead upon the cross, His arms extended to embrace us, His head bowed down to give us the kiss of peace, and His Sacred Heart open to receive us, that Symbol of His love having literally emptied itself for our sakes, for, as the Gospel of to-day relates, "one of the soldiers with a spear opened His side, and immediately there came out blood and water." Truly, as St. John says, "Jesus, knowing that His hour was come, that He should pass out of this world to the Father: having loved His own who were in the world, He loved them unto the end." (John xiii. 1.)

The heart has ever been regarded as the seat of all human emotions. Whether this be physiologically true, or not, matters little when we refer to this particular portion of the human organism in order to graphically express our love or our sympathy for others. It is no less expressive a sign or symbol of such emotions, and is frequently made use of in this connection in Holy Scripture, where it is said to dilate with joy, contract with sadness, break with sorrow, grow fat and hard in prosperity. Whilst our divine Lord Himself says: "Learn of Me, because I am meek and humble of heart." (Matt. xi. 29.)

In the feast which our holy mother the Church celebrates to-day she proposes for the object of our devotion the actual, living Heart of our divine Lord and Master Jesus Christ, hypostatically united to the divinity, as the most adorable Symbol of His love for us. With her usual regard for what is appropriate and helpful, she ordains that this solemn commemoration of the love of Jesus for men shall take place on the same Sunday on which she recalls to our minds the parables of the lost sheep and of the lost coin, in which the Saviour's attitude of kindness and mercy toward poor sinners is so strikingly and beautifully shown.

As is related in the Gospel, the most holy Heart of Jesus was pierced by the spear of the Roman centurion and there immediately came forth a miraculous issue of blood and water. This was the literal fulfilment in Christ of two ancient prophecies concerning the Messias—"You shall not break a bone of Him" (Ex. vii. 46.), and "They shall look upon Him whom they have pierced." (Zach. xii. 10.) The first fruits of this miraculous manifestation of the love of the Sacred Heart for men were soon made apparent in the conversion of the centurion, who, according to St. Luke, "seeing what was done, glorified God, saying: Indeed this was a just man." (Luke xxiii. 47.) Moreover, "all the multitude of them that were come together to that sight, and saw the things that were done, returned striking their breasts." (xxiii. 48.)

Devotion to the Sacred Heart is no new devotion, then, for ever since that day Holy Church has honored that Sacred Symbol of the love of our divine Master for sinful men. Even during His mortal life Our Lord Jesus Christ frequently drew the attention of sinners to the love and kindness of His Sacred Heart. "Learn of Me," He said, "because I am meek and humble of heart." (Matt. xi. 29.) And He only asks for our love in return: "My son, give Me thy heart: and let thy eyes keep My ways." (Prov. xxiii. 26.)

Many Popes and Councils of the Church have in all ages recommended to the faithful the Most Sacred Heart of Jesus as an object of adoration and imitation. But it was not till the time of the special revelation of our divine Lord Himself to Blessed Margaret Mary Alacoque, toward the close of the seventeenth century, when the love of Jesus had grown cold in the ungrateful hearts of men, that the devotion was spread and practised in a special manner, according to the divine directions, and confraternities were established all over the world. Now the Sacred Heart has assumed for us that personal and intimate expression of the love of Jesus for us in His sacred passion, and in the Most Holy Sacrament of the Altar, where His abiding presence is both the example and the cause of our intimate union with Him in the charity born of Christian imitation and perfection.

And what a lovable character the Sacred Heart of Jesus is, as all devout Catholics know Him! Truly He is one of ourselves, in all things like us except in sin, and therefore possessing as man that intimate knowledge and personal experience of all our trials, temptations, sorrows, and sufferings which creates between Him and us that true bond of sympathy with all our feelings and emotions. The word "sympathy" literally means "suffering together with," and is consequently eminently characteristic of the Sacred Heart of Jesus, which experienced the highest possible degree of human suffering. "O all ye that pass by the way, attend, and see if there be any sorrow like to My sorrow" (Lam. i. 12.), He says by the mouth of His prophet

Jeremias. Hence St. Paul says: "We have not a high priest, who can not have compassion on our infirmities: but one tempted in all things like as we are, without sin." (Heb. iv. 15.)

The greatest suffering which afflicted the Sacred Heart was the knowledge of the base ingratitude of men, for whose sakes He had exhausted all the treasures of His mercy and love. As He complained to Blessed Margaret Mary when He revealed Himself to her, showing His Sacred Heart encircled with thorns, surmounted by a cross, and on a throne of fire: "Behold this Heart that has loved men so much, and which has spared itself nothing, not even to consuming itself to give them pledges of its love; but which, in return receives from the greater number no other recompense than ingratitude and insults offered to Me in this Sacrament of Love; and what grieves me most is that these hearts are consecrated to Me." He then directed her as to the establishment of a special feast in honor of His Sacred Heart in order to remind Christians of His love for them, especially in the Blessed Sacrament of the Eucharist, and thus to lead them to make some reparation by their increased love and devotion for the ingratitude and insults so frequently offered to Him by those upon whom His great love had been wasted. In return for which He promised to shed an abundance of grace, mercy, and love upon all those who should thus honor Him, making special reference to the blessings He had in store for all poor sinners who were anxious for the grace of conversion.

And time has proved the truth of His promises, for ever since sinners have indeed found in His Sacred Heart an ocean of mercy, and holy souls have been consumed by the fire of His divine love, thus literally fulfilling the prophecy contained in those words in the Lesson of to-day's feast: "I will give thanks to Thee, O Lord, for Thou wert angry with me; Thy wrath is turned away, and Thou hast comforted me. Behold, God is my Saviour, I will deal confidently, and will not fear; because the Lord is my strength, and my praise, and He is become my salvation. You shall draw waters with joy out of the Saviour's fountains."

But in order to enjoy the fulfilment of that prophecy in our own regard we must strive as far as we can to realize our personal obligation to do our share in the fulfilment of the command and prophecy contained in the words immediately following: "You shall say in that day: Praise ye the Lord, and call upon His name; make His works known amongst the people; remember that His name is high. Sing ye to the Lord, for He hath done great things; show this forth in all the earth. Rejoice, and praise, O thou habitation of Sion; for great is He that is in the midst of thee, the Holy One of Israel."

The very best way to accomplish this is by joining the Confraternity of the Sacred Heart in our parish, faithfully attending all its meetings, and carefully discharging all its duties. We shall then be in a position to make use with profit of the means employed in every such organization for the spiritual benefit of its members; namely, prayer, preaching and the sacraments, not to speak of the innumerable indulgences and other spiritual favors, such as the encouragement and good example which we mutually afford one another in such a pious union of earnest souls.

If private prayer is so powerful a means of obtaining favors from Almighty God, how much more efficacious is prayer in common, especially public prayer. "Where there are two or three gathered together in My name, there am I in the midst of them" (Matt. xviii. 20.), says Christ. What an extraordinary power do we not possess, then, when assembled as members of the Confraternity, under the guidance of Holy Church, in God's own house of prayer, and in His sacramental presence.

At every meeting there will be a short instruction on some article of faith, some doctrine, practice, or feast of the Church, to increase our knowledge of God's holy Word, our love for His holy Law, and our activity in His holy service. The practical result of this will be to awaken in us a strong desire to draw nearer to the Sacred Heart, to "taste and see that the Lord is sweet" (Ps. xxxiii. 9.) by more frequent and devout reception of the holy sacraments. Prayer and preaching would be alike useless if we neglected these great and necessary means of salvation. But as members of the Confraternity we shall be reminded of our duty and helped to fulfil it.

Thus we shall live in the presence of the Sacred Heart, consoled by His love, cheered by His promises, and make some reparation for the ingratitude of sinners, whilst for ourselves we shall surely "draw waters with joy out of the Saviour's fountains."

XL

FOURTH SUNDAY AFTER PENTECOST

HIS WORD

"The creature shall be delivered from the servitude of corruption."
(Epistle: Rom. viii. 18–23.)

"Master . . . at Thy word I will let down the net." (Gospel: Luke v. 1–11.)

THE Epistle and Gospel of to-day are together an epitome of all that we have been taught since the feast of the Ascension about the personality of our divine Master Himself and of His relations with the chosen laborers in His vineyard.

The Old Law was a law of fear. The New Law instituted by Our Lord Jesus Christ is a law of love. "This is My commandment, that you love one another, as I have loved you. Greater love than this no man hath, that a man lay down his life for his friends. You are My friends, if you do the things that I command you. I will not now call you servants: for the servant knoweth not what his lord doth.

But I have called you friends: because all things whatsoever I have heard of My Father, I have made known to you. You have not chosen Me: but I have chosen you, and have appointed you, that you should go, and should bring forth fruit; and your fruit should remain; that whatsoever you shall ask of the Father in My name, He may give it you" (John xv. 12–16) were His own words to His disciples, in which He clearly laid down the position proposed by the Church for our consideration to-day. And St. Paul expresses the same idea when he says: "He that is called in the Lord, being a bondman, is the freeman of the Lord. Likewise he that is called, being free, is the bondman of Christ. You are bought with a price; be not made the bond-slaves of men." (1 Cor. vii. 22, 23.)

The argument is made clear in the Epistle. As creatures we are subservient to the laws of the flesh. We must suffer all manner of hardships—"For we know that every creature groaneth and travaileth in pain even till now." We must work anyhow: either according to the exigencies of merely human necessities, without any reference to Almighty God—in "the servitude of corruption"; or as faithful children of our Heavenly Father, in "the liberty of the glory of the children of God." In the former case we must seek our reward in the empty honors and material advantages which the world may offer—"for the creature was made subject to vanity." In the latter case we can look forward to a great, glorious, and eternal reward from our divine Master, a reward so far surpassing in value the labors and trials undertaken in view of it that St. Paul "reckons, that the sufferings of this time are not worthy to be compared to the glory to come, that shall be revealed to us."

That even the transient reward for which men labor without thought of Almighty God is as doubtful as the pain and suffering connected with it is certain is made beautifully evident in the Gospel. There we are told that St. Peter and some of his brethren had been out fishing all night, without any result from their labors. In the morning Our Lord came to them and said to St. Peter: "Launch out into the deep, and let down your nets for a draught. And Simon answering, said to Him: Master, we have labored all the night and have taken nothing: but at Thy word I will let down the net. And when they had done this, they enclosed a very great multitude of fishes, and the net broke."

How many there are who spend all their lives in fruitless toil and suffering, aiming at the acquisition of the false honors, riches, and pleasures of this world, only to be disappointed in the end. For even if they succeed in attaining the objects of their ambition they shall find only what Solomon found in everything but work for God—"vanity and vexation of spirit." (Eccles. i. 14.) Like St. Peter in the Gospel they may well say: "We have labored all the night and have taken nothing."

As no one could be so foolish as to labor in vain from a matter of principle, but as many act accordingly through ignorance, or forgetfulness, or through some mistaken idea, it is very necessary for each and every one of us, both good and bad alike, to examine our work, our motives, the nature of our servitude; whether we are slaves of the flesh, subject to vanity, or whether we are serving our Heavenly Father as free children of His kingdom of love, working always in His presence and at His word with true generosity of mind and complete sacrifice of self, "launching out into the deep" to do the Master's work cheerfully and well.

To begin with, we must labor for success in the bark of Peter, as true children of Holy Church, ever and always guided aright under the divine direction of the Vicar of Jesus

Christ, obedient to the laws and listening with docility to the teachings of our divine Master, who said to His Church—"He that heareth you, heareth Me." (Luke x. 16.) If we are faithful in keeping the commandments of God and His holy Church, we shall be in the state of grace, and so be in a position to merit the heavenly reward of our labors. A soul in mortal sin is dead to God, and can do nothing to merit a reward in the next life, whilst a soul in the state of grace is intimately united with Jesus Christ and shares in His merits so that by virtue of them its work becomes meritorious in the sight of God.

In the next place, we must labor whilst it is day; that is, whilst we have time and opportunity, which is here and now, not waiting in the hope of labor in the future or of a deathbed repentance, for, as St. John says: "I must work the works of Him that sent Me, whilst it is day; the night cometh, when no man can work." (John ix. 4.)

We must labor with great zeal, earnestness, and generosity. We must "launch out into the deep," avoiding all dangers of shoals and reefs and hidden rocks of temptation, which lie near to the shore of this treacherous world. We must despise the world and its vanities and, placing ourselves under the direction and protection of our divine Master, work hard for our heavenly reward. "Whatever thy right hand is able to do, do it earnestly," says Holy Scripture, "for neither work, nor reason, nor wisdom, nor knowledge, shall be in hell, whither thou art hastening" (Eccles. ix. 10.), and where your spiritual shipwreck will surely bring you if you work in the dark, without the light of God's presence, or near the shore of the world's dangers and temptations, from which He warns you to keep clear.

Finally, we must labor at "the Master's Word." When the apostles had acknowledged that they had labored all the night and had taken nothing, St. Peter said to Jesus: "At Thy word I will let down the net." Then he was so wonderfully successful that "he was wholly astonished, and all that were with him." We must then have a pure intention of doing everything because it is the will of Almighty God. Otherwise all our labors will avail us nothing. This is what St. Paul means when he says: "If I should distribute all my goods to feed the poor, and if I should deliver my body to be burned, and have not charity, it profiteth me nothing." (1 Cor. xiii. 3.) For the charity of which he speaks is that pure and sincere love of God by which we do everything for His sake.

This divine charity should, therefore, be the motive of all our actions, the aim, end and object of all our desires. The Pharisees, who prayed frequently, gave alms, and were to all outward appearance holy men, were entirely wanting in this most necessary disposition. They practised a certain amount of virtue in order to gain the applause of men, but they could never hope for a spiritual reward, as Our Lord Himself often declared—"Amen, I say to you, they have received their reward." (Matt. vi. 16.) So St. Paul advises us to keep constantly before our minds a pure and sincere motive, a holy spiritual intention of pleasing God in everything, no matter how humble or how unspiritual the work itself may appear to be. "Whether you eat, or drink," he says, "or whatsoever else you do, do all to the glory of God." (1 Cor. x. 31.)

Thus God will reward us for doing His work. He will bless our labors and make them fruitful of life everlasting. For even though we labor whilst it is day, in the presence and under the direction of Jesus, and with the right intention, it is the Master's blessing that brings the reward exceeding great. "I have planted," says St. Paul, "Apollo watered, but God gave the increase. Therefore neither he that planteth is anything, nor he that watereth, but God that giveth the increase." (1 Cor. iii. 6, 7.)

Hence we should labor with true humility, and with full dependence, trust, and confidence in the assisting grace of Almighty God, saying with the Psalmist: "Not to us, O Lord, not to us; but to Thy name give glory." (Ps. cxv. 1.) For we never can know for certain to what merit of ours the apparent result of our efforts is due. It may not be the will of Almighty God to reward us in this life by the sight of the results of our labors made profitable by His holy blessing. Besides, what may appear to be the fruit of our labor under the divine guidance and blessing may be due to the meritorious work of those who have gone before us in the vineyard, and who are now enjoying the eternal reward of their labors, the visible results of which they were not allowed to see or to enjoy in this life. As our divine Master Himself said to His disciples on one occasion: "He that reapeth, receiveth wages and gathereth fruit unto life everlasting: that both he that soweth, and he that reapeth, may rejoice together. For in this is the saying true: That it is one man that soweth, and it is another that reapeth. I have sent you to reap that in which you did not labor: others have labored, and you have entered into their labors." (John iv. 36–38.)

"This same," then, "shall comfort us from the works and labors of our hands on the earth, which the Lord hath cursed" and, like Noe, we shall "find grace before the Lord." (Gen. v. 29.) With God alone rests the blessing of our labor and its reward. For us it is enough to know that we do His will. Let us cheerfully and generously devote ourselves to the Master's service, launching out into the deep without fear, and without misgiving as to the result, looking to our dear Lord and Master Jesus Christ for His guidance and example, as well as for His blessing on our work. He says of Himself: "My meat is to do the will of Him that sent Me, that I may perfect His work." (John iv. 34.) Thus we shall ever labor in the deep and in the day, laying up for ourselves a great and eternal reward in the kingdom of heaven where we shall hear that best of all the Master's words: "Well done, thou good and faithful servant, because thou hast been faithful over a few things, I will place thee over many things: enter thou into the joy of thy Lord." (Matt. xxv. 21.)

PART V

THE RESULTS

"They received every man a penny."
(Matt. xx. 9.)

XLI

FIFTH SUNDAY AFTER PENTECOST

ENEMIES

"If also you suffer anything for justice' sake, blessed are ye."
(Epistle: 1 Peter iii. 8–15.)

"Except your justice abound more than that of the scribes and Pharisees, you shall not enter into the kingdom of heaven."
(Gospel: Matt. v. 20–24.)

WHEN our divine Master was sending forth His disciples on their mission of preaching and teaching He warned them that one of the results of their loyalty and devotion to Him and His holy doctrine would be to bring upon themselves the hatred of the world; that is, of sinners. "Because you are not of the world," He said to them, "but I have chosen you out of the world, therefore the world hateth you. Remember My word that I said to you: The servant is not greater than his master. If they have persecuted Me, they will also persecute you." (John xv. 19,

20.) "And these things they will do to you; because they have not known the Father, nor Me." (xvi. 3.) And as hatred was to be a sign of the enemies of Christ, so love was to be a proof of His true disciples. "By this shall men know that you are My disciples, if you have love one for another." (John xiii. 35.)

The great distinction between true and false Christians, then, is that the latter hate and persecute the former as their inveterate enemies. We were told the same truth some time ago when we were taught that the test of the true disciples of our divine Master was that of the virtue of charity toward all. But to-day our attention is drawn to the matter more particularly. In the first place, to remind us that even in our own days the words of Christ still hold true, and that though the just still suffer persecution they ought to be prepared for it, and feel consoled by the promise made in the Epistle—"If you also suffer anything for justice' sake, blessed are ye. And be not afraid of their fear, and be not troubled." And in the second place, that we might carefully examine ourselves in order to find out to which of these two classes we belong—whether we are, though Christians in name, in reality enemies of Christ and His followers; and that by the test of fraternal charity referred to in the Epistle: "Having compassion one of another, being lovers of the brotherhood, merciful, modest, humble: not rendering evil for evil, nor railing for railing, but contrariwise, blessing"; as well as in the light of the warning given by our Lord Jesus Christ Himself in the Gospel: "Except your justice abound more than that of the scribes and Pharisees, you shall not enter into the kingdom of heaven."

The scribes were the recognized teachers and expounders of the Old Law among the Jews, and the people naturally looked up to them for guidance in the ways of truth and justice. The Pharisees were men who made it their great object to observe the outward details of the Law, especially in small matters, in order to gain the respect of the people. That they could never be accused of openly breaking any of its precepts is abundantly clear from what Our Lord Himself said of them. They prayed long and frequently; they fasted often; they gave their due proportion of alms to the poor; they had the words of the Law inscribed on their forehead-bands, and scrupulously observed every little exterior ceremony. But our Blessed Saviour openly and vehemently denounced them as unworthy to enter into the kingdom of heaven. He called them hypocrites, deceivers, "whited sepulchres, which outwardly appear to men beautiful, but within are full of dead men's bones, and of all filthiness." (Matt. xxiii. 27.) And the reason He gave was that whilst they observed the outward appearances of religion in order to appear virtuous before men, they neglected "the weightier things of the law; judgment, and mercy, and faith." (Matt. xxiii. 23.) In other words, they were wanting in that motive of true charity which is necessary in order to make our actions pleasing to God and deserving of a spiritual reward. Their want of this virtue showed itself particularly in their words and actions against their neighbor, for they were full of pride and vainglory in their estimate of themselves, but full of hatred, unjust judgment, and evil speaking against others.

There are even at the present day many apparently good Christians, as far as keeping the laws of Church and State is concerned, so that they can not be accused of the open or serious breach of any of them. They dare not break the laws of the State with impunity. Therefore they do not commit murder or theft or other serious crime. They are careful not to render themselves liable to the penalty of the law for slander or calumny. They discharge their outward duties to the Church by hearing

Mass, approaching the sacraments, contributing to the support of their pastors, giving their children a good Catholic education, and generally leading a respectable life. But do they, like the Pharisees, "outwardly appear to men just; but inwardly are full of hypocrisy and iniquity"? (Matt. xxiii. 28.) The test is, are they charitable in spirit, in word, and in deed? Or do they merely keep the letter of the law and injure their neighbor's character as far as they dare without danger of punishment?

This is the test as to whether they are friends or enemies of Christ, as given by our divine Master Himself in to-day's Gospel, where He explains what He means by His warning: "Except your justice abound more than that of the scribes and Pharisees, you shall not enter into the kingdom of heaven." "You have heard that it was said to them of old," He says, "Thou shalt not kill. And whosoever shall kill shall be in danger of the judgment. But I say to you, that whosoever is angry with his brother, shall be in danger of the judgment." Here He shows the great difference between the Old Law and the New Law. In the former it was forbidden to commit murder, but in the latter not only the exterior effectual action but also the inward desire, and that anger from which such desires proceed, is also prohibited. Then He goes on to say that "whosoever shall say to his brother, Raca, shall be in danger of the council." The word "Raca" was an injurious and contemptuous epithet among the Jews: and the "Council" was a court of justice at Jerusalem in which all serious charges were tried by an assembly of seventy-two judges. "Whosoever shall say, Thou fool, shall be in danger of hell fire." The term "fool" in Holy Scripture signifies "a sinner, an injurious man," and "hell fire" was the name given to a place near Jerusalem where a constant fire was kept burning by the worshipers of Moloch. This was often referred to by Our Lord as a symbol of the eternal fire by which the damned are punished in the hell of eternal torments.

All which goes to prove that when our Blessed Saviour denounced the Pharisees He did so because all their apparent religion was mere outward form and ceremony and had no real, internal, supernatural foundation. Unless we are very different from them, therefore, the same woe is pronounced against us. Let us, then, examine ourselves and see whether we are "not like the rest of men, extortioners, unjust, adulterers" (Luke xviii. 11.) merely because we are afraid of legal punishment and penalties; whether we are only apparently religious in our attendance at Church and in our frequentation of the sacraments; or whether we are careful to be as correct in our thoughts and desires, and in our very heart, as we are in our outward actions.

Are we, then, enemies or friends of Christ? The answer to this all-important question is found in the concluding words of this day's Gospel: "If therefore thou offer thy gift at the altar, and there thou remember that thy brother hath anything against thee; leave there thy offering before the altar, and go first to be reconciled to thy brother: and then coming thou shalt offer thy gift." Have you by uncharitable thoughts, unkind or unjust remarks, or injurious actions caused any one to suffer serious loss in his property or character? Have you grievously injured the good name of any of your neighbors by rash judgment, by repeating and spreading anything you may have heard to his discredit, whether true or false? Have you by word or action caused him much pain, anxiety, loss of position or of friends, or even tribulation of spirit? It does not matter whether he deserves it or no, you have thereby under the very cloak and appearance of virtue ranged yourself on the side of the enemies of Christ. You are worse than the Pharisees, for, as our divine Master said when He spoke of such to His disciples: "All these things they will do to you for My Name's sake: because they know not Him that sent Me. If I had not come, and spoken to them, they would not have sin; but now they have no excuse for their sin." (John xv. 21, 22.) What a dreadful character for a professed follower of Christ! What a terrible condemnation such a one will have to suffer at the judgment-seat of an angry God!

Let us, then, in fervent prayer ask Almighty God to open our eyes to our true condition. The Pharisees were spiritually blind. So are many Christians. But we have been warned, and we have been provided with a sure test and a certain remedy—in the test of charity in thought, word, and deed; and in the remedy of a complete and perfect change of heart, "having compassion one of another, being lovers of the brotherhood, merciful, modest, humble," with the love, mercy, and compassion, with the meekness and humility of Jesus, the friend rather than the judge of sinners.

If we have anything to suffer from others through their harsh, unkind judgments, unjust or uncharitable remarks, injurious words, or bitter expressions, we should feel happy that we are accounted worthy to suffer for the sake of our divine Master, for such crosses are proofs that we are His friends. How consoling to our hearts should be those words in to-day's Epistle: "Who is there that can hurt you, if you be zealous of good? But if also you suffer anything for justice' sake, blessed are ye. And be not afraid of their fear, and be not troubled. But sanctify the Lord Jesus Christ in your hearts." Let us, as an act of thanksgiving to our dear Lord and Master for giving us this proof of His love and token of His friendship, resolve to "sanctify Him in our hearts" by imitating His charity, mercy, meekness, and humility in our whole lives, but particularly in our conversation, by never criticizing, condemning or even examining in our own minds through mere curiosity the actions, opinions, or motives of our neighbor which do not concern us; for "He that will love life, and see good days, let him refrain his tongue from evil, and his lips that they speak no guile."

XLII

SIXTH SUNDAY AFTER PENTECOST

LIFE

"You are dead indeed to sin, but alive unto God in Christ Jesus our Lord."
(EPISTLE: Rom. vi. 3–11.)
"If I shall send them away fasting to their home, they will faint in the way, for some of them came from afar off."
(GOSPEL: Mark viii. 1–9.)

ONE of the chief results of faithfulness to our divine Master in thought, word, and work is that promised to His faithful children as the chief object of His coming upon earth to live amongst them: "I am come," He says, "that they may have life, and may have it more abundantly." (John x. 10.)

Our holy mother the Church wishes us to consider to-day what this *life* really means, so that we might be grateful to Almighty God for what He has already done for us in the past, and that we might be led to further and fresher efforts to increase, strengthen and preserve by His gracious assistance that most precious of all the treasures the divine bounty has enriched us with or promised to us.

The word "life," as used in Sacred Scripture, has a variety of meanings. It is used to signify the natural course of man's existence upon earth from His birth to His death: "They shall add to thee length of days, and years of life and peace." (Prov. iii. 2.) It refers to the physical power of performing the actions of life: "Why is life given to them that are in bitterness of soul?" (Job iii. 20.) It includes the means of subsistence and the blessings accompanying it: "Be not solicitous for life, what you shall eat . . . the life is more than the meat." (Luke xii. 22, 23.)

Whilst all these various gifts are, as it were, the natural results of God's providence we have every reason to be grateful for them. God created us to His own image and likeness and continues to preserve us every moment of our existence: "Who hath set my soul to live: and hath not suffered my feet to be moved." (Ps. lxv. 9.) He has endowed us with an immortal soul, with the faculties of intelligence and free will and has given us the earth to be our portion. He supplies all the wants of our body with a loving Father's care, and if we trust in Him we need never be afraid: "The Lord is the protector of my life: of whom shall I be afraid?" (Ps. xxvi. 2.)

That Almighty God is most anxious to supply all the wants of our bodies is shown in the story of the miraculous multiplication of the loaves and fishes in the Gospel of to-day. Our divine master had on a previous occasion told the people who listened to His preaching that if they made it their first and chief business to attend to the wants of their souls, all things necessary for their bodies would in due course be supplied by the watchful and gracious providence of their Heavenly Father: "Be not solicitous, therefore, saying, What shall we eat, or what shall we drink, or wherewith shall we be clothed? For after all these things do the heathens seek. For your Father knoweth that you have need of all these things. Seek ye therefore first the kingdom of God, and His justice, and all these things shall be added unto you." (Matt. vi. 31–33.) So when the multitudes, who were anxious to listen once more to the Master's words of heavenly wisdom, heard that Jesus was in a distant part, their only thought was to set out and find Him, abandoning their worldly pursuits and not stopping even to provide themselves with the necessary food for the journey. So, as the Gospel relates, "When there was a great multitude with Jesus, and had nothing to eat; calling His disciples together, He saith to them: I have compassion on the multitude, for behold they have been with Me three days and have nothing to eat. And if I shall send them away fasting to their home, they will faint in the way, for some of them came from afar off."

Our divine Master, pleased with their zeal for hearing the words of life, and with their faith and trust in Him, determined to supply their bodily necessities by performing a most wonderful miracle. By this He wished not merely to show His power and prove His divinity, but also to foreshadow to them the heavenly food of the Blessed Eucharist which He was afterward to give them. The only provisions available were seven loaves and a few small fishes. These Jesus blessed and told His disciples to distribute them to the people, of whom there were about four thousand. And so it was done, the food miraculously multiplying during the process of distribution, until all were satisfied: "and they took up that which was left of the fragments, seven baskets."

But whilst Almighty God is ever anxious to supply the wants of the body and to preserve the natural life of His creatures, He created man for a higher purpose; namely, to know, love, and serve Him here on earth and afterward to see and enjoy Him forever in heaven. Man has therefore a higher and nobler life than that of a mere creature. He has the supernatural life of his immortal soul. And this Almighty God likewise sustains, strengthens, nourishes, and perfects by His ever watchful providence and abounding grace. Hence we have in Holy Scripture frequent references to another kind of life—a spiritual, supernatural, heavenly life, by which we live to God in His grace and love during our short sojourn in this vale of tears with the hope and promise of that eternal life in His heavenly kingdom which we hope to obtain through the infinite merits of our Lord and Saviour Jesus Christ.

By the sin of our first parents we lost all right to eternal life in heaven. But by the gracious mercy of our Heavenly Father, who loved us so much that He "spared not even His own Son, but delivered Him up for us all and hath also with Him given us all things" (Rom. viii. 32.), we were "born again" by virtue of the merits of our dear Redeemer applied to our souls in holy Baptism. And as God watches over and preserves the natural life of the body by His all-wise providence, so He watches over the spiritual welfare of the soul. Our Divine Lord and Master Jesus Christ,

AFTER PENTECOST

who fed the multitude in the wilderness with corporal food, will nourish our souls with the grace and merits purchased for us by the sacrifice of His own most precious body and blood. As St. Peter says: "The God of all grace, who hath called us unto eternal glory in Christ Jesus, after you have suffered a little, will Himself perfect you, and confirm you, and establish you" (1 Peter v. 10.); and St. Paul: "He who hath begun a good work in you, will perfect it unto the day of Christ Jesus" (Philipp. i. 6.).

Hence in the Epistle of to-day we are told that "all we who are baptized in Christ Jesus, are baptized in His death. For we are buried together with Him, by baptism unto death." That is, we are enabled by the merits of Jesus Christ to begin a new spiritual life after Baptism, as children restored to their lost inheritance, as dead in sin, risen to a new life with hope of eternal happiness.

But the goodness of Almighty God did not stop here. Even after our redemption and regeneration by the saving waters of Baptism we proved false to our regained friendship with our Creator and offended Him by actual sin. Once more we became dead to eternal life. Again we lost all right to heaven and deserved to be forever cut off from all hope of eternal happiness. But our good God "the same kindness which He showed to the living, He hath kept also to the dead" (Ruth ii. 20.), and Jesus Himself "hath appeared for the destruction of sin, by the sacrifice of Himself" (Heb. ix. 26.). This our divine Master accomplished by teaching us His love and mercy for the sinner and His desire for our conversion; by offering us His grace and help to rise from death to life by penance and mortification; and by His sweet forgiveness of us in His Sacrament of Reconciliation, where the merits of His sacred passion and death are applied to our souls by the words of absolution pronounced by His sacred minister, so that, as the Epistle says, "we may walk in newness of life . . . knowing that our old man is crucified with Him, that the body of sin may be destroyed, to the end that we may serve sin no longer."

Having once more, then, become "dead to sin, but alive unto God in Christ Jesus our Lord," our spiritual life must be preserved by proper nourishment. And the same divine Master who fed the multitude in the desert with bodily food, will feed us with His own body and blood in Holy Communion, for some of us, like some of them, have come to Jesus "from afar off," for we had strayed a great distance along the paths of sin. But now we are in His holy presence and under His protecting care. Let us listen to His teaching, act upon His advice, and endeavor to do His holy will in all things. Thus we shall be strong to walk in the path to our true home in His eternal kingdom and we shall not "faint in the way," for He has compassion on our weakness and will not send us on our journey fasting, but nourished to the full with the Bread of the strong, as the prophet Elias was nourished by an angel in the desert, "and walked in the strength of that food forty days and forty nights, unto the mount of God, Horeb" (3 Kings xix. 8.), where he had a vision of God.

The happy result of this zeal will be for us true life in the highest and best sense. For though Almighty God sometimes promises a long and happy life to those who serve Him faithfully in this world, He by no means gives us to understand that all virtuous and holy people shall be blessed with length of days and temporal prosperity. In His divine providence He foresees that such would not conduce to the ultimate benefit of many souls, the spiritual welfare of which is His supreme care. Neither does true happiness consist in length of days, or in temporal peace and prosperity, but in the knowledge, love, and service of Almighty God. In other words, the true disciple of Jesus Christ is supremely happy in spite of all the trials, temptations, troubles, and sufferings that surround Him, for He has the consciousness of doing His duty for the love of His divine Master and with the hope of an eternal reward for it. He experiences the truth of the Psalmist's promise: "O taste, and see that the Lord is sweet: blessed is the man that hopeth in Him" (Ps. xxxiii. 9.), as well as that of the promise of Jesus Himself: "Come to Me, all you that labor, and are burdened, and I will refresh you. Take up My yoke upon you, and learn of Me, because I am meek, and humble of heart: and you shall find rest to your souls. For My yoke is sweet, and My burden light" (Matt. xi. 28–30.). He can say with the Master Himself: "Now this is eternal life: That they may know Thee, the only true God, and Jesus Christ whom Thou hast sent. I have glorified Thee on the earth; I have finished the work which Thou gavest me to do." (John xvii. 3, 4.)

XLIII

SEVENTH SUNDAY AFTER PENTECOST

FRUITS

"What fruit therefore had you?"
(EPISTLE: Rom. vi. 19-23.)
"By their fruits you shall know them."
(GOSPEL: Matt. vii. 15-21.)

LAST SUNDAY we saw that one of the chief results of faithful and persevering labor in the service of our divine Master was true life and real happiness both in this world and in the next. To-day our holy mother the Church endeavors to warn us against mistaking the apparent for the true result by drawing our attention to those very signs and proofs of what is true and what is false religion, as given by our divine Master Himself. In the Gospel we are told to beware of false teachers, who have all the outward appearance of true followers of Christ, but whose real character is exposed by the nature of the results accruing from their teaching and principles—"By their fruits you shall know them." And in the Epistle we are warned against ourselves, so as to avoid even in our own case the error of confounding true and false virtue.

One of the greatest dangers against which the true Christian has to contend is that of error regarding the maxims and principles of the true Faith. Hence our divine Master was careful to warn the people of His own time against the false principles which ruled the conduct of the scribes and Pharisees. "Beware," He said to His disciples, "of the leaven of the Pharisees." (Matt. xvi. 6.) For, although the body of doctrine which they taught and explained to the people with due authority was literally correct according to the law of Moses, their interpretation of it in their own conduct was vitiated and corrupted by their evil intention. Hence Our Lord said: "The scribes and the Pharisees have sitten in the chair of Moses. All things whatsoever they shall say to you, observe and do; but according to their works do ye not; for they say and do not . . . And all their works they do for to be seen of men." (Matt. xxiii. 2–5.)

But if the Pharisees had the authority of God through Moses for the truth of the doctrines which they taught, what is to be said about the false teachers of the present day, who have neither authority, nor doctrine, nor principles admitted by Our Lord Jesus Christ?

No wonder, then, we are warned in to-day's Gospel to "Beware of false prophets, who come to you in the clothing of sheep, but inwardly they are ravening wolves," for the prophecy of our divine Master has come to pass: "There shall arise false Christs and false prophets, and shall show great signs and wonders, inasmuch as to deceive (if possible) even the elect." (Matt. xxiv.) These "false Christs and false prophets" come to seduce us not merely in person, but in the guise of interesting, instructive, and entertaining literature; in allegedly virtuous and helpful theatrical shows and moving-picture productions, where virtue always triumphs and vice is punished, but where vice is shown nevertheless in all its dangerous and seductive surroundings and circumstances; and in up-to-date theories in which a new era of peace, liberty of thought and action, happiness and plenty is speciously promised. But "by their fruits you shall know them," says Christ. They have nothing in common with the teachings of Jesus, and the fruits of their doctrines are seen in what St. Paul calls "the works of the flesh, which are fornication, uncleanness, contentions, emulations, wraths, quarrels, dissensions, sects, envies, murders, drunkenness, revelings and such like: Of the which I foretell you, as I have foretold to you, that they who do such things shall not obtain the kingdom of God." (Gal. v. 19–21.) A terrible but realistic picture of the state of those who listen to the teachings and poison their minds with the principles of our modern false prophets! How different is the condition of a peaceful, holy, Christlike Catholic community! "The fruit of the spirit," continues the same Apostle, "is charity, joy, peace, patience, benignity, goodness, longanimity, mildness, faith, modesty, continency, chastity." (v. 22–23.)

This warning of Jesus Christ is useful in helping us to distinguish false from true virtue not only in others but even in ourselves. "Not every one that saith to Me, Lord, Lord, shall enter into the kingdom of heaven," says our divine Master in the Gospel of to-day; "but he that doeth the will of My Father who is in heaven, he shall enter into the kingdom of heaven." There are some who fondly flatter themselves with hopes of eternal salvation because they consider themselves good Catholics and are not guilty of the more serious crimes: whilst at the same time they are guilty of some habit of secret sin which they lightly refer to as merely a weakness of theirs. The drunkard thinks he is not so bad because he is generous to his friends and charitable to the poor.

The impure man flatters himself that he is honest, sober, and upright in all his dealings. The dishonest man persuades himself that all is right because he gives a certain percentage of his ill-gotten gains to the Church. But are these valid titles to the possession of the kingdom of heaven? Our divine Master says emphatically that they are not, and that no one can be saved unless his justice is greater than that of the scribes and the Pharisees, whose ideas of virtue were much the same as the self-justifiers and eye-servers of the present day. It is not enough to keep only some of the commandments. We must keep them all without exception, as the Lord commanded Moses to tell the people—"That they may remember all the commandments of the Lord, and not follow their own thoughts and eyes going astray after divers things." (Deut. xv. 39.) This is what St. James means when he says: "Whosoever shall keep the whole law, but offend in one point, is become guilty of all. For He that said, Thou shalt not commit adultery, said also, Thou shalt not kill. Now if you do not commit adultery, but shalt kill, thou art become a transgressor of the law." (James ii. 10, 11.)

In the next place we must be doers of good works, for "every tree that bringeth not forth good fruit shall be cut down, and shall be cast into the fire." Hence St. Peter says: "If these things be with you and abound, they will make you to be neither empty nor unfruitful in the knowledge of our Lord Jesus Christ. For he that hath not these things with him is blind and groping!" (2 Peter i. 8, 9.) And St. James: "What shall it profit, if a man say he hath faith, but hath not works? Shall faith be able to save him? . . . But wilt thou know, O vain man, that faith without works is dead?" (James ii. 14–20.)

Are these the principles which have hitherto guided us? If so, we are "blind leaders of the blind," false prophets of our own salvation, clothed in the name only of that Christianity which we pretend to profess, but the unfortunate victims of self-destruction. Where are our fruits of holiness and justice? "I have appointed you," says Christ, "that you should go, and should bring forth fruit " (John xv. 16.). The only results we can show are useless and misspent lives, full of wasted opportunities, neglected graces, and criminal omissions, even of positive sin. As the Epistle says: "Do men gather grapes of thorns, or figs of thistles? Even so every good tree bringeth forth good fruit, and the evil tree bringeth forth evil fruit."

In order to encourage us to a complete change of life, that we might "now yield our members to serve justice unto sanctification" we are told in the Epistle to compare the personal fruits yielded respectively by a life of sin and a life of virtue. Even in the midst of so-called delights the sinners are not happy. Their false teacher the devil deceives them by promising them pleasure and contentment in the indulgence of their sensual appetites, but when they have followed his advice and abandoned true happiness for the sake of a fleeting pleasure, misery enters their breast and they feel the truth of those words of Holy Scripture: "There is no peace to the wicked, saith the Lord." (Isaias xlviii. 22.) And again: "Destruction and unhappiness in their ways: and the way of peace they have not known." (Ps. xiii. 3.) King David acknowledged his misery even in the midst of sensible delights, when he was at enmity with God and leading a life of sin: "My tears have been my bread day and night, whilst it is said to me daily: Where is thy God?" (Ps. xl. 4.) And King Solomon, who says he denied himself nothing, confesses the same truth: "And whatever my eyes desired, I refused them not: and I withheld not my heart from enjoying every pleasure, and delighting itself . . . and I saw in all things vanity and vexation of mind." (Eccles. ii. 10, 11.) So it is with all sinners, if they would only acknowledge it to themselves. But they try to deceive even themselves—"They have deceived my people, saying: Peace, and there is no peace." (Ezech. xiii. 10.) No wonder then St. Paul asks in the Epistle: "What fruit had you then in those things, of which you are now ashamed?"

But if the temporal happiness of the sinner is so illusory, the eternal misery which he earns for himself is as sure as the Word of God itself, which says: "Every tree that bringeth not forth good fruit shall be cut down, and shall be cast into the fire"—the everlasting fire of hell. No wonder such a one is called a "fool" in Holy Scripture: "Take thy rest," said the rich man to his soul, "eat, drink, make good cheer. But God said to him: Thou fool, this night do they require thy soul of thee." (Luke xii. 19, 20.) Truly, "the wages of sin is death."

What a different spirit possesses the souls of those who live orderly lives and work for God! "Delight in the Lord and He will give thee the requests of thy heart" (Ps. xxxvi. 4.), says the Psalmist. In spite of the storms that rage around them their hearts are filled with genuine peace and solid happiness, which is built on the consciousness of God's abiding presence with them, bringing them His "peace which surpasseth all understanding, keeping their hearts and minds in Christ Jesus." (Philipp. iv. 7.) And the only desire of their hearts is to be united forever with their divine Master in the kingdom of heaven. Which for them is a sure and certain hope, resting on the sacred promise of Almighty God Himself. They have indeed their "fruit unto sanctification, and the end life everlasting. For the wages of sin is death. But the grace of God, life everlasting, in Christ Jesus our Lord."

XLIV

EIGHTH SUNDAY AFTER PENTECOST

FRIENDS

"If you mortify the deeds of the flesh, you shall live." (EPISTLE: Rom. viii. 12–17.)
"Make unto you friends of the mammon of iniquity." (GOSPEL: Luke xvi. 1–9.)

WHEN two nations are at war it is the ardent endeavor of each to secure as many others as possible on its side, to make friends of those who might otherwise be enemies, or to cause them at least to remain neutral. In our struggle for salvation we have many enemies to contend against. As St. Paul says: "Our struggling is not against flesh and blood; but against principalities and powers, against the rulers of the world of this darkness, against the spirits of wickedness in the high places." (Eph. vi. 12.) With such we can never hope to make peace. There can be no truce with Satan and his followers. Their kingdom is the "unclean land" spoken of by the prophet Esdras, who warns us: "Seek not their peace, nor their prosperity for ever: that you may be strengthened, and may eat the good things of the land." (Esdras ix. 12.) Other spiritual kingdoms there are which by God's grace we may hope to keep as it were neutral, such as those referred to by St. John as "the concupiscence of the flesh, the concupiscence of the eyes, and the pride of life." (1 John ii. 16.) But there are kingdoms which by their very nature and constitution are opposed to us, but which we can make our friends and allies if we by God's help manage them properly. Such are the "deeds of the flesh" and the "mammon of iniquity" referred to in the Epistle and Gospel of to-day.

It is clearly laid down in the Epistle that man, who is composed of a body and soul and made to God's likeness, should be ruled by the higher and nobler spiritual part of his nature; for, as God is a spirit, and as we have been redeemed by the merits of our Lord Jesus Christ from the bondage of sin, and regenerated as children of Our Father in heaven, "we are the sons of God. And if sons, heirs also: heirs indeed of God, and joint heirs with Christ." So we should live according to the spirit and make a friend and ally of that body which otherwise would be our deadly and successful enemy—"For if you live according to the flesh you shall die. But if by the spirit you mortify the deeds of the flesh, you shall live."

This helps to explain the extraordinary parable of the unjust steward made use of by our divine Master in the Gospel, and His advice to us to be as careful and provident in making use of all the means at our disposal in order to secure our eternal salvation as wicked men are foreseeing and clever in securing the worldly advantages they propose to themselves. This steward was employed by a rich merchant to manage his business. Like many in similar positions at the present day, he was extravagant and wasteful and lived far beyond his income. To meet his expenses he applied to his own use a considerable amount out of his master's funds. And the latter came to hear of it. So he sent for him immediately, demanded the accounts and summarily dismissed him. Whereupon he realized the seriousness of his position. He could not hope for another similar engagement. He was unfitted for hard manual labor, and his pride prohibited him from depending on mere charity. He foresaw that unless he acted promptly he would be reduced to a very distressful condition. So he evolved an ingenious plan. He went round to each of his master's debtors and wrote off large amounts from their bills. They were as dishonest as he was himself in agreeing to such a proposal, but by his action he made them his friends and reasonably hoped that when he could no longer earn his own living they would all help to support him. When his master heard of his action he praised him for his wisdom and ingenuity, though of course he naturally felt strongly resentful at the dishonesty and injustice of his procedure. So our divine Master concludes that if such wickedness has such rare wisdom and sense to protect and provide for itself so securely, how much more ought not true virtue make use of all the lawful means within its power to secure for itself eternal life in the kingdom of heaven. But it is not so, He says, "for the children of this world are wiser in their generation than the children of light." And so he advises us to make friends of all those natural endowments which would otherwise become our enemies, making special reference to those material gifts of worldly riches and possessions which cause the ruin of so many souls and which He here calls "the mammon of iniquity."

Whatever gifts we possess, whether of nature or of grace, are given to us in trust by Almighty God, to be administered by us for His greater glory and for our own salvation and sanctification—"Every best gift, and every perfect gift, is from above, coming down from the Father of lights," says St. James. (i. 17.) And St. Peter clearly says we are merely "stewards of the manifold grace of God." (1 Peter iv. 10.) Hence it is our duty to make the most profitable use not only of the spiritual favors with which Almighty God in His gracious mercy endows us, but also of all those natural qualities of mind and body and other temporal blessings with which we are enriched. We must trade with our talents and take care not to hide them in the earth like the wicked and slothful servant who was cast out into exterior darkness; not, indeed, for wasting his master's goods, but for being an "unprofitable servant." (Matt. xxv. 14-30.) To us also when we least expect it the Master will come and demand an account of our stewardship. "Watch ye therefore," says Christ, "because you know not the day nor the hour." (Matt. xxv. 13.)

Our holy mother the Church calls our attention particularly to-day to the necessity of not merely employing our best and most perfect gifts to our greater spiritual advantage, but also of making friends of—(that is, of turning to useful account, according to the advice of our divine Master in the Gospel)—our own bodies, which, through the corruption of human nature by the fall of Adam, became as it were our natural enemies. According to Holy Scripture "a man's enemies are those of his own household" (Micheas vii. 6.) : "the corruptible body is a load upon the soul, and the earthly habitation presseth down the mind that museth upon many things." (Wis. ix. 15.) Hence, although by natural antipathy "the flesh lusteth against the spirit: and the spirit against the flesh: for these are contrary one to another: so that you do not the things that you would" (Gal. v. 17.), we can by God's grace make the enemy of the flesh a helpful and useful friend to the soul in assisting us to attain our eternal salvation.

And how is this to be accomplished? The answer is given in the Epistle: "If by the spirit you mortify the deeds of the flesh, you shall live."

In the state of innocence in which man was originally created, all the lower faculties of his carnal nature were in complete subjection to his spirit. But the soul having revolted against its Creator by sin, the body in turn revolted against the soul, and still urges it to evil even against its own reason. "The good which I will, I do not; but the evil which I will not, that I do," says St. Paul. (Rom. vii. 19.) Thus man's body by its sensual appetites rises against his spirit and is a source of continual trial and danger to him. Hence he is under the necessity of constantly subduing his lower nature if he wishes to avoid sin, not to say advance in virtue.

How utterly foolish it would be, then, to pamper that body which by its inordinate craving for the pleasures of the flesh is never satisfied—"The eye is not filled with seeing, nor is the ear filled with hearing" (Eccles. i. 8.), says Holy Scripture. Hence there is only one way to act, and that is to keep the body and the senses under control; to subdue them, train them, and make them the servants rather than the masters of the soul by constant self-denial and mortification, so that, as Holy Scripture says, "the lust thereof shall be under thee, and thou shalt have dominion over it." (Gen. iv. 7.) Thus what would otherwise be our most dangerous enemy—for it is always with us—will become our constant and faithful friend and ally. What would otherwise "serve uncleanness and iniquity, unto iniquity" will now "serve justice unto sanctification" (Rom. vi. 19.), and become "a living sacrifice, holy, pleasing unto God." (Rom. xii. 1.)

Such is the teaching of all the saints and

spiritual writers. Such was ever the precept and practice of our divine Master Himself, whose life was made for our encouragement and example one long course of mortification and suffering. He Himself had no need of it, for sin of any kind never had the slightest dominion over Him, and His most pure and holy body was always in complete and perfect subjection to His most holy soul. "Christ also suffered for us, leaving you an example that you should follow His steps. Who did no sin, neither was guile found in His mouth" (1 Peter ii. 21, 22.), says St. Peter, who proceeds with the advice: "Christ therefore having suffered in the flesh, be you also armed with the same thought: for He that hath suffered in the flesh, hath ceased from sins." (iv. 1.) Thus it was that the great Apostle of the Gentiles armed himself. "I chastise my body, and bring it into subjection," he says: "lest, perhaps, when I have preached to others, I myself should become a castaway." (1 Cor. ix. 27.)

Hence St. Paul exhorts us that "as we have borne the image of the earthly [Adam], let us bear also the image of the heavenly [Christ]" by constant mortification, for "flesh and blood can not possess the kingdom of God" (1 Cor. xv. 19, 20.) if allowed to take the upper hand. But if brought into subjection to the spirit we can truly say with St. Paul: "I live, now not I; but Christ liveth in me. And that I live now in the flesh: I live in the faith of the Son of God, who loved me, and delivered Himself for me." (Gal. ii. 20.)

The result will be that out of old enemies we shall have made new and steadfast friends that will help us on to final victory in the great struggle for salvation and will not only win for us the crown of eternal life but will make our lives really happy in this world also. "And when this mortal hath put on immortality, then shall come to pass the saying that is written: Death is swallowed up in victory . . . But thanks be to God, who hath given us the victory through our Lord Jesus Christ." (1 Cor. xv. 54, 57.)

XLV

NINTH SUNDAY AFTER PENTECOST

FAILURE

"Neither let us tempt Christ."
(EPISTLE: 1 Cor. x. 6–13.)
"Seeing the city, He wept over it."
(GOSPEL: Luke xix. 41–47.)

WHEN our divine Master was about to make His triumphant entry into Jerusalem, the Holy City came into view as He rested for a moment on the road from Bethany where it winds round the Mount of Olivet. As He stood in contemplation over the past glories of the favored race whom it represented, and saw in the holy temple, glittering in all its marvelous beauty, the expression and proof of the unlimited wonders of grace, mercy, and protection with which His Heavenly Father had cared for His chosen people, no sentiments of pleasure pervaded His divine bosom, no feelings of joy lit up His holy countenance, but His eyes became dimmed with tears, His Sacred Heart became filled with sorrow and regret, and, as the Gospel of to-day briefly relates, "seeing the city, He wept over it."

Why should Jesus weep on such a day, when He was actually about to enter the Holy City in triumph, to be received with joyful greetings by the populace, and to be hailed as the Son of David, as the promised Messias who was coming to save and sanctify them in the name of the Lord? It was because as God He knew the evils that were so soon to come upon it, and because as man, as the Son of David according to the flesh, He had a tender regard for it as representing His own people, the descendants of Abraham, to whom God had promised a blessed posterity, specially cared for and protected as His own people, of whom the Messias was to be born. But now He foresaw the failure of all the divine plans in their regard and He foretold the destruction of their city and temple, the pride and glory of their race—"For the days shall come upon thee: and thy enemies shall cast a trench about thee, and compass thee around and straiten thee every side, and beat thee flat to the ground, and thy children who are in thee: and they shall not leave in thee a stone upon a stone."

But there was a sadder and a deeper reason for the tears of Jesus than the forthcoming destruction of the mere material city and temple of Jerusalem. He knew that in spite of their joyful greetings to him of "Hosanna to the Son of David" those very same people would in a few days more cry out: "Away with Him! Away with Him! Crucify Him! Crucify Him!" They were His own people. He had come to save them, but they were, after acknowledging Him for a brief period, afterward finally to reject Him. "He came unto His own, and His own received Him not." (John i. 11.) Their approaching ruin, then, was to be the punishment of their own unfaithfulness, ingratitude, and hardness of heart—"Because thou hast not known the time of thy visitation."

Ever since Almighty God chose Abraham to be the father of the whole Israelite nation and promised that it should be a great nation and that from it should come the Redeemer and Saviour of all mankind, He lavishly showered upon His chosen people such a multitude of graces, blessings, and special favors of every kind as have no parallel in the history of the world. And neither is there any parallel in the history of any nation to the blindness, ingratitude, hard-heartedness, and obstinacy to the divine grace as that perverse and wicked people.

To Abraham and his descendants God gave as their special possession the land of Chanaan, which, on account of its beauty and fertility, is referred to in Holy Scripture as "a land that floweth with milk and honey" (Ex. iii. 8.), saying to him: "All the land which thou seest, I will give to thee, and to thy seed forever" (Gen. xiii. 15.), and assuring him: "Fear not, Abram, I am thy protector, and thy reward exceeding great." (Gen. xv. 1.)

Afterward, when the Jews were in bondage in Egypt, God raised up their great leader Moses who, by a succession of most amazing miracles, led them by the power of God from the hands of their oppressors; and God maintained them for many years in the desert, guiding them by means of a cloud by day and a pillar of fire by night, feeding them with food miraculously sent from heaven, quenching their thirst by water obtained from a rock by the mere touch of the rod of Moses, and giving them every proof of His divine care and protection.

But they were forgetful of and ungrateful for all God's care and kindness in their regard. They were constantly murmuring against Him in every little difficulty and even grievously insulting and offending Him in spite of all His favors, threats, and punishments, as is partly related in the Epistle of to-day: "Neither let us covet evil things, as they also coveted. Neither become ye idolaters, as some of them; as it is written: The people sat down to eat and drink, and rose up to play. Neither let us commit fornication, as some of them committed fornication, and there fell in one day three and twenty thousand. Neither let us tempt Christ: as some of them tempted, and perished by the serpents. Neither do you murmur: as some of them murmured, and were destroyed by the destroyer."

Nor did the mercies of God to His people cease even then. He sent them great kings, wise judges, mighty warriors to rule, guide, defend and protect them; holy prophets to make known to them His will, to warn them against their evil ways and to assure them of His continued Fatherly care. But all in vain. At last He sent His own divine Son, who appeared in the flesh amongst them as their promised Messias, healing their sick, curing their blind, raising their dead to life, and shedding all over their nation the rays of His divine presence and holy blessing. But Him also they rejected. This was their last great grace—"the time of their visitation." No wonder, then, that our Lord Jesus Christ, on the day of His entry into Jerusalem, paused to weep over the coming destruction of the Holy City and its temple. No wonder His human heart was stricken with grief, for His divine mind foresaw the ruin for them not only of these sad reminders of His love for them, but also of His last hopes for their redemption as a nation, and of all His plans for their temporal and eternal happiness which were but to end in failure.

Not many years afterward the sad prophecy of Jesus was fulfilled to the very letter. The emperor of Rome laid siege to the Holy City, conquered it, demolished it, and reduced its temple to such complete destruction that "not even a stone was left upon a stone." In the meantime, worse calamity had befallen the people themselves, for they had not only rejected their Saviour but had blasphemed, mocked, spat upon, scourged and crucified Him, and had called down the curse of His precious blood from heaven upon their nation —"And the whole people, answering, said: His blood be upon us and upon our children." (Matt. xxvii. 25.)

As the Epistle says: "All these things happened to them in figure: and they are written for our correction, upon whom the ends of the world are come." The chosen people of Israel, favored though they were by God's most special care, are but a figure of us enriched as we have been by God's choicest favors. The city and temple of the Holy City, rich, glorious, and beautiful though they were, are but figures of the human soul, the City of God, the temple of the Holy Ghost, shining under the light of God's grace, "bought with a great price" (1 Cor. vi. 20.)—the most precious blood of Our Lord Jesus Christ. Our Promised Land is heaven itself: our great leader is Jesus; our guide by day and by night is our holy Faith; our nation is the holy Church; our food and drink is the body and blood, soul and divinity of Our Lord Jesus Christ Himself.

Therefore, before we condemn the Jews for their cruel ingratitude, let us examine ourselves and see if when Jesus was about to enter the holy city of our soul in triumph on the day of our Baptism, of our first confession, of our first holy communion, of our Confirmation, or on any other of those wonderful occasions when He pays us a special and official visit, He could foresee any signs of future ruin and destruction to grieve His Sacred Heart. Alas! If the sight of Jerusalem and its temple drew from Him tears of pity, the sight of the holy city and temple of our soul caused Him to suffer a sweat of blood when in the garden of Gethsemani He foresaw its future fate through our ingratitude and sin! If the Jews were instructed and warned by the prophets about the consequences of sin, we have been taught by Jesus Himself. "God," says St. Paul, "who at sundry times and in divers manners, spoke in times past to the Fathers by the prophets, last of all in these days hath spoken to us by His Son." (Heb. i. 1.) If His own people rejected Him in favor of the wicked Barabbas, we have by sin despised Him for the sake of a vile passion, a little gain, a filthy pleasure. They in their blindness and ignorance put Him to death. We by sin "crucify again to ourselves the Son of God, and make a mockery of Him." (Heb. vi. 6.)

"Jerusalem, Jerusalem, thou that killest the prophets, and stonest them that are sent unto thee, how often would I have gathered together thy children, as the hen doth gather her chickens under her wings, and thou wouldest not!" (Matt. xxiii. 37.), said our divine Master to them and to us. And again: "Hear, O ye heavens, and give ear, O earth, for the Lord hath spoken. I have brought up children, and exalted them; but they have despised Me. The ox knoweth his owner, and the ass

AFTER PENTECOST

his master's crib; but Israel hath not known Me, and My people hath not understood. . . . They have forsaken the Lord, they have blasphemed the Holy One of Israel, they are gone backwards." (Isaias i. 2–4.)

Thanks be to the good God, who still speaks such words to us! It shows that even yet "the time of our visitation" has not passed; for every such message as that given to us to-day is a visit from the Master. He has often before called us to repentance but we have "gone backwards." If we refuse Him now He may never call us again. "When tribulation and distress shall come upon you: then shall they call upon Me and I will not hear," He says. Neither will He then weep over us, but "will laugh in our destruction." (Prov. i.)

Let us, then, try to realize to-day "the things that are to our peace" and so prevent the eternal ruin of our soul. Let us purify that holy temple by casting out all affection for sin and its occasions. It will then be for us once more our "Father's house, a house of prayer," where we shall evermore harken to the voice of Jesus our divine Master "teaching daily in the temple" how to make certain future success out of past miserable failure.

XLVI

TENTH SUNDAY AFTER PENTECOST

SUCCESS

"No man can say, the Lord Jesus, but by the Holy Ghost."
(Epistle: 1 Cor. xii. 2–11.)
"This man went down into his house justified rather than the other."
(Gospel: Luke xviii. 9–14.)

WE saw last Sunday something of what failure means. But who can judge of success? The very word itself has such a variety of meanings, depending upon the point of view from which one considers the matter—whether one takes up a spiritual or a material attitude; whether one looks for present and immediate results, or is prepared to wait longer for more valuable and far-reaching effects; whether one seeks his own glory or that of God; his own profit or that of others; whether he is satisfied with what is really valuable, though not brilliant or conspicuous; or prefers what strongly appeals to the multitude—that it is impossible for us to form a correct estimate from the weak and fallible standard of poor human ideals. Even in the same individual these are constantly changing. The young man on the threshold of life, who sets forth to carve out for himself a successful career, is often bitterly disappointed when in maturer years he actually attains the object of his youthful ambition, which now appears to be totally unworthy of all his previous labor and solicitude. Having grasped the rosy apple for which he reached, he finds in his hands nothing but ashes. No; the matter must be examined in the light of man's superior spiritual destiny, for, as St. Paul says: "The sensual man perceiveth not these things that are of the Spirit of God; for it is foolishness to him, and he can not understand, because it is spiritually examined." (1 Cor. ii. 14.)

From the point of view of many, Christ's mission was a failure. From the personal and human standpoint of Christ Himself as man, His life and work would indeed in one sense appear at first sight to be a failure, for He died as a criminal on the cross, His work not completed, His mission unaccomplished, nay, not even acknowledged by those for whom it had been undertaken. Thus as man He wept over Jerusalem and deplored in accents of human grief His failure to accomplish the things that were to bring it peace, for He foresaw not only its spiritual but even its material destruction.

We all know, however, that the mission of our divine Master was not only a success but a triumph. For even though He died as a criminal on Good Friday, He rose in glory on Easter Sunday. And though His human life was ended in the knowledge of His failure to convert His chosen people, yet it began again and furnished by the wonderful mystery of His resurrection an indisputable proof of His divine authority to attempt it. Ever since, by the marvelous spread and wonderful success of the Christian religion all over the world— in itself the greatest of all the miracles which so abundantly support its truth and its divinity—the work of Our Lord Jesus Christ upon earth is daily more and more being acknowledged even by His enemies as a magnificent and unqualified success.

Our holy mother the Church to-day, therefore, wishes to show us that we are to judge of success from a higher standpoint than that of mere material and present effects. That, being children of a spiritual kingdom, we must look to the real result of our efforts, not considering the material praise or profit they may bring us here and now or at any time in this life from the opinions of men, but the eternal reward which they will merit for us in the sight of Almighty God, who alone can judge aright, for He alone knows all the circumstances. Even if we should gain all the honor and glory and all the material rewards possible, but did not please God, our work would be a failure. "What shall it profit a man, if he gain the whole world, and suffer the loss of his soul?" says St. Mark (viii. 36.).

Nor are we to judge of our success even from a spiritual point of view by what can be observed in us either by ourselves or by others. "To me," says St. Paul, "it is a very small thing to be judged by you or by man's day; but neither do I judge my own self. For I am not conscious to myself of anything, yet am I not hereby justified; but he that judgeth me is the Lord. Therefore judge not before the time; until the Lord come, who both will bring to light the hidden things of darkness and will make manifest the counsels of the hearts; and then shall every man have praise from God." (1 Cor. iv. 3–5.)

What the amount of that praise will be will depend upon the share which we shall have taken in co-operating with the grace which Almighty God dispenses in varying measure to each one, and not upon the results alone, for He does not expect equal results from all. As the Epistle of to-day points out: "To one, indeed, by the Spirit, is given the word of wisdom; and to another, the word of knowledge, according to the same Spirit: to another, faith in the same Spirit: to another, the grace of healing in one Spirit: to another, the work of miracles: to another, prophecy: to another, the discerning of spirits: to another, divers kinds of tongues: to another, interpretation of speeches. But all these things one and the same Spirit worketh, dividing to every one according as He will." Hence the brilliant results of some of our actions may be due entirely to the work of God, whilst we as His humble instruments for its accomplishment may deserve blame rather than praise for our share in it. Thus our divine Master on one occasion said to His disciples: "Many will say to Me in that day: Lord, Lord, have we not prophesied in Thy name, and cast out devils in Thy name, and done many miracles in Thy name? And then will I profess unto them, I never knew you: depart from Me, you that work iniquity." (Matt. vii. 22, 23.)

That God does not expect equal results from all is therefore clear, seeing that the effects of such divers gifts are themselves so totally different. This is also shown in the parable of the talents. To one man his master gave five talents; to another, two; and to another, one. The first gained five others by trading with them. The second gained two others in like manner. But the third hid his talent in the earth and gained nothing. When the master returned he rewarded and praised equally the first and second, saying to each: "Well done, good and faithful servant: because thou hast been faithful over a few things, I will place thee over many things: enter thou into the joy of thy Lord." (Matt. xxv. 23.) But the third he punished because, though he restored his talent, he had neglected to trade with it and had gained nothing.

The parable of the laborers in the vineyard proves the same thing. The master of the vineyard hired laborers at different hours during the day—some early in the morning, some at the third hour, some at the sixth, some at the ninth, and some even at the eleventh hour. At the end of the day he paid them all alike a day's wages, though those who had worked all day complained, saying: "These last have worked but one hour, and thou hast made them equal to us, that have borne the burden of the day and the heats." (Matt. xx. 12.)

That we are able to merit any reward at all in the supernatural order is entirely due to the grace and assistance of the Holy Ghost and the merits of Our Lord Jesus Christ. As St. Paul says in the Epistle, "no man can say, the Lord Jesus, but by the Holy Ghost." And again: "We are not sufficient to think anything of ourselves as of ourselves: but our sufficiency is from God." (2 Cor. iii. 5.) And Christ Himself says: "Without Me you can do nothing." (John xv. 5.) Yet we can not only resist temptation, but merit grace and eternal life by the help of "the same God, who worketh all in all," if we only pray. "If you shall ask Me anything in My name, that I will do," says Christ Himself (John xiv. 14.); and so St. Paul assures us: "I can do all things in Him who strengtheneth me" (Philipp. iv. 13.), "who will render to every man according to his works." (Rom. ii. 16.)

We are, therefore, entirely incapable of judging of the degree of success or failure in which the work of any one results in the sight of God. "All is not gold that glitters," and the most apparently successful results are often only the saddest failure, just as the most shining piety, which obtains for a man the respect of his neighbors, is not always the most solid or the most perfect in the sight of God, as is clear from the story of the Pharisee and the publican in the Gospel of to-day.

These two men went up to the same place to perform the same good work of prayer. The Pharisee was an apparently virtuous and holy man and highly respected as such. The publican was quite the opposite. He was indeed "an extortioner, unjust, and an adulterer." The Pharisee told the truth about himself too, for in reality he did fast and give tithes and was not guilty of those serious crimes to which he called attention in the case of the poor publican. But which of them was successful in his work of prayer? Our divine Master Himself tells us that "this man went down into his house justified rather than the other." That is, the sinner obtained grace, mercy, and forgiveness before God; but the proud and haughty self-justifier only rendered himself more guilty in His sight.

Would not the world have naturally thought the opposite? But "shall not God search out these things: for He knoweth the secret of the heart," says the Psalmist. (Ps. xliii. 22.) God saw in the Pharisee pride, vainglory, and above all want of charity. He saw in the publican humility, self-abasement, and the good intention. Which teaches us that no matter how sinful we may have been in the past, no matter how our lives have been withered by failure, God is ever ready to raise the fallen, to succor the sinner and by His grace lead him to true success. Whilst they who by their outward appearance of virtue have gained the good opinion of their neighbors and rejoiced in apparent success will gain very little praise or reward from God unless their actions are accompanied by that inward spirit of faith, humility, and trust in God by which they do all for His sake and give Him thanks for the success, for "Unless the Lord build the house, they labor in vain that build it." (Ps. cxxvi. 1.)

Let us, then, in such a spirit of faith and confidence look to our divine Master alone for true success. If we achieve anything of good in this life, let us humbly say: "Not to us, O Lord, not to us: but to Thy name give glory." (Ps. cxiii. 1.) At the last day Christ will show to all men not only the success of His own divine mission but likewise that of all His true disciples, whose lives were perhaps thought a failure by those who, in spite of apparent success, will then stand condemned, like those who will claim to have worked even miracles but whom the Lord will profess never to have known (Matt. vii. 22, 23.). Looking at the glory of the just they will sadly acknowledge: "These are they, whom we have had some time in derision, and for a parable of re-

AFTER PENTECOST

proach. We fools esteemed their lives madness, and their end without honor. Behold how they are numbered among the children of God, and their lot is among the saints." (Wis. v. 2–5.)

XLVII

ELEVENTH SUNDAY AFTER PENTECOST

MIRACLES

"His grace in me hath not been void."
            (EPISTLE: 1 Cor. xv. 1–10.)
"He hath done all things well."
            (GOSPEL: Mark vii. 31–37.)

LEST any of her children should be discouraged by past failure, and lest the difficulty of the work of their future salvation should lead them to abandon all hope of success, our holy mother the Church to-day endeavors to renew our courage and strength, and to infuse into our souls trust and confidence in God's mercy and power. For our dear Redeemer has the most loving and sincere desire to save all sinners, especially those who are conscious of their miserable state, as the prophet Ezechiel explains: "Thou, therefore, O son of man, say to the house of Israel: Thus you have spoken, saying: Our iniquities and our sins are upon us, and we pine away in them. How then can we live? Say to them: As I live, saith the Lord God, I desire not the death of the wicked, but that the wicked turn from his way and live. Turn ye, turn ye from your evil ways: and why will you die, O house of Israel?" (Ezech. xxxiii. 10, 11.) He has at the same time the power of a God to help us, which will stop at nothing and will accomplish even miracles in order to assist us, as is shown in the Epistle and Gospel of to-day.

In the latter is related the story of the miraculous cure of the deaf and dumb man. He was brought to our divine Master by his friends, who asked with beautiful and simple faith that the Saviour would "lay His hand upon him." This He not only did but "taking him from the multitude apart, He put His fingers into his ears, and spitting, He touched his tongue; and looking up to heaven, He groaned, and said to him: Ephpheta, which is, Be thou opened." And the result was a perfect cure, so that all who witnessed it acknowledged the divine power of Jesus, saying: "He hath done all things well."

This was a miracle in the natural order, performed by Jesus for the cure of a bodily infirmity. In the Epistle reference is made to a miracle in the supernatural order; namely, the conversion of St. Paul and his wonderful success in the ministry of Christ, for he was changed from being a notorious persecutor of the Christians to become the great Apostle of the Gentiles. This wonderful transformation St. Paul himself attributes to the grace of God and his co-operation with it—"By the grace of God I am what I am: and His grace in me hath not been void." The same result he promises to those who like himself receive the Gospel in the proper spirit and mold their lives upon its teaching—"By which also you are saved, if you hold fast after what manner I have preached unto you, unless you have believed in vain." And as firm faith in the divinity of Jesus Christ is the chief doctrine of that Holy Gospel, he briefly refers to the principal proofs of it by quoting the authority of many of those who had seen our Blessed Saviour after His resurrection, as well as by adducing his own personal proof of it: "And last of all, He was seen also by me, as by one born out of due time. For I am the least of the apostles, who am not worthy to be called an apostle, because I persecuted the Church of God. But by the grace of God I am what I am; and His grace in me hath not been void."

Paul was a young man from Asia who had come to Jerusalem to study the law. He was highly respected by the Jews on account of his great zeal for their faith and his fierce hatred of Christianity. He was one of those who ad-

AFTER PENTECOST 165

vised the execution of St. Stephen, the first martyr, and actually held the outer garments of the executioners while they were carrying out the sentence of stoning the saint to death. He continued his work of persecution with great zeal and went from house to house dragging out Christians for punishment on account of their holy Faith. Because of this numbers of them fled from Jerusalem to Damascus. So Paul volunteered to pursue them, and was accordingly commissioned to do so, being supplied with a band of armed men to assist him. On the road to Damascus a great light suddenly appeared from heaven, and Paul was struck to the ground, blinded, whilst a voice cried to him: "Saul, Saul, why persecutest thou Me?" And he answered: "Who art Thou, Lord?" And the Lord said: "I am Jesus of Nazareth whom thou persecutest." And when Paul asked "What shall I do, Lord?" he was told to go to a holy man named Ananias, in Damascus. He was accordingly led thither and shortly afterward received his sight and his holy faith and became "a vessel of election, to carry the name of the Lord before the Gentiles, and kings, and the children of Israel." (Acts ix. 15; xxii.) If our ears have been stopped so that we can no longer hear the voice of God calling us to repentance;

if our tongues have been tied so that we no longer ask Him for mercy and forgiveness, our condition is indeed serious. It shows that Almighty God has abandoned us—"We would have cured Babylon," He says by the mouth of His prophet, "but she is not healed: let us forsake her." (Jer. li. 9.) When God abandons the sinner on account of his repeated refusals to listen to the call of divine grace, the unfortunate soul is lulled into a kind of false security. He does not consider the next life, death, judgment, hell, or heaven, and is as content in the enjoyment of his unlawful pleasures as if it had been specially revealed to him that his soul was predestined for eternal happiness in spite of sin. This condition is caused chiefly by the withdrawal of the grace of the fear of God's punishments, which is in itself the greatest punishment. "For, because sentence is not speedily pronounced against the evil, the children of men commit evils without any fear" (Eccles. viii. 11.), says Holy Scripture. And again: "The wicked man when he is come into the depth of sin contemneth." (Prov. xviii. 3.) This is because God in His anger has taken away the hedge of His holy fear from the vineyard of the soul—"I will take away the hedge thereof, and it shall be wasted." (Isaias v. 5.)

No matter what our condition may be, however, we must never despair of God's mercy, for "the Lord is sweet to all: and His tender mercies are over all His works" (Ps. cxliv. 9.), so that the sinner who despairs actually deprives God of His dearest attribute and prerogative. Let us, then, have great confidence in our good God, who says of the sinner: "Because he hoped in Me I will deliver him: I will protect him because he hath known My Name. He shall cry to Me, and I will hear him: I am with him in tribulation, I will deliver him, and I will glorify him" (Ps. xc. 14, 15.); and who has promised by the mouth of His prophet to heal all his infirmities—"God Himself will come and will save you. Then shall the eyes of the blind be opened, and the ears of the deaf shall be unstopped. Then shall the lame man leap as a hart, and the tongues of the dumb shall be free." (Isaias xxxv. 4, 5.) The miracle of the cure of the deaf and dumb man in the Gospel is but a figure of the greater miracle God will perform in the soul of the sinner. He who "hath done all things well" will still continue to exercise His divine power in favor of those who most require it. When the grace of God touches the sinner's heart, tears of repentance will follow—"Waters are broken out in the desert, and streams in the wilderness," says the prophet. (Isaias xxxv. 6.) Then, like St. Paul, the poor sinner will hear the voice of the Master saying to him: "Why dost thou persecute Me?" Then he will be able to say with confidence: "Lord, what wilt Thou have me to do?" for he will be able once more to hear and speak aright, and to act aright also, realizing that he "can do all things in Him that strengtheneth him." (Philipp. iv. 13.)

Whilst we must never despair of God's mercy, neither must we ever presume upon it. As St. Paul says in the Epistle: "I make known unto you the Gospel which I preached to you, which also you have received, and wherein you stand; by which also you are saved, if you hold fast after what manner I preached unto you, unless you have believed in vain." This is the unchanging and unchangeable gospel of true repentance for our past sins and a firm resolution of sinning no more. He who delays his conversion in the hope of at length obtaining God's mercy will surely be deprived of it. "Say not, The mercy of the Lord is great, He will have mercy on the multitude of my sins. For mercy and wrath quickly come from Him, and His wrath looketh upon sinners, Delay not to be converted to the Lord, and defer it not from day to day. For His wrath shall come on a sudden, and in time of vengeance He will destroy thee." (Ecclus. v. 6–9.) St. Paul also warns us of this dangerous error: "Be not deceived, God is not mocked. For what things a man shall sow, those also shall he reap" (Gal. vi. 7, 8.): and again: "Despisest thou the riches of His goodness, and patience, and long-suffering? Knowest thou not that the benignity of God leadeth thee to penance?" (Rom. ii. 4.) This very benignity of God leads many to presume still further, and because He does not immediately punish them they continue still further to offend Him. Hence He says to such: "These things hast thou done, and I was silent. Thou thoughtest unjustly that I should be like to thee: but I will reprove thee, and set before thy face. Understand these things, you that forget God; lest He snatch you away, and there be none to deliver you." (Ps. xlix. 20–23.)

Yes. The benignity of God will lead us to penance rather than to despair or presumption by which we should despise the riches of His goodness and mercy. "He hath done all things well; He hath made both the deaf to hear, and the dumb to speak." "To-day," then, "if you shall hear His voice, harden not your hearts" (Ps. xciv. 8.), but with all the powers of your soul humbly beseech your divine Master "that

He would lay His hand upon you." He will "take you from the multitude apart" and touch not only your ears and your tongue but your heart and your soul. "I will lead her into the wilderness," He promises, "and I will speak to her heart." (Osee ii. 14.) He will take you away from the dangers that surround you and make your past experience of failure and sin a source of your greatest strength and most solid virtue, by leading you to trust entirely in Him. "Be you humbled, therefore, under the mighty hand of God," says St. Peter, "that He may exalt you in the time of visitation: casting all your care upon Him, for He hath care of you." (1 Peter v. 6.)

Then indeed will take place in your favor the greatest miracle of all, for by the grace of God "Waters are broken out in the desert, and streams in the wilderness. And that which was dry land, shall become a pool, and the thirsty land springs of water . . . and a path and a way shall be there, and it shall be called the holy way . . . And the redeemed of the Lord shall return, and shall come into Sion with praise, and everlasting joy shall be upon their heads." (Isaias xxxv. 6–10.)

XLVIII

TWELFTH SUNDAY AFTER PENTECOST

PRIVILEGES

"How shall not the ministration of the Spirit be rather in glory?"
(Epistle: 2 Cor. iii. 4-9.)

"Many prophets and kings have desired to see the things that you see, and have not seen them: and to hear the things that you hear, and have not heard them."
(Gospel: Luke x. 23-37.)

WHEN Moses went up into the mountain to speak with the Lord he remained there forty days and forty nights and returned with the Tables of the Law. God had promised him among other things that He would do wonderful things for His people; that He would be "merciful and gracious, patient and of much compassion, and true, keeping mercy unto thousands: taking away iniquity, and wickedness, and sin" (Ex. xxxiv. 6, 7.); that He would "do signs such as were never seen upon the earth, nor in any nations." (10.) And when the great leader returned to announce the Word of the Lord to the people "they could not steadfastly behold his face for the glory of his countenance," as the Epistle of to-day relates, because his face was shining so brightly "from the conversation of the Lord." That was under the Old Law, the law of fear and servitude. And God kept His promise, for, as we know, He performed such wonders for His chosen people in delivering them out of the hands of their enemies—miraculously supporting them in the desert and giving them such constant and forceful reminders of His personal care of them—that it could be truly said that such signs of His love "were never seen upon the earth, nor in any nations." (Ex. xxxiv. 10.)

But the Old Law has passed away and the holy countenance of the great lawgiver, which shone with the glory of the Lord, is also "made void." Great as were the proofs of God's fatherly care of the Jews, and wonderful as were the manifestations of His regard for the chosen people, they fade into comparative insignificance when we consider what He has done for those children whom He has begotten in His love rather than in His fear, "by the word of truth" rather than by threats of punishment.

Hence our attention is called to-day to the

wonderful privileges which we possess as Christians and Catholics, as the loving friends of our divine Master, as faithful children of His holy Church. "Blessed are the eyes that see the things that you see," says the Gospel, "for I say to you that many prophets and kings have desired to see the things that you see, and have not seen them; and to hear the things that you hear, and have not heard them."

What have we seen? And what have we heard? We have seen "the glory of the Lord with open face" (2 Cor. iii. 18.) and we have heard the voice of God speaking to us in accents of love and sympathy in the person of His own Divine Son, our Lord and Saviour Jesus Christ. We have received the gift of faith, by which we see everything in its true light. It is more to us than the cloud by day and the pillar of fire by night which guided the Israelites through the desert on their way to the Promised Land, for it guides us with unerring certainty through the desert of this world with all its snares and dangers to our true home in heaven. It shows us God Himself ever present with us—Jesus, "the way, and the truth, and the life" (John xiv. 6.), ever ready to provide us with the food and drink of our souls which will strengthen them unto life everlasting. "Your fathers did eat manna in the desert," He said, "and are dead. . . . If any man eat of this bread, he shall live forever; and the bread that I will give, is My flesh, for the life of the world." (John vi. 49–52.)

Born in the bosom of the holy Catholic Church, we have ever been favored children of Almighty God. We have been made to realize the real value of life, the emptiness of the world, and its vanities, and the true happiness of serving God here for a time so as to enjoy His presence afterward in heaven forever. If God promised to do great things for the Jews and miraculously led them to the Promised Land after wandering for forty years in the desert, He has done more for us by calling us from our earliest years to enjoy in His holy House on the holy mount the favor of His intimate presence. "I will bring them into My holy mount, and will make them joyful in My house of prayer: their holocausts and their victims shall please Me upon My altar; for My house shall be called the house of prayer for all nations." (Isaias lvi. 7.) In the holy Catholic Church we have met our God without fear, as a dear and familiar friend. There we have made the acquaintance of Jesus Himself in person, and have obtained that personal and intimate knowledge of Him such as His holy Mother and St. Joseph were privileged to enjoy during His residence with them in the holy house at Nazareth. There we have learned to love His holy Mother as our own, for there it was that Jesus gave us to her as her dear children. And there we have learned to admire and be comforted by the example of the devoted, lowly Joseph, the faithful guardian of the Holy Family.

What love we have learned at the foot of the cross on which our divine Master died to show us His love! What grace and mercy we have experienced when in the sacred tribunal of penance our sins were blotted out by the merits of His precious blood! What feelings of peace we enjoyed, what strength to our souls we obtained when we knelt at the altar and received the precious food of His body and blood! What odors of sweetness we were able to send up to heaven in the sight of the Divine Majesty when we devoutly and reverently assisted at the holy sacrifice of the Mass! What favors and blessings we received through the intercession and merits of that spotless and holy Victim! What instruction and advice, what consolation and hope, what warning and help we received when we listened to the very words of the Master Himself from the lips of His anointed minister! What help in our difficulties, what relief in our sufferings, what trust in God's care of us we feel when, in a spirit of love and union with all the angels and saints in heaven, we kneel in His presence before the Blessed Sacrament of His love and with lively sentiments of faith, adoration, humility, and thanksgiving send up our petitions in the very presence of our divine Master ever present in the tabernacle of the altar! And even when that great privilege is denied to us, how glad we feel as we say our morning and evening prayers, recite the holy Rosary of His blessed Mother, wear her scapular, or gaze with affection upon her picture! Truly we may say, in the words of God Himself: "Neither is there any other nation so great, that hath gods so nigh them, as our God is present to all our petitions. What other nation is there so renowned, that hath ceremonies, and just judgments, and all the law, which I will set forth this day before your eyes?" (Deut. iv. 7, 8.)

But Almighty God continues: "Keep thyself, therefore, and thy soul carefully. Forget not the words that thy eyes have seen, and let them not go out of thy heart all the days of thy life." (Deut. iv. 9.) For, as the Epistle says: "If the ministration of death, engraved with letters upon stones, was glorious . . . how shall not the ministration of the Spirit be rather in glory?" That is, if the Old Law was accompanied by such visible manifestations of God's presence as appeared upon the face of Moses, how should not the New Law engraven in our hearts by God show forth in our lives the bright results of His holy presence! We ought to be like our divine Master, for we are "predestinated to be made conformable to the image of His Son." (Rom. viii. 29.) Every thought, every word, and every action of ours, then, should be worthy of His teaching and example. Our whole lives should be formed according to His model of perfection; not merely carrying out the letter of His precepts in a grudging fashion but doing everything according to His spirit—"Who hath made us fit ministers of the new testament, not in the letter, but in the spirit. For the letter killeth: but the spirit quickeneth."

An instance of this proper spirit is given in the Gospel of to-day in the story of the Good Samaritan, related by our divine Master as an answer to a Jewish lawyer who had questioned Him concerning the law of charity. The Samaritans were despised by the Jews because they did not profess the true faith. Yet when a certain man was wounded and robbed he found only a Samaritan to assist him. The priest and the Levite, who knew the exact letter of the law, both passed him by. But he who was ignorant of its letter possessed its proper spirit, for the Samaritan charitably attended to the unfortunate man, dressed his wounds, and paid for his care and keep at an inn. In this he showed real love of his neighbor, and our divine Master advised the lawyer to "Go, and do in like manner," although the latter had previously acknowledged and repeated the precept of charity to God and the neighbor.

Hence it is not enough to be born in the true Faith, to be regular in attendance at Church, or even at the sacraments, to pray much, to give alms, to keep the commandments according to the letter. We must perform all these good works with the right intention and in the proper spirit; that is, for the pure and sincere love of God. Many have done these things, and more, but God has said to them, "You have received your reward." Many have enjoyed the privileges which we enjoy, and have done the works which we do, and greater, but they have never heard the consoling words: "Well done, thou good and faithful servant." Nay, Our Lord Himself tells us that at the last day "Many will say to Me in that day: Lord, Lord, have we not prophesied in Thy name, and cast out devils in Thy name, and done many miracles in Thy name?

And then will I profess unto them, I never knew you: depart from Me, you that work iniquity." (Matt. vii. 22, 23.)

What a pity that such immense and wonderful privileges as we enjoy should be wasted or unappreciated! How little we can depend upon ourselves for the fruit of them! Let us, then, humbly acknowledge our weakness and ingratitude. "We are not sufficient to think anything of ourselves, as ourselves, but our sufficiency is from God." Let us depend with great confidence on the grace and assistance of Almighty God, doing everything for His sake, showing charity to all in thought, word, and deed. If we thus labor in His service we can confidently say with St. Paul: "I can do all things in Him who strengtheneth me." (Philipp. iv. 13.) He will make us "fit ministers of the new testament, not in the letter, but in the spirit." And "as to the rest, there is laid up for us a crown of justice, which the Lord the just judge will render to us in that day." (2 Tim. iv. 8.)

XLIX

THIRTEENTH SUNDAY AFTER PENTECOST

GRATITUDE

"That the promise by the faith of Jesus Christ might be given to them that believe."
(Epistle: Gal. iii. 16–22.)

"There is no one found to return and give glory to God, but this stranger."
(Gospel: Luke xvii. 11–19.)

WHEN we consider the many wonderful privileges which we enjoy under the New Law of grace and love and liberty, we may perhaps be inclined to imagine that it is, as it were, a piece of so-called good fortune to have been born in these happy days of greatest favors. And lest we might accordingly be wanting in gratitude to the Giver of all good gifts, our holy mother the Church to-day wishes to impress upon us the great necessity for personal thankfulness to Almighty God, whose special mercies we enjoy not through any chain of accidental circumstances but through the personal love which He has for the soul of each one of us in sending His only-begotten Son to redeem and save us, according to His express promise.

Our attention is therefore drawn in the Epistle to the fact which St. Paul endeavored to impress upon the members of the Church in Galatia, namely, that although the Old Law intervened between the promise of God to Abraham and the coming of Our Lord Jesus Christ upon earth, it has nothing to do with our relations to God regarding the same promise. To us in Abraham, therefore, was promised remission of sin, grace, mercy, and salvation through the merits of our Blessed Saviour and our faith in Him. How grateful we should be, then, when each of us can truly say that our divine Master "for us men and for our salvation came down from heaven, and became incarnate by the Holy Ghost of the Virgin Mary, and was made man."

In the story of the healing of the ten lepers, as related in to-day's Gospel, our Blessed Lord, whilst paying a compliment to the Old Law by saying to the afflicted creatures: "Go, shew yourselves to the priests," at the same time proved the superiority of the New Law by curing them before they had time to report themselves, for "it came to pass that, as they went, they were made clean." And this signal and miraculous favor was conferred upon them on account of their faith in Christ as the Mediator of the New Testament—"Go thy way, for thy faith hath made thee whole."

But the point to which the Church wishes to draw our particular attention to-day is the fact that ten were made clean, whereas only one returned to thank our Blessed Saviour, who said: "Were not ten made clean? And where are the nine? There is no one found to return and give glory to God, but this stranger," for, "this was a Samaritan" and not one of the chosen people.

As no one is so contemptible amongst men as an ungrateful man amongst his benefactors, so nothing is so displeasing to the Sacred Heart of Jesus as the ingratitude of the sinner: and nothing increases the rich flow of His grace and love to us so much as our humble thankfulness for and acknowledgment of His mercy and kindness. "For the earth that drinketh in the rain which cometh often upon it," says St. Paul, "and bringeth forth herbs meet for them by whom it is tilled, receiveth blessing from God. But that which bringeth forth thorns and briers, is reprobate, and very near unto a curse, whose end is to be burnt." (Heb. vi. 7.)

When one is guilty of ingratitude for favors

received, it is a proof that he has not sufficiently appreciated their value. This is to despise the kindness and generosity of their benefactor, than which there can be no greater insult. This is why Almighty God complains so bitterly of the ingratitude of men: "Hear, O ye heavens, and give ear, O earth, for the Lord hath spoken. I have brought up children, and exalted them: but they have despised me" (Isaias i. 2.) Almighty God so loved man as to create him to His own image and likeness, to give him the earth for his portion, and heaven for his inheritance—"Thou hast made him a little lower than the angels: Thou hast crowned him with glory and honor, and hath set him over the works of Thy hands: Thou hast subjected all things under his feet." (Heb. ii. 7, 8.) What a deep debt of gratitude he owes his Creator! But what a crime of deeper ingratitude he has committed by sin! He has not only despised God by failing to thank Him for His benefits, but he has added insult to injury by offending Him!

If, after the right to inheritance in the kingdom of heaven had been restored to us by the merits of Christ applied to our souls in the holy sacrament of Baptism, we failed to express our deep sense of gratitude to Almighty God for so signal a favor by devoting our whole lives to His love and service, we should be deserving of the greatest contempt. But when, after being cleansed from original sin and freed from the power of the devil by God's holy grace, we deliberately renounce allegiance to our Creator by the commission of mortal sin, no expression can be used to adequately describe the enormity of our crime. In Baptism we answered the challenge of the Church thrice successively to "renounce Satan and all his works and pomps." When we commit mortal sin we expressly prove ourselves traitors of the deepest dye, and insult God's goodness by preferring the kingdom of Satan and of darkness to His holy kingdom of grace and light.

But yet—O incomprehensible mystery of the love of God!—Jesus seeks us once more and promises us pardon in the sacrament of Penance if we repent of our crime and return to His allegiance! "I will forgive their iniquity," He says, "and I will remember their sin no more." (Jer. xxxi. 34.) Again He receives back the traitor; once more He receives his assurance of future allegiance and re-admits him to a share in the privileges He has prepared for the children of His kingdom—"For the Lord hath redeemed Jacob, and delivered him out of the hand of one that was mightier than he. And they shall come, and shall give praise in Mount Sion: and they shall flow together to the good things of the Lord . . . and their soul shall be as a watered garden, and they shall be hungry no more." (Jer. xxxi. 12.)

Once by Baptism, and again by Penance, the soul recovers its lost grace and is restored to the friendship of God. Surely no thought of further sin will ever disturb the peace which it feels in the sweetness, in the knowledge, and in the service of Christ, compared to the slavery it experienced in the service of Satan. Surely no rational being could be guilty of such perfidy, not to speak at all of ingratitude, as to relapse of his own free will into his former miserable condition; of trampling upon all God's mercies and making a mockery of His kindness, His grace, and His sacraments. Surely if he does, the very "stone shall cry out of the wall: and the timber that is between the joints of the building shall answer" (Hab. ii. 11.) in the Church where he swore his renewed allegiance! Yet so, alas, it is. And this is how the relapsing sinner wipes out from his heart all sense of gratitude, for such an estimable quality is altogether beyond the pale of such a nature. But he does more, for "when the unclean spirit is gone out of a man, he walketh through places without water, seeking rest:

and not finding, he saith: I will return into my house whence I came out. And when he is come, he findeth it swept and garnished. Then he goeth and taketh with him seven other spirits more wicked than himself, and entering in they dwell there. And the last state of that man becomes worse than the first." (Luke xi. 24-26.)

Of such sinners our divine Master says that they are not merely unworthy of heaven, but they are *unfit* for it—"No man putting his hand to the plow, and looking back, is fit for the kingdom of God." (Luke ix. 62.) And St. Paul accordingly holds out very little hope of true conversion for such on account of the small effect the ordinary means of God's grace have upon them. "It is impossible," he says, "for those who were once illuminated, have tasted also the heavenly gift, and were made partakers of the Holy Ghost, have moreover tasted the good word of God, and the powers of the world to come, and are fallen away: to be renewed again to penance, crucifying again to themselves the Son of God, and making Him a mockery." (Heb. xvi. 4-6.)

But with God all things are possible. The lepers in the Gospel of to-day were afflicted with a horrible, revolting, and humanly incurable disease, which was so dreaded by the people that those who suffered from it were not allowed to live with, or mix with, or even come near their fellow-men. Hence, when the unfortunate ten met our divine Master in Samaria on His way to Jerusalem, they "stood afar off; and lifted up their voices, saying: Jesus, Master, have mercy on us." Their disease was incurable, but not by the hand of God, for Jesus in His mercy made them clean—"Whom when He saw, He said: Go, shew yourselves to the priests. And it came to pass that, as they went, they were made clean."

Leprosy is a figure of sin, and is particularly a type of the relapsing sinner, whose sores and wounds rot in the sight of God and become covered with the foul and filthy incrustations of depraved passions, so that his case seems hopeless and incurable. But through the infinite mercy of God and by the merits and intercession of that same kind and loving Jesus, even they will be made clean if only they will pray earnestly for the grace of conversion, crying out with a sincere and anxious heart: "Jesus, Master, have mercy on us." They must pray with great humility, "standing afar off." They must call upon God with great zeal and earnestness and with firm and lively faith, "lifting up their voices" in strong and fervent petition.

As our Blessed Saviour said to the lepers: "Go, shew yourselves to the priests," so He says to all poor sinners: "Go, and show the state of your soul to My priest in the sacrament of Penance. He has the power which I gave him of curing all your infirmities. He will advise you, and, above all forgive you, for I have said to him: 'Whose sins you shall forgive, they are forgiven them.'" Then, "if your sins be as scarlet, they shall be white as snow: and if they be red as crimson, they shall be white as wool" (Isaias i. 18.), according to the prophet Isaias.

Let us have great courage and confidence then in the infinite mercy of God. He is far more anxious to cure the spiritual leprosy of sin than He was even to cure the bodily disease of those ten poor afflicted ones who besought His mercy. And when we shall have been restored to fresh and healthy vigor, once more able to associate with the "children of the household of the faith," let us not forget to show our gratitude for such a wonderful favor by devoting all the powers of our souls to the love and service of our divine Master, by whose kindness and power we have been made clean.

L

FOURTEENTH SUNDAY AFTER PENTECOST

LOYALTY

"These are contrary one to another."
         (Epistle: Gal. v. 16–24.)
"No man can serve two masters."
         (Gospel: Matt. vi. 24–33.)

THE interests of our immortal souls are ever and always in direct opposition to the interests of our bodies. The law of God is not the law of the world: "the flesh lusteth against the spirit: and the spirit against the flesh; for these are contrary one to another." Where the law of the flesh is ease, comfort, and the indulgence of the passions, the law of the spirit is self-denial, mortification, and suffering. "If any man will come after Me," says Christ, "let him deny himself, and take up his cross, and follow Me." (Matt. xvi. 25.) Charity is ever opposed to enmities, contentions, wraths, and quarrels: modesty, continency, chastity to immodesty, uncleanness, luxury, as is clearly explained in the Epistle of to-day.

Hence we must serve either God or the world. "You can not serve God and Mammon," says our divine Master in to-day's Gospel, for "no man can serve two masters" whose interests are so diametrically opposed to one another. As Christians and Catholics, who have already experienced the ineffable joy of laboring in the vineyard of the Lord, and who know the value of the promised reward in the kingdom of heaven of serving Him whose "yoke is sweet and whose burden light" (Matt. xi. 30.), there can be no possible doubt as to which master we ought to serve with loyalty and affection in our own best interests, for, as St. Paul says: "We have not received the spirit of bondage again in fear; but have received the spirit of adoption of sons" (Rom. viii. 15.); and again: "The wages of sin is death. But the grace of God, life everlasting in Christ Jesus our Lord." (Rom. vi. 23.)

Whilst we live in this world, however, we are surrounded by the dangers of the "servitude of corruption," because God has placed us here to make use in His service as means of salvation of the very instruments of the slavery of the flesh. We are not angels but men. And so it becomes necessary for us to become delivered from the slavery of the world and the flesh and to make them our servants rather than our masters. Composed of a body and soul, man must devote his energy to the care of the higher and nobler portion of his nature; but he must also, in due order and subordination to it, support the necessities of his frail mortal body. "For we know that every creature groaneth, and travaileth in pain even till now," says St. Paul, "and not only it, but ourselves also, who have the first fruits of the Spirit, even we ourselves groan within ourselves, waiting for the adoption of the sons of God, the redemption of our body." (Rom. viii. 22, 23.)

Hence we must be thoroughly loyal in the service of God. As soon as any of His enemies are at all inclined to assert their mastery over us, or interfere in the slightest degree with His best interests, we must exert to the utmost our spirit of loyalty and at any sacrifice and at any cost reduce them to subjection, saying with our divine Master: "Go behind me, Satan; thou art a scandal unto me: because thou savorest not the things that are of God, but the things that are of men." (Matt. xvi. 23.)

That we may be on our guard against the specious pretexts of such dangerous and persevering enemies, our holy mother the Church to-day warns us against a very common, a very constant and a very insidious method of attack by which our loyalty to our divine Master might be placed in jeopardy. And that is the necessity under which we are burdened of providing for the natural wants of the body, such as food, clothing, and shelter. For which purpose she quotes in the Gospel the words of our divine Master Himself on the subject.

He tells us that our Heavenly Father, who feeds the birds of the air and clothes the lilies of the field, also provides for the natural wants of mankind. He has given us life and strength, and is also prepared to give us the lesser gifts of food and clothing, for "Is not the life more than the meat: and the body more than the raiment?" We should not, therefore, be unduly solicitous or inordinately anxious for the acquisition of temporal comforts lest we endanger the welfare of our souls.

In any case it is Almighty God who provides for our temporal wants, even though we may think that because we work hard—labor, spin, sow, plow, and reap—that we obtain the necessaries of life by our own efforts, unaided by the special providence of Almighty God. If God does not wish to provide us with food and raiment, of what use will be our plowing, and sowing, and reaping? "In the morning sow thy seed," says Holy Scripture, "and in the evening let not thy hand cease:

for thou knowest not which may spring up, this or that." (Eccles. xi. 6.) And St. Paul expresses the same idea of our ultimate dependence on God's providence no matter what strenuous efforts we may make ourselves—"I have planted, Apollo watered, but God gave the increase. Therefore, neither he that planteth is anything, nor he that watereth; but God that giveth the increase." (1 Cor. iii. 6, 7.)

How foolish, then, are those who not only labor all their lives without any thought of God, as if God would have neglected them, but who even put aside His holy Law and strive to secure for themselves and their families riches, honor, glory, position, power, and every kind of temporal success and prosperity. They work for them, as it were, in spite of God. They serve Mammon straight out. They say they have no time for prayer or sacrifice, for Church, chapel, or meeting, and that religion will not earn their bread for them or make a success of their business.

But this is just where they make the mistake. They would labor just as strenuously and much more successfully if they followed the advice of our divine Master in the Gospel: "Seek ye therefore first the kingdom of God, and His justice, and all these things shall be added unto you." Which does not mean that if a man spends all his time in the Church, or in private prayer, he will find himself miraculously provided with all that he wants for soul and body, his business prospering and his store increasing. No, but it means that one of the very first things he must do in order to serve God rather than Mammon is to attend to his business—to faithfully discharge the duties of his state in life. For the same God who said "Thou shalt not have strange gods before Me" (Ex. xx. 3.), also said "In the sweat of thy face shalt thou eat bread." (Gen. iii. 19.) The law of God's providence is that we should lead lives of useful activity in His service and for His sake in the sphere of life in which He has placed us. The faithful discharge of such duty to God automatically includes the discharge of all our duties to our neighbor and to ourselves. It gives us an exalted idea of our responsibility and consequently encourages us in the pursuit of those material advantages as means to salvation which the worshipers of Mammon propose to themselves as their end, their object, and their only god.

Who is such a conscientious and trustworthy servant as the good Catholic, who neither wastes his master's goods, steals his money, nor squanders his time away, because the Law of God says to him "Thou shalt not steal"?

Who is so sought after, even by infidels, as the business or professional man whose uprightness and honesty and proved worth are built on the solid principles of conscientious religious convictions? Men who boast of having no religion at all are the very first to acknowledge the certificate of worth which the possession of such sacred convictions brings to their happy possessor, even from these very men who despise their origin, because, perhaps, such know best how crooked is the path in which they themselves must walk in order to follow their false god of Mammon to his unholy shrine.

Whilst Catholics are in the main true to their principles of faithful service of their divine Master, there are some who, for the sake of a little gain, a little fame, a little business profit or professional advancement, sometimes pay court to this false usurper and sink their principles temporarily on the cowardly plea of expediency, or prudence, or what they are pleased to term "broad-mindedness." If so, they are guilty of disloyalty to the God whom they profess to serve. And He will not suffer them to offer a divided service. "You can not serve God and Mammon," He says. And again: "Thou shalt not have strange gods before Me . . . I am the Lord thy God, mighty, jealous." (Ex. xx. 3, 5.) We should therefore never diverge one iota from loyalty to Him who has created us, redeemed us, and given us the privilege of being His beloved subjects.

If Almighty God promises us the necessaries of life, and at the same time expects us to perform our daily duties in order to obtain them, so also He promises what is really essential to our temporal support and welfare. He does not promise riches, or luxury, honors, success, or a constant flow of prosperity. Our divine Master Himself was born in poverty, and lived a life of suffering, in order to show us by His example how to conquer the flesh and the world. Divine Providence knows what is best for each one of us, and He knows that we are drawn nearer to Him by failure than by success, by poverty than by prosperity. For many, prosperity and riches would be the most dangerous enemies of their souls, and would lead them to forget God—"The prosperity of fools shall destroy them," says the Wise Man, "but he that shall hear me shall rest without terror, and shall enjoy abundance, without fear of evils." (Prov. i. 32, 33.)

Let us, then, cultivate the spirit of loyalty to our true and only Master. Let us discharge faithfully and well all the duties of our state of life and trust to Almighty God to provide for all our necessities. Let us avoid all undue anxiety and inordinate care about the things of this life and the wants of ourselves and our families, for "Your Father knoweth that you have need of all these things: Seek ye therefore first the kingdom of God, and His justice, and all these things shall be added unto you." "Be nothing solicitous," therefore, "but in everything, by prayer and supplication, let your petitions be made known to God." (Philipp. iv. 6.) For, although Almighty God knows all our wants, like a loving Father He likes us to show our trust in Him by asking Him for all that we stand in need of for soul and body. Although the wants of the soul are more serious than those of the body, yet the latter are more sensibly and more keenly felt. Hence it is a useful adjunct to fervent prayer if we mingle with our petitions for light and grace some request for temporal favors such as our divine Master Himself has taught us in the words: "Give us this day our daily bread."

PART VI

THE DUTIES

"We have borne the burden of the day and the heats." (Matt. xx. 12.)

LI

FIFTEENTH SUNDAY AFTER PENTECOST

OF ENERGY

"Whilst we have time, let us work good."
(EPISTLE: Gal. v. 25–vi. 10.)
"I say to thee, Arise."
(GOSPEL: Luke vii. 11–16.)

NOW THAT we have seen the nature of the work which we have to accomplish as laborers in the vineyard of the Lord, and have also been taught something concerning ourselves as workers, the helps we have been provided with by the kind and generous disposition of the Master Himself, and have been notified and encouraged regarding the results we may expect from a faithful devotion to duty, our Holy Mother the Church begins to-day to point out to us some of our first and most necessary duties, thereby summing up, as it were, the practical advice which she has been giving us ever since the beginning of the year.

She places before us in the Gospel of to-day the story of the raising to life of the son of the widow of Naim. It is the second of those three classes of similar miracles performed by our divine Master, which are types or figures of the restoration to spiritual life, by God's clemency and grace, of those who are dead in sin. The first class is that represented by the daughter of Jairus. His daughter had just died when Jesus "took her by the hand. And the maid arose." (Matt. ix. 25.) When a soul first falls into sin and quickly repents, God immediately pronounces its pardon. The second class is that represented by the widow's son. He had been dead some time, had already been removed from the house and was being carried to the grave when Jesus met him. Such are they who remain in sin for a considerable time without repentance, but who have not yet abandoned themselves to vice altogether. These also God in His mercy meets on the road to perdition and restores them to His grace. The third class of sinner is typified by Lazarus. He had died and had been buried. Nay, he had been four days in the grave and had already begun to show signs of corruption. "Lord, by this time he stinketh, for he is now of four days" (John xi. 39.), said his sister Martha to Jesus, who, on arriving at the sepulcher, "cried with a loud voice; Lazarus, come forth. And presently he that had been dead came forth, bound feet and hands with winding bands." (John xi. 43, 44.) Even to souls that are corrupt in sin and rendered apparently helpless by the strong bands of temptation and of habit God does not refuse His mercy and assistance.

In the miracle of to-day's Gospel the widow of Naim is a figure of our holy mother the Church, from whom "the bridegroom has been taken away." (Matt. ix. 15.) Her mourning over her separation from her divine Spouse is increased by the spiritual death of her child, who is as precious to her as an only son. But the grace of God and the divine compassion of our Lord Jesus Christ saves him in time and restores him to his mother in the full strength and vigor of youth with the words: "Young man, I say to thee, Arise."

Let us then be up and doing. The Master's Work is waiting for us, and our holy mother the Church is watching anxiously to help us to perform it with energy and devotion. She overlooks our past faults "in the spirit of meekness" of the Master Himself and urges us to "work good whilst we have time" without failing.

One of the greatest dangers that can beset a soul in the spiritual life is the evil of sloth. It is akin to death and is followed by similar consequences. It is defined by theologians to be "a torpor of mind and weakness of will which engenders a dislike for spiritual things on account of the labor and trouble connected with them." (Gury. i. 179.) If it cause neglect of serious obligations it is a mortal sin, one of the "seven deadly sins." It behooves us, therefore, as laborers in the vineyard of the Lord, to be ever on our guard against it, for the Master Himself warns us: "Cursed be he that doth the work of the Lord deceitfully." (Jer. xlviii. 10.) If, however, sloth does not lead us to the neglect of those duties necessary for salvation, but even of those which are greatly conducive to that end, it may on account of particular circumstances be a mortal sin for some, but it is certainly a most dangerous disposition for all, as it leads to tepidity and want of zeal—"deceit" in God's service. The natural difficulty and repugnance which we feel in the discharge of our duties is not sinful provided it does not cause us to neglect them, for the flesh will ever struggle against the spirit—"The flesh lusteth against the spirit: and the spirit against the flesh; for these are contrary one to another: so that you do not the things that you would." (Gal. v. 17.) Even the greatest saints have experienced this difficulty. As St. Paul says: "Every creature groaneth, and travaileth in pain even till now. And not only it, but ourselves also, who have the first fruits of the Spirit, even we ourselves groan within ourselves." (Rom. viii. 22, 23.)

We must carefully distinguish sloth from idleness, and spiritual energy from fruitless, or rather useless and unnecessary labor. There is a laziness of body and a laziness of spirit, an energy of mind and an energy of soul. As our divine Master said to Martha: "Thou art careful, and troubled about many things: But one thing is necessary." (Luke x. 41.) So there are many who are naturally endowed with great bodily energy and mental activity. These gifts they may apply either to the good of their souls by doing their duty faithfully and well, and with the right intention, thus "proving their own work" to be that which "works good to all men" as well as to themselves: or they may use them in the pursuit of the things that please them, attending to a multitude of various pursuits, but neglecting their proper business. There are others again who are naturally indolent, being of a slow and sluggish disposition. These may plod on in their own slow way for God's sake and so fulfil the law successfully: or they may give in to their laziness and spend their time unprofitably, doing nothing. It is, therefore, one thing to engage in no employment at all. This is rather to be called indolence. It is another to neglect one's proper business and devote one's self to other and useless employments. And this is the most dangerous kind of idleness, for such people, being of an active disposition, will expend their natural energy in dangerous pursuits. Many of them, according to St. Paul, "being idle they learn to go about from house to house: and are not only idle, but tattlers also, and busybodies, speaking things which they ought not." (1 Tim. v. 13.) Notice that according to St. Paul one may be an "idler" and a "busybody" at the same time. Others are entirely taken up with the care of their bodies and the pleasures of sense. Their only occupation seems to be to discover new dishes, new fashions, new novels, new plays, new friends, and new pleasures of every kind. Some of them go so far as to seek variety under the appearance of religion by seeking new churches, new choirs, new music, new preachers, and even new confessors! It would not be without profit to such to meditate seriously upon the punishment of the rich Dives, who was buried in hell for no other crime than that he "was clothed in purple and fine linen, and feasted sumptuously every day." (Luke xvi. 19.)

The chief malice of spiritual sloth lies in the fact that it destroys the principle of spiritual life in the soul, which is the motive of divine charity, by which we do all our duties faithfully for the love of God. Our great duty is to save our souls. This is a work of much difficulty and uncertainty on account of the dangers by which we are surrounded and the corruption of our nature—"With fear and trembling work out your salvation" (Philipp. ii. 12.), says St. Paul. "The kingdom of heaven suffereth violence, and the violent bear it away." (Matt. xi. 12.), says St. Matthew. It is not enough, then, merely to refrain from evil, even if that were possible, we must occupy ourselves in the practice of good works, especially and before all in the energetic discharge of the duties of our state in life, faithfully attending to our own business and thus avoiding the expenditure of much misdirected energy in minding what does not concern us. "And you," says St. Peter, "employing all care, minister in your faith, virtue; and in virtue, knowledge; and in knowledge, abstinence; and in abstinence, patience; and in patience, godliness; and in godliness, love of brotherhood; and in love of brotherhood, charity. For if these things be with you and abound, they will make you to be neither empty nor unfruitful in

the knowledge of Our Lord Jesus Christ. . . .
Wherefore, brethren, labor the more, that by
good works you may make sure your calling
and election. For doing these things, you
shall not sin at any time." (2 Peter i. 5–10.)
"For he that hath not these things with him, is
blind, and groping, having forgotten that he
was purged from his old sins." (i. 9.)

Yes, we have been "purged from our old
sins" by the grace of Almighty God. We have
been raised from death to life by the voice of
our divine Master saying to us: "Arise."
He has restored us to our holy mother the
Church in all the strength of our youth and
vigor in the spiritual life. Let us, then, be
very active in her service and that of the Master. He will help us to overcome all dangers
and difficulties. The slothful man is afraid
of everything, imagines the task more difficult
than it really is, and foresees trouble where
none exists. "Desires kill the slothful," says
Holy Scripture: "for his hands have refused to
work at all. He longeth and desireth all the
day." (Prov. xxi. 25.): and again: "The
slothful man saith: There is a lion without,
I shall be slain in the midst of the streets."
(xxii. 13.)

"Hast thou seen a man swift in his work?"
says the Sacred Writer, "he shall stand before

kings, and shall not be before those that are obscure." (Prov. xxii. 29.) The man of energy trusts in Almighty God, saying with St. Paul: "I can do all things in Him who strengtheneth me." (Philipp. iv. 13.) He is not afraid to exert himself, and is ever willing to make sacrifices and put up with difficulties. He is not a coward and does not therefore allow imaginary troubles or dangers to frighten him. Like St. Paul he perseveres in spite of all: "As dying, and behold we live; as chastised, and not killed; as sorrowful, yet always rejoicing; as needy, yet enriching many; as having nothing, and possessing all things." (2 Cor. vi. 9, 10.) With God's help all is easy. "My yoke is sweet and My burden light." (Matt. xi. 28.) Let us, then, devote all our energy to the service of the Master—"and in doing good, let us not fail, for in due time we shall reap, not failing. Therefore, whilst we have time let us work good to all men, but especially to those who are of the household of the faith."

LII

SIXTEENTH SUNDAY AFTER PENTECOST

OF HUMILITY

"For this cause I bow my knees to the Father of our Lord Jesus Christ."
(EPISTLE: Eph. iii. 13–21.)
"He that humbleth himself shall be exalted."
(GOSPEL: Luke xiv. 1–11.)

THE GREAT prayer of St. Paul for his people, as quoted in to-day's Epistle, was that they should possess the spirit of Christ, by which they were to be made rich and "strengthened with might unto the inward man." This is the spirit of meekness and humility, according to our divine Master Himself, who says: "Learn of Me, because I am meek and humble of heart." (Matt. xi. 29.) And as humility is the foundation of all virtue it is especially the foundation and root of "the charity of Christ which surpasseth all knowledge." Thus by their humility they were to be exalted; nay, "filled unto all the fulness of God," according to the promise made by Our Lord Jesus Christ in the Gospel of to-day: "Every one that exalteth himself shall be humbled: and he that humbleth himself shall be exalted."

Humility is defined by St. Bernard as "a true knowledge of ourselves by which we become sincerely contemptible in our own eyes." It consists, therefore, in having in our own hearts a true knowledge of our own nothingness, founded not on mere sentiment but on the plain fact of who and what we are. "Let, therefore," says St. Jerome, "all feigned and affected language be dropped." It is customary for people to speak in humble accents about themselves, to show the shadow and appearance of humility, to say that they are nothing, that they are but poor and miserable creatures and ungrateful sinners, deserving of nothing but contempt. But if any one else expresses such an opinion of them the difference is at once apparent. The proud man can not brook insult or disparagement or even honest criticism. If anything is said to hurt his feelings or cause him to be lessened or despised in the opinion of others even by justly correcting him, you will immediately see him throw off the mask and appear unconsciously in his true colors.

"If any man think himself to be something," says St. Paul, "whereas he is nothing, he deceiveth himself." (Gal. vi. 3.) Hence no man is anything of himself. "What hast thou that thou hast not received," says the same Apostle. "And if thou hast received, why dost thou glory, as if thou hadst not received?" (1 Cor. iv. 7.) It is because we do not know ourselves as we really are. And this ignorance arises from want of due consideration of our own nothingness and worthlessness, just as pride arises from a false estimation of our own good qualities due to similar ignorance. "Why is earth and ashes proud?" says the Preacher. (Ecclus. x. 9.) We are, as it were, blinded by our natural conceit and desire to think much of ourselves. Whereas the man enlightened by divine faith knows that all that he possesses, whether by nature or by grace, gifts of body, mind or soul, are all the gratuitous gifts of God—that "every best gift, and every perfect gift, is from above, coming down from the Father of lights," (James i. 17.), and that therefore to God alone belongs the credit of whatever physical or moral perfections he may possess. "Not to us, O Lord, not to us; but to Thy name give glory," (Ps. cxiii. 1.), and "Unless the Lord build the house, they labor in vain that build it" (Ps. cxxvii. 2.), says the Psalmist.

Pride, then, is utterly foolish, as all must acknowledge when they perceive it in others.

But we can not so easily see this in ourselves, for pride has the peculiar faculty of blinding those who possess it, so that the proud man is the most indignant of all others at being accused of it. Like the ostrich which hides its head in the sand of the desert and imagines that its great body is thereby concealed, so the proud man deceives himself. "Behold I have made thee a little one among the nations, despicable among men," says Holy Scripture, "Thy arrogancy hath deceived thee, and the pride of thy heart." (Jer. xlix. 15, 16.) But this foolishness is criminal and has a special malice of its own which makes it most hateful to God. For by all other crimes the sinner turns his back upon God but by pride he sets himself up before Him and declares war to His very face, attempting, as it were, to dethrone Him, like Lucifer of old, who said: "I will ascend above the height of the clouds, I will be like the Most High." (Isaias xiv. 14.) Hence Almighty God throughout Holy Scripture continually denounces this contemptible crime. He curses the proud and says they are an abomination to Him. Thus, for example: "Pride is hateful before God and men." (Ecclus. x. 7.) "Pride is the beginning of all sin: he that holdeth it, shall be filled with maledictions." (Ecclus. x. 15.) "I hate arrogance and pride, and every wicked way." (Prov. viii. 13.) "The soul that hath committed anything through pride . . . because he hath been rebellious against the Lord shall be cut off from amongst his people." (Num. xv. 30.)

As Almighty God hates pride and punishes it, so He loves humility and rewards it. "God resisteth the proud, but to the humble He giveth grace" (1 Peter v. 15.), says St. Peter. And by a strange dispensation of Providence also, the very means by which the proud seek to obtain for themselves honor and glory before men are the very means best calculated to bring them dishonor and contempt instead, as our divine Master explains very clearly in the Gospel of to-day. He had been invited to dine with some of the Pharisees, who had evidently sought His company for no other reason than that they might exalt themselves at His expense, for "they watched Him" to see if they could catch Him in any breach of the Law, about which they claimed to be so particular. There was a man there who had the dropsy, and as it was the Sabbath day they were ready to accuse Our Lord of breaking its observance if He attempted to cure him, as they expected. But Jesus anticipated their objection and put the question to themselves: "Is it lawful to heal on the Sabbath day?" This they did not answer. But Our Lord healed the man first and then answered the question by calling their attention to the fact that if it were lawful according to them to assist even an animal on the Sabbath, it was much more lawful to assist a human being by curing his disease, as He had done. Thus He humbled their pride by His action and His reason for it, and then explained the natural results of humility to the assembled guests by showing how he who sought to exalt himself by taking a higher seat at table than was due to him was humbled by being asked to sit lower down, whereas he who humbly took a lower place than he was entitled to was honored by being told: "Friend, go up higher."

But whilst "every one that exalteth himself shall be humbled: and he that humbleth himself shall be exalted" is true in fact, we must remember that hope of such exaltation should not be our motive of humility, which is founded on a true appreciation of our own real character in the sight of Almighty God rather than on that apparent character which we hold in the eyes of men, known as "reputation." We may have a good "reputation" but a bad "character" which apparent paradox is due to the ignorance of others with regard to our real qualities. But no man can have such similar ignorance with regard to himself unless, blinded by pride, he is either ignorant or forgetful of how much he is indebted to God for the good and to himself for the bad that is in him. So St. Paul advises us: "Let nothing be done through contention, neither by vainglory. But in humility, let each esteem others better than themselves: each one not considering the things that are his own, but those that are other men's. For let this mind be in you, which was also in Christ Jesus." (Philipp. ii. 3–5.)

The "mind which was in Christ Jesus" was the spirit of humility, who, though He was God, became the least of all in order to show us, not only by His word but also by His example, that the foundation of all virtue lies in humility. "Who being in the form of God, thought it not robbery to be equal with God. But emptied Himself, taking the form of a servant, being made in the likeness of men, and in habit found as a man. He humbled Himself, becoming obedient unto death, even to the death of the cross." (Philipp. ii. 6–8.) He was born in poverty and lived in poverty all His life. He chose the poor for His companions. When honors were offered to Him He fled. When He was accused He was silent. "When He was reviled He did not revile; when He suffered He threatened not" (1 Peter ii.

23.), but was always of a meek, mild, kind, gentle, loving, and forgiving disposition, as was foretold by the prophet: "He shall not contend, nor cry out, neither shall any man hear His voice in the streets. The bruised reed He shall not break: and smoking flax He shall not extinguish." (Matt. xii. 19, 20.)

How different the heart of the proud man! He is blind to his own faults but keen to observe and criticize those of others, rashly condemning and despising them, like the Pharisees in the Gospel who "trusted in themselves and despised others." (Luke xviii. 9.) He is vain and presumptuous, ambitious, overbearing, boastful, and intolerant, saying in effect: "Is not this the great Babylon which I have built, to be the seat of the kingdom, by the strength of my power and the glory of my excellence?" (Dan. iv. 27.) The proud seek and swallow flattery with an eagerness that makes them ridiculous. They pretend to be greater than they even think themselves and so become abominable hypocrites. They will brook no opposition or correction, and are contentious, jealous, hard-hearted, and unmerciful.

They are fools indeed. But let us be wise. "Unless you become as little children, you shall not enter into the kingdom of heaven," (Matt. xviii. 3.), says Christ. How easy it ought to be to think little of ourselves! If, in order to merit heaven, God commanded us to become great, mighty, learned, powerful, and successful in great undertakings, it would be different. But all He asks us to do is to lie low and be "as little children," not thinking much of ourselves, meek, obedient, forgiving, and thankful for what we get.

Let us, then, first learn to know ourselves by praying to our heavenly father for light to know our little worth. Let us study the life and character of our divine Master and strive to imitate Him in His meekness and humility of heart, saying with St. Paul: "I bow my knees to the Father of Our Lord Jesus Christ, of whom all paternity in heaven and earth is named, that He would grant according to the riches of His glory, to be strengthened by His Spirit with might unto the inward man." This is the spirit of humility which will make us like our divine Master and cause us to be recognized as His spiritual brethren and His coheirs to the kingdom of heaven, where He will exalt us forever and confirm us forever in glory.

LIII

SEVENTEENTH SUNDAY AFTER PENTECOST

OF CHARITY

"Supporting one another in charity."
(EPISTLE: Eph. iv. 1–6.)
"Thou shalt love the Lord thy God."
(GOSPEL: Matt. xxii. 35–46.)

THE PRECEPT of charity is so important that our holy mother the Church wishes to-day to sum up all her past teaching on the subject, even as our divine Master in the incident related in the Gospel of to-day epitomized "the whole law and the prophets" in the words: "Thou shalt love the Lord thy God with thy whole heart, and with thy whole soul, and with thy whole mind. This is the greatest and the first commandment. And the second is like to this: Thou shalt love thy neighbor as thyself."

"That day there came to Him the Sadducees, who say there is no resurrection," says the Gospel, and they asked Jesus what they considered to be an unanswerable question. A woman had had seven husbands in succession—

"At the resurrection, therefore, whose wife of the seven shall she be?" Our Lord's answer was that "in the resurrection they shall neither marry nor be married; but shall be as the angels of God in heaven"; and He added a few pertinent remarks concerning their error and their ignorance of God and the Scriptures so convincingly that "the multitude hearing it, were in admiration at His doctrine."

"But the Pharisees hearing that He had silenced the Sadducees came together," and tried to score a success. They sent a lawyer to ask Him: "Which is the greatest commandment in the law?" The answer of Christ is that recorded in the Gospel of to-day relating to divine charity. In order to complete their discomfiture and show His authority for this "new commandment" of brotherly love, He proved His own divinity by showing that if Christ was the Son of David He was also his Lord and Master, "and no man was able to answer Him a word."

It seems strange that there should be any necessity for a law commanding us to love God, seeing how infinitely lovable He is on account of His divine perfections. "In the Old Law," says St. Alphonsus, "men might doubt whether God loved them with a tender love; but, after seeing Him dying on a cross for us, how can we doubt of the tenderness and the ardent affection with which He loves us?" But either in the Old Law or in the New Law who could doubt as to the love God deserves from us? Who could fail to love Him if they only knew Him? The answer is, only those who do not know Him; only those who are either ignorant or forgetful of His divine perfections. There are many who do not know God at all, "like the Gentiles that know not God." (1 Thess. iv. 5.) There are even many professed Christians who do not know Him—"For some have not the knowledge of God, I speak it to your shame" (1 Cor. xv. 34.), says St. Paul to the Corinthians. But there are many more who are careless or forgetful of Him on account of the pleasures of the world and the flesh in which they are wholly engaged, like the Israelites of old who ungratefully forgot their Creator amongst the false gods of other nations. Hence God was forced continually to remind them of His supreme dominion over them and of their duty to serve Him alone. To us as well as to them He has to say: "Take heed diligently lest thou forget the Lord, who brought thee out of the land of Egypt, out of the house of bondage. Thou shalt fear the Lord thy God, and shalt serve Him only." (Deut. vi. 13.)

But now God wishes us to love rather than fear Him. And so our divine Master frequently reminded us of the precept of charity and of our obligations to know God that we might be led to love and serve Him. Thus it was that He became man for our sakes in order to make His great love known to us and so in a manner force us to love Him—"The charity of Christ presseth us" (2 Cor. v. 14.), says St. Paul—for Almighty God Himself, who is so anxious to provide for our happiness, could not in His infinite justice admit us to the kingdom of His love if we did not love Him and prove it by keeping the commandments—"If any one love Me he will keep My word." (John xiv. 23.)

The precept of charity, then, binds us to love God above all things for His own sake, because He is infinitely good in Himself. It must be a love of *preference*—"He that loveth father or mother more than Me, is not worthy of Me" (Matt. x. 37.), says Christ. It need not necessarily be more *felt* than love for our relations or our friends, for a person may weep more easily for the loss of these than for the loss of God and at the same time be prepared to sacrifice them and everything else dear to them rather than offend the Divine Majesty or lose His love.

Many say, and even think, that they love God; but they deceive themselves. The only real proof is our hatred of sin and our sincere desire to keep all His commands. Our charity, therefore, must be *interior,* that is, from the heart; and *sovereign,* that is, above all things. If our love of God is thus perfect and unselfish it will embrace all that He expects of us and will answer above all to the great test of charity toward our neighbor. "By this shall all men know that you are My disciples," says Christ, "if you have love one for another." (John xiii. 35.) "If any man say, I love God, and hateth his brother; he is a liar" (1 John iv. 20.), says St. John.

Thus "the second is like to the first: thou shalt love thy neighbor as thyself." The same precept which binds us to love God also binds us to love our neighbor. "And this commandment we have from God," says St. John, "that he who loveth God, love also his brother." (1 John iv. 21.) We are bound to love our neighbor in thought, word, and deed, from the motive of divine charity, that is, for God's sake rather than his own. For there is the natural and human love which we feel for another on account of merely natural and human motives, such as his estimable qualities, his goodness to us, or for our own interest in any way. But there is a superior love and a higher order of charity grounded on faith and on the motive of the love of God, who wishes us to love also our neighbor, because it is His holy will and He loves him Himself with an everlasting love. "If you love them that love you what reward shall you have? Do not even the publicans this? And if you salute your brethren only, what do you more? Do not also the heathens this?" (Matt. v. 46, 47.), says Christ, who tells us plainly: "I say to you: Love your enemies: do good to them that hate you: and pray for them that persecute and calumniate you." (Matt. v. 44.)

We must, then, for God's sake love our neighbor in thought, word, and deed. In thought, by never judging anything evil of him, particularly on uncertain grounds, for "charity thinketh no evil." (1 Cor. xiii. 5.) It is best not to judge him at all. "Judge not," says Our Saviour Himself, "that you may not be judged. For with what judgment you judge, you shall be judged." (Matt. vii. 1, 2.) Therefore we should avoid all curiosity about the affairs of others which do not concern us. As a rule people who are very anxious to find out all they can about their neighbor's business, especially his faults and failings, are the very last we should expect to keep the knowledge to themselves. In this matter as in everything else they find they must pay for what they get; and they accordingly barter their news of the affairs of one in exchange for news of another. Hence when we find any one professing to know a great deal about the character of a neighbor we may well ask: "With whose character did they purchase their information?"

Which goes to prove that we must love our neighbor in word by carefully abstaining from all calumny and detraction. By the former we tell something about him that is not true—a most grievous sin. By the latter we reveal a fault that he has actually committed—a mortal sin if the matter be serious. Such sins can never be forgiven unless we make reparation for the injury done, as far as is possible. But it is to be feared that such reparation is not always made. After the sin has been confessed and absolution received some do not trouble further about the matter. Indeed, there are many who never think of confessing such sins in their true and proper light and fondly look upon them as merely little acts of uncharitable conversation.

Some spend most of their time in these hateful practices, and although they always find many to encourage them they are detested and feared by everybody. "The tale-bearer shall defile his own soul and shall be hated by all" (Ecclus. xxi. 31.), says Holy Scripture. Their excuse generally is that they merely repeated the secret to a friend or two. But Holy Scripture says: "If a serpent bite in silence, he is nothing better that backbiteth secretly." (Eccles. x. 11.); and we are accordingly advised by the Holy Ghost: "Hast thou heard a word against thy neighbor? Let it die within thee" (Ecclus. xix. 10.); and again: "Strive not in a matter which doth not concern thee." (Ecclus. xi. 9.) "He that loveth his neighbor hath fulfilled the law" (Rom. xiii. 8.), says St. Paul; and so St. James says: "If any man offend not in word, the same is a perfect man." (iii. 2.)

We must also be charitable in our actions. "Let us not love in word, nor in tongue," says St. John, "but in deed and in truth." (1 John iii. 18.) We must relieve our neighbor in his spiritual and corporal necessities. "Pray for them that persecute and calumniate you," says Christ. (Matt. v. 44.) Help them when they are ill or in want. "Alms delivereth from death, and the same is that which purgeth away sins, and maketh to find mercy and life everlasting" (Job xiii. 9.), says Holy Scripture. Such charity, therefore, is very pleasing to God and will be the standard by which Jesus Christ will judge us at the last day, for He will say to the just: "Come, ye blessed of My Father. ... For I was hungry, and you gave Me to eat; I was thirsty, and you gave Me to drink; I was a stranger, and you took Me in; naked, and you covered Me; sick, and you visited Me; I was in prison, and you came to Me ... [for] as long as you did it to one of these my least brethren, you did it to Me." (Matt. xxv. 34-40.)

Above all we must be charitable to our enemies, for in being charitable to our friends there is always the danger of the personal human motive spoiling the full fruit of the spiritual reward. "Do not also the heathens this?" Nothing is so pleasing to Almighty God as charity to our enemies in thought, word, and deed, for nothing makes us so like our divine Master and Model, the meek, gentle, and forgiving Jesus, who says to us: "Forgive and you shall be forgiven." (Luke vi. 37.)

Therefore "walk worthy of the vocation in which you are called. With all humility and mildness, with patience, supporting one another in charity."

LIV

EIGHTEENTH SUNDAY AFTER PENTECOST

OF PENANCE

"Who will confirm you unto the end without crime." (EPISTLE: 1 Cor. i. 4–8.)
"Be of good heart, son, thy sins are forgiven thee." (GOSPEL: Matt. ix. 1–8.)

HAD MAN, after being restored by the merits of Our Lord Jesus Christ in the holy sacrament of Baptism to his lost inheritance in the kingdom of heaven, remained faithful to the commands of Almighty God, and thus placed no obstacle to his eternal enjoyment of the bliss of paradise, how grateful he should be to the Giver of all good gifts. But, alas, he not only proved ungrateful to his Creator, but offended Him still more by actual sin, and thus brought upon himself once more the loss of all his spiritual possessions and earned for himself eternal damnation.

But God, pitying his weakness and misery, again places within his reach the means of further reconciliation. He offers him a second plank by which to save himself from the shipwreck of sin. "He who hath begun a good work in you," says St. Paul, "will perfect it unto the day of Christ Jesus" (Philipp. i. 6.), "so that," as the Epistle of to-day says, "nothing is wanting to you in any grace, waiting for the manifestation of Our Lord Jesus Christ. Who also will confirm you unto the end without crime."

This promise was faithfully and wonderfully kept by our divine Master by the institution of the holy sacrament of Penance. It is related in the Gospel of to-day that on one occasion a man suffering from a disease which caused complete paralysis and consequent loss of all movement and sensation in his limbs was brought to Jesus in rather extraordinary circumstances, as St. Mark relates—"And they came to him, bringing one sick of the palsy, who was carried by four. And when they could not offer him unto Him for the multitude, they uncovered the roof where He was; and opening it, they let down the bed." (Mark ii. 3, 4.) Our Lord, admiring their faith and perseverance, immediately consoled the sick man by saying. "Be of good heart, son, thy sins are forgiven thee." Which remark caused the scribes and Pharisees to think that He was blaspheming. But Jesus knew their thoughts and wished to let them know that He could see the secrets of their hearts as well as cure the sick man and even forgive sins. So He said to them: "Why do you think evil in your hearts?" Do you not know that I can as easily forgive sin as I can presently cure this disease by the divine power which I possess? And to prove the truth of His assertions He miraculously cured the poor man, who immediately "arose and went into his house." "And the multitude seeing it, feared and glorified God, who had given such power to men."

This power of forgiving sins our divine Master communicated to His apostles, and their successors, the bishops and priests of the Church. On the very day of His resurrection, as St. John relates, He appeared to His apostles assembled in the upper room in Jerusalem, and said to them: "As the Father hath sent Me, I also send you. When He had said this, He breathed on them, and He said to them: Receive ye the Holy Ghost. Whose sins you shall forgive, they are forgiven them; and whose sins you shall retain, they are retained." (John xx. 21–23.) On another occasion He had said to them: "Whatsoever you shall bind upon earth, shall be bound also in heaven; and whatsoever you shall loose upon earth, shall be loosed also in heaven." (Matt. xviii. 18.) This is such a clear and definite power of dealing with sinners in the sacrament of Penance given to the Church that no comment is necessary except to consider how best we may make use of such a wonderful privilege.

Had Our Lord Jesus Christ merely given to His Church the power of *loosing* and of *forgiving,* her sacred ministers might exercise it indiscriminately on the multitude, allowing its effects to operate upon those individuals who might happen to be disposed for their reception. But Christ also gave the Church the power of *binding* and of *retaining.* This makes all the difference, and thereby constitutes the exercise of such powers a *judicial act.* So that before the priest pronounces sentence either of binding or loosing, of forgiving or retaining, he must hear the cause and try the case according to its merits. This proves the absolute necessity of an honest and full confession on the part of the penitent who seeks absolution for his sins.

As the penitent himself, from the very nature of the case, must be at once the accuser and the witness against himself, it is easy to see that his confession must be humble, sincere, and complete. It must be humble, because as a sinner he seeks pardon; and "God resisteth the proud, and giveth grace to the humble." (James iv. 6.) It must be sincere because the witness must be truthful and give evidence even against himself without exaggeration or equivocation of any kind—"The deceitful man God will abhor." (Ps. v. 7.) From which it follows that his confession must be complete; that is, it must embrace all mortal sins and any seriously aggravating circumstances connected with them, as, for example, an unfortunate *habit* of a certain sin.

As even Almighty God Himself can not forgive sin unless the sinner truly repents, the first and most important disposition necessary for obtaining pardon in the sacrament of Penance is a sincere sorrow for having offended God; which includes logically a firm resolution of sinning no more and a willing intention of satisfying God's justice for past sins. Whilst through want of a confessor we may obtain pardon by an act of charity or of perfect contrition, coupled with the will to confess our sins if possible, we can obtain forgiveness in the sacrament of Penance by contrition of a lower or less perfect kind, which must, however, have a *supernatural* reason or motive. Such, for example, is the motive of the fear of hell or of the loss of heaven. But no merely *natural* reason for sorrow will be of any avail before God, such as, for example, the loss of health, property, reputation, or friends, caused by our sins.

As Penance is a true sacrament, we must be extremely careful to supply the proper *necessary matter,* otherwise we shall render it invalid and lose the grace attached to its worthy reception. It was instituted by Christ to restore to the friendship of God the soul separated from Him by mortal sin. This it accomplishes by the infusion of sanctifying grace through the mercy of God and the merits of our Holy Redeemer. Venial sin is also remitted by the sacrament because of the increase of God's grace and our removal of obstacles to it by our exercise of good dispositions.

Hence the *necessary matter* of the sacrament consists of all mortal sins committed after Baptism and not previously remitted in confession. If we have no such sin to confess we must at least confess either a mortal sin of our past life already remitted, or some venial sin or sins for which we are truly sorry. If we merely confess some venial faults which we habitually commit it shows that we are not confessing any sin for which we are truly sorry, and consequently we expose the sacrament to the danger of invalidity and profanation, and so abuse the grace of God which is offered to us. It is to be greatly feared that many are guilty of such abuse and that they continually and frequently run to confession without ever making a good one or obtaining any grace whatever from the sacrament.

We should, therefore, pray fervently every time we desire to approach the sacred tribunal for the grace to make a good confession, and by the light of God's grace carefully examine our conscience. We should at the same time refrain from over-anxiety or unnecessary scrupulosity regarding the number and the nature of our sins, but honestly devote as much care and attention to the matter as we should give to any serious worldly business. The most important matter to concern ourselves with is the sincerity of our contrition and the firmness of our purpose of amendment. If we forget to confess a sin, or any of our past sins have escaped our memory, God in His mercy forgives them. If we afterward remember them we are bound to submit them to "the power of the keys" at our next confession. But if we are not sorry for our sins we render Almighty God Himself powerless to forgive us.

No doubt the obligation of confession is difficult to human nature and a source of shame and confusion to us. But, as Holy Scripture says, "There is a shame that bringeth sin, and there is a shame that bringeth glory and grace." (Ecclus. iv. 25.) It is said that the devil restores to us at confession that shame which he took from us when he caused us to commit sin. Let it, then, be a cause of our grace and glory in the sacred tribunal, where we must expose our weakness and misery not to angels but to men, not to the saints in heaven but to sinners like ourselves, "who can have compassion on them that are ignorant and that err: because they themselves also are compassed with infirmity." (Heb. v. 2.)

The man in the Gospel who was suffering from paralysis is a true figure of the soul in mortal sin, which is deprived of all spiritual motion and is incapable of any meritorious action. It is in a pitiful state, but still Jesus has mercy on it; and when its good angel and its own ardent desire to be cured from its infirmity cause it to be brought into the presence of our dear Saviour in the holy sacrament of Penance, He immediately says "Be of good heart, son, thy sins are forgiven thee. . . . Arise, and walk"; for the priest, His representative, has not only the mind and the spirit which animated our divine Master in His merciful dealings with sinners—"we have the mind of Christ" (1 Cor. ii. 16.), says St. Paul—but he has also His power to say: "I absolve thee from thy sins."

How grateful we should feel, then, that the love of Jesus has left us this wonderful means of peace and reconciliation! How frequently and how devoutly we should make use of it! What obstacles we should overcome to secure its advantages! If we were as anxious to approach our divine Master with the burden of our sins as the poor man in the Gospel with his infirmity, we should easily find ways and means, time and opportunity to seek His mercy in the holy sacrament of Penance. We should, too, be more grateful than we are, and more anxious to express our "thanks to our God always for the grace that is given us in Christ Jesus. That in all things we are made rich in Him, in all utterance, and in all knowledge . . . so that nothing is wanting to us in any grace, waiting for the manifestation of Our Lord Jesus Christ. Who also will confirm us unto the end without crime, in the day of the coming of our Lord Jesus Christ."

LV

NINETEENTH SUNDAY AFTER PENTECOST

OF GOOD WILL

"Be renewed in the spirit of your mind."
(Epistle: Eph. iv. 23-28.)
"Friend, how camest thou in hither not having on a wedding-garment?"
(Gospel: Matt. xxii. 2-14.)

THE PARABLE of our divine Master in the Gospel of to-day is a beautiful and instructive synopsis, in figurative language of Christian teaching. It is an abridgment of our holy religion which shows at once the merciful designs of Providence in our regard, the means He employs to accomplish them, the strange perversity of the human heart in refusing or neglecting to comply with His wishes, the happiness of those who conform to His holy will, and the misery and punishment of those who oppose it.

Our holy mother the Church in proposing the teachings of the parable for our instruction to-day wishes us particularly to observe its chief conclusion; namely, the necessity for a complete reformation of heart and conscience and a sincere desire or good will to conform to the holy will of God in everything after the example of our divine Master Himself, whose spirit was always that of perfect conformity with the wishes of His Heavenly Father— "My meat is to do the will of Him that sent Me" (John iv. 34.); and again: "He that sent Me, is with Me, and He hath not left Me alone: for I always do the things that please Him." (John viii. 29.) And this desire she expresses in the Epistle: "Be renewed in the spirit of your mind: and put on the new man, who according to God is created in justice and holiness of truth"; not forgetting to mention as usual our great obligation of brotherly love in all things as the most potent and necessary proof of our sincerity.

The kingdom of heaven in the parable is the True Church, which is compared to a marriage-feast. The guests originally invited were the Jews. But they refused God's call and rejected the teaching and religion of Jesus Christ. His servants, the prophets and apostles, and even Jesus Himself, they, "having treated contumeliously, put to death." The result was the rejection of the Jews, the destruction of Jerusalem and the call of the Gentiles, "both bad and good." Even of these many "neglected and went their ways, one to his farm, and another to his merchandise," and some treated the servants of the Master, the sacred ministers of the Gospel, just as the Jews treated the prophets and apostles and Jesus Himself. But many also accepted the invitation and sat themselves down at the Master's table, professing to be faithful friends and followers of Christ. But some were discovered without the necessary wedding-garment of sanctifying grace, or of real desire or good will to please and honor the King, who accordingly ordered them to be bound and cast out forever "into the exterior darkness. There shall be weeping and gnashing of teeth."

Whilst many of those who are desirous of a place in the real kingdom of heaven have necessarily accepted a place in the spiritual kingdom of Christ's Church and have at some time or another freely embraced the Holy Catholic Faith, we must ever remember that mere desires will not suffice for salvation. "Desires kill the slothful." (Prov. xxi. 25.) Not only will the unrepentant sinner be found without the wedding-garment of sanctifying grace, but the weak and careless Catholic, who thinks that because he is a member of the True Church, has accepted the teachings of Christ, and thus finds himself seated as a guest at the table of the King, will also be noticed as an unworthy intruder without the garment of good will, without the spirit of Christ, without the good works which must always accompany true faith. "For even as the body without the spirit is dead," says St. James, "so also faith without works is dead." (James ii. 26.) And Our Lord Himself has said: "Not every one that saith to Me, Lord, Lord, shall enter into the kingdom of heaven: but he that doth the will of My Father who is in heaven, he shall enter into the kingdom of heaven." (Matt. vii. 21.)

Many have the desire to become saints. They would *like* to be saints. But how few saints there are! No wonder the saints performed miracles, because to be a saint is in itself a miracle—a miracle of God's grace by which, notwithstanding all the vicissitudes of gifts, graces, fortune, and circumstances, they are as true to their God as the needle is true to the pole in all changes of temperature, wind, and weather. And yet it is only what we should expect from one who has accepted Christ and His teaching and has guaranteed to adore, love, and serve God alone. For, just as two and two make four not only sometimes, or frequently, but *all the time,* so should we be in the state of grace and engaged in the active service of Almighty God not only generally, as some even boast of, but *always*. Not only should we carry out the holy will of God in many or in most things, but in all and in everything. How one single act of unfaithfulness or ingratitude destroys years of friendship! Why should we expect God to treat us as His choicest friends when we even once betray Him by preferring a miserable creature, a little gain, a vile pleasure, to His eternal love? Do we think God is satisfied to be despised or set aside for the rest of the year provided we profess our friendship for Him at Christmas or Easter, at the death of a friend or relative, on the occasion of our marriage, in a dangerous illness, or at the mission or retreat in our parish? "Be not deceived," says St. Paul, "God is not mocked. For what things a man shall sow, those also shall he reap." (Gal. vi. 7, 8.)

And yet God is prepared to forego, forgive, and even forget the past, if we only repent of our unfaithfulness and sincerely desire to serve Him faithfully for the future: "I will forgive their iniquity, and I will remember their sin no more" (Jer. xxxi. 34.); and again: "Thou hast cast all my sins behind thy back." (Isaias xxxviii. 17.) He says through His prophets.

This sincere desire must be genuine good will and not a mere velleity, which signifies a merely indolent, or inactive, wish or inclination. He who desires the end must also desire and use the means to that end—"Not every one that saith to Me, Lord, Lord, . . . but he that doth the will of My Father." Our salvation, of course depends upon Almighty God, but it also depends upon ourselves. Whilst we can not perform even the slightest meritorious act without the assistance of God's grace inclining the will and supplying the spiritual energy—"for it is God who worketh in you both to will and to accomplish, according to His good will" (Philipp. ii. 13.)—we must at the same time co-operate with the divine assistance and *"work out our salvation."* (Philipp. ii. 12.)

The first great essential in this important work is of course faith in God and in the promises of Jesus Christ. "Without faith it is impossible to please God," says St. Paul, "for he that cometh to God, must believe that He is, and is a rewarder to them that seek Him." (Heb. xi. 6.) The next is to engage in the work with the proper motive and in the proper spirit. This is the motive of divine charity by which we do and suffer everything for the pure love of God. This is the spirit of **Jesus Christ**, the spirit of humility by which we are led to realize that of ourselves we can do nothing, but that with God's grace we can do anything. "I can do all things in Him who strengtheneth me." (Philipp. iv. 13.) Which leads us to a great confidence in God and diffidence in ourselves; so that we pray for help and guidance and are always resigned to God's holy will in everything, making His will our will, living in Him and for Him alone, so that we can say with St. Paul: "I live, now not I; but Christ liveth in me." (Gal. ii. 20.)

Whilst there are many Christians but few saints, then, whilst "many are called but few are chosen," and whilst "wide is the gate and broad is the way that leadeth to destruction, and many there are who go in thereat; how narrow is the gate, and strait is the way that leadeth to life: and few there are that find it." (Matt. vii. 13, 14.) Whilst we are seated as guests at the marriage-feast in the Master's House there are some who have not on the wedding-garment of grace and good will. Let us make it our business to be amongst the number of those who are not only "called to be saints," but who also "are sanctified in Christ Jesus" (1 Cor. i. 2.), to "enter in at the narrow gate" that leads to life eternal, and to provide ourselves with the garment of good will.

To accomplish this we must make a radical and complete change in all our ways. We must be entirely "renewed in the spirit of our minds and put on the new man, who according to God, is created in justice and holiness of truth." We may have performed many good actions, we may have lived what is called a generally virtuous life; but if we had had the proper spirit and the proper motive it would have made all our actions great and holy and would have rendered our lives perfect in the sight of Almighty God, no matter how humble or insignificant they may have been in the eyes of men. As our divine Master explains, "The kingdom of heaven is like to leaven, which a woman took and hid in three measures of meal, until the whole was leavened." (Matt. xiii. 33.) Perhaps we have not even done as much as King Amasias, of whom Holy Scripture says: "He did what was good in the sight of the Lord: but yet not with a perfect heart" (2 Paral. xxv. 2.), for which he was punished by being slain by his own people.

We must give our whole hearts to the service of Almighty God, who says to us: "My son, give Me thy heart: and let thy eyes keep My ways." (Prov. xxiii. 26.) Let us, then, with great humility and keen desire pray with the Psalmist: "Create a clean heart in me, O

God, and renew a right spirit within me" (Ps. l. 12.); with St. Paul, saying, "Lord, what wilt Thou have me to do?" (Acts ix. 6.); and with the Master Himself: "Thy will be done." Let us give ourselves with great generosity to God, without reserve and without any exceptions, "not serving to the eye, as it were pleasing men, but as the servants of Christ doing the will of God from the heart, with a good will serving as to the Lord, and not to men." (Eph. vi. 6, 7.)

The result will be perfect peace of heart and soul amidst all the trials and temptations that surround us, for God's will being our will we can say with St. Paul, "Who, then, shall separate us from the love of Christ? Shall tribulation? or distress? or famine? or nakedness? or danger? or persecution? or the sword? . . . But in all things we overcome because of Him that hath loved us. For I am sure that neither death, nor life, nor angels, nor principalities, nor powers, nor things present, nor things to come, nor might, nor height, nor depth, nor any other creature, shall be able to separate us from the love of God, which is in Christ Jesus our Lord." (Rom. viii. 35–39.) No, because, as the Psalmist says: "O Lord, Thou hast crowned us, as with a shield of Thy good will." (Ps. x. 13.)

LVI

TWENTIETH SUNDAY AFTER PENTECOST

OF ZEAL

"Redeeming the time."
(EPISTLE: Eph. v. 15-21.)
"And himself believed and his whole house."
(GOSPEL: John iv. 46-53.)

CONSIDERING how ungrateful we have been in the past, what a lot we have to answer for, and what a complete change we must effect in our whole course of action, our holy mother the Church urges us to-day to be wise and to begin at once our reformation with great zeal and earnestness—"not as unwise, but as wise: redeeming the time" and carrying out the holy will of God with joy, gratitude, and in the fear of the Lord.

In the Gospel is related the story of the fervent zeal of a certain ruler, or petty king, in coming personally to our divine Master to ask Him to restore to health his son who was even then dying. Notwithstanding the fact that Our Lord refused him, he repeated his request. And his zeal was rewarded by the consoling words of Jesus: "Go thy way, thy son liveth," as well as by the gift of the true Faith, which through his zeal and example was also bestowed on his entire household, for "himself believed and his whole house."

The principle which animated the ruler to make such determined and persistent efforts in spite of all difficulties to secure the Saviour's assistance was his great love for his son. Love conquers all difficulties and makes all labor for the beloved sweet and easy. Thus the love of a mother for her child causes her to accomplish with pleasure and without exception the multitude of what seem to others disagreeable and sometimes even unnecessary tasks. So St. Paul says of the love which we should have for Almighty God as the principle of all our actions—"Charity is patient, is kind; charity envieth not, dealeth not perversely; is not puffed up, is not ambitious, seeketh not her own, is not provoked to anger, thinketh no evil, rejoiceth not in iniquity, but rejoiceth with the truth: beareth all things, believeth all things, hopeth all things, endureth all things. Charity never falleth away." (1 Cor. xiii. 4–8.)

Love, then, is the secret of zeal. If we loved Almighty God perfectly, according to His commandment: "Thou shalt love the

Lord thy God, with thy whole heart, and with thy whole soul, and with thy whole mind" (Matt. xxii. 37.), we should be filled with a burning zeal for His honor and glory, for the salvation of all men and for our own sanctification and perfection; with such an ardent desire to see Him more known and better loved that we should be prepared to attempt all projects, overcome all difficulties and accomplish all things by His grace and assistance. All sin would be hateful to us, even the slightest, and all suffering would seem sweet, as has been proved and experienced by all the saints, as St. Paul testifies when he says: "In all things let us exhibit ourselves as the ministers of God, in much patience, in tribulation, in necessities, in distresses, in stripes, in prisons, in seditions, in labor, in watchings, in fastings, in charity, in knowledge, in long-suffering, in sweetness, in the Holy Ghost, in charity unfeigned, in the word of truth, in the power of God; by the armor of justice on the right hand and on the left; by honor and dishonor, by evil report and good report; as deceivers, and yet true; as unknown, and yet known; as dying, and behold we live; as chastised, and not killed; as sorrowful, yet always rejoicing; as needy, yet enriching many; as having nothing, and possessing all things." (2 Cor. vi. 4–10.)

Want of true zeal on our part, then, is due to want of perfect charity, which is ultimately due to our want of a lively faith. As St. Paul explains, the Gentiles attained to justice but the Jews failed to do so "because they sought it not by faith, but as it were of works." (Rom. ix. 30–32.) "Being justified therefore by faith," he says, "let us have peace with God, through Our Lord Jesus Christ: by whom also we have access through faith into this grace wherein we stand, and glory in the hope of the glory of the sons of God. And not only so; but we glory also in tribulations, knowing that tribulation worketh patience; and patience trial; and trial hope. And hope confoundeth not: because the charity of God is poured forth in our hearts by the Holy Ghost, who is given to us." (Rom. v. 1–5.)

Just as energy in our divine Master's service is opposed by sloth, so zeal in His service is opposed by tepidity, or lukewarmness. Of the two vices tepidity is by far the more dangerous and is the more displeasing to God, who says to the lukewarm soul: "I would thou wert cold or hot. But because thou art lukewarm, and neither cold nor hot, I will begin to vomit thee out of My mouth." (Apoc. iii. 15, 16.) That tepidity is a most dangerous vice is clear also from the fact that it generally indicates a state of hidden mortal sin, the poor soul being spiritually blind to its miserable condition: and also from the words of God Himself to such a soul: "Thou sayest: I am rich, and made wealthy, and have need of nothing; and knowest not that thou art wretched, and miserable, and poor, and blind, and naked." (Apoc. iii. 17.) And the cure He advises is the pure and perfect love of Himself: "I counsel thee to buy of Me gold fire tried, that thou mayest be made rich; and mayest be clothed in white garments, and that the shame of thy nakedness may not appear; and anoint thy eyes with eyesalve, that thou mayest see. Such as I love I rebuke and chastise. Be zealous, therefore, and do penance. Behold I stand at the gate and knock." (Apoc. iii. 18–20.)

What a privilege for us that we are thus visited by our dear Master! To-day He stands at our door and knocks. He warns us of our danger and bids us examine our condition. And He suggests the remedies of penance for the past and great zeal for the future.

The chief danger of tepidity arises from the fact that it is looked upon as anything but dangerous; and this from a mistaken idea as to what it really is. Many look upon it as a mere negation, a want of perfection, a kind of spiritual relaxation from constant work, a weariness in well-doing, and so confuse it with weariness of mind, spiritual dryness, or want of sensible feelings of devotion, which are not in themselves sins any more than temptations to which we do not wilfully consent. Tepidity is a positive state of sin, for the lukewarm soul is one that does not scruple about committing venial sins, though it tries to avoid mortal sins. It is a mean vice, because it bargains with God, as it were, as to how far it may dare to offend Him without losing Him altogether. It wishes to buy heaven, that "pearl of great price," as cheaply as possible; to win it, as it were, on a mere technicality. Thus it approaches nearer and nearer to mortal sin until eventually the border is passed and the poor, blind, deluded soul finds itself in the pit which it so fondly imagined it was avoiding.

There are two classes of venial sins—those of surprise and those of full deliberation. The former are the result of human frailty, and no one can be entirely free from them, "for there is no just man upon the earth, that doth good, and sinneth not" (Eccles. vii. 21.), says Holy Scripture. And St. John tells us that "if we say that we have no sin, we deceive ourselves, and the truth is not in us." (1 John i. 8.) But the just man soon discovers and repents of such faults and recovers himself by the grace of God with even increased strength, being led to depend more upon God and less upon himself in future. A tepid soul, on the contrary, often commits deliberate venial sins which it could easily avoid if it had the good will to serve God sincerely and with true love. Indeed, it is just the want of perfect love that kills true zeal; and it is remarkable that such souls generally begin their unfaithfulness by little breaches of the virtue of charity in their conversation. If "charity covereth a multitude of sins" (1 Peter iv. 8.), surely the want of it exposes them. Little things always lead to greater, and "he that contemneth small things shall fall by little and little" (Ecclus. xix. 1.); and "Behold, how small a fire, what a great wood it kindleth" (James iii. 5.), says Holy Scripture.

Thus the love of God becomes gradually supplanted by the love of sin, venial at first, but ultimately mortal. For he who desires to serve God in such a poor fashion can not expect to be enriched in great measure by His grace, for "he who soweth sparingly, shall also reap sparingly." (2 Cor. ix. 6.) So when the temptation to mortal sin takes hold of him, although God will still not withhold sufficient grace to overcome it, He will withhold His special grace. For such a sinner a fall is almost certain and a recovery very difficult, for he has already abused the very helps which are most necessary for him, such as prayer, acts of contrition, horror of sin, the love of God, self-examination, and humility.

Whilst the cure of tepidity is difficult, it is not impossible, by the grace of God, to be obtained by fervent prayer. The first great step toward a recovery is the realization of our condition. This, thank God, we now see, for our divine Master Himself has supplied us with the eye-salve which cures our spiritual blindness. The next is a strong desire to be relieved from our miserable condition, which should lead us to the throne of God's grace and mercy, where by fervent prayer we shall obtain all the help we require. "Let us go, therefore, with confidence to the throne of grace: that we may obtain mercy, and find grace in seasonable aid." (Heb. iv. 16.) Then we must remove all occasions of sin, particularly of habitual sin, however venial. We must "catch the little foxes that destroy the vines" (Cant. ii. 16.)—the deliberate venial faults which eat away the spiritual life of the soul.

And finally, we must devote ourselves with our whole heart and soul in a spirit of perfect generosity to the love and service of Almighty God, counting no price too much, no sacrifice too great, no detail of too little importance, in order to secure that "pearl of great price" which our divine Master has in store for us. "The kingdom of heaven is like to a merchant seeking good pearls. Who when he had found one pearl of great price, went his way, and sold all that he had and bought it." (Matt. xiii. 46.) This is the pearl of the precious love of God which is for us our dearest and most valued treasure, to procure and preserve which will be our chief delight in our zealous work for the Master, who will help us to make up for the past and redeem the time by sanctifying with the gifts of His faith and His love the whole household of our soul.

LVII

TWENTY-FIRST SUNDAY AFTER PENTECOST

OF DEFENSE

"Put you on the armor of God."
(EPISTLE: Eph. vi. 10–17.)
"So also shall My Heavenly Father do to you." (GOSPEL: Matt. xviii. 23–35.)

"THE LIFE of man upon earth is a warfare" (Job vii. 1.), says holy Job. On the one side are ranged the world, the flesh, and the devil, and on the other heaven, the soul, and Jesus Christ. The battle is for a kingdom. The one side fights for hell and the ruin of souls, the other for the kingdom of God and the salvation of men. The leader on the one side "goeth about like a roaring lion, seeking whom he may devour" (1 Peter v. 8.), saying to his army: "Let us lie in wait for blood, let us hide snares for the innocent without cause; let us swallow him up alive like hell, and whole as one that goeth down into the pit." (Prov. i. 11, 12.) The leader on the other side goes about doing good, "virtue and power going out from Him, and healing all" (Luke vi. 19.), saying: "The Son of man is come to seek and to save that which was lost" (Luke xix. 10.), "The thief cometh not, but for to steal and to kill and to destroy. I am come that they may have life and may have it more abundantly. I am the good shepherd. The good shepherd giveth his life for his sheep." (John x. 10, 11.)

There can be no doubt as to which army we shall join, for which leader we shall fight. So our holy mother the Church wishes us to-day to provide ourselves with all possible means of defense against the enemy, so that we may fight manfully and with every hope of complete and final victory. But, as St. Paul says, "though we walk in the flesh, we do not war according to the flesh. For the weapons of our warfare are not carnal." (2 Cor. x. 3, 4.) Hence the Epistle of to-day advises us: "Put you on the armor of God, that you may be able to stand against the deceits of the devil. For our wrestling is not against flesh and blood, but against principalities and powers, against the rulers of the world of this darkness, against the spirits of wickedness in the high places." And the armor of God which we must put on consists of "truth," "justice," "the gospel of peace," "faith," and "the word of God."

AFTER PENTECOST

We must put on the armor of God and not trust to ourselves. "No man can say the Lord Jesus, but by the Holy Ghost" (1 Cor. xii. 3.), says St. Paul, and "Without Me you can do nothing" (John xv. 5.), says Christ Himself. Hence we must have great confidence in the power and assistance which God will give us, and be very humble and diffident in ourselves. "Blessed is the man that is always fearful" (Prov. xxviii. 14.), says Holy Scripture. We must therefore "work out our salvation with fear and trembling" (Philipp. ii. 12.), expecting nothing but disaster from our own unaided efforts and nothing but victory from God, for "no one hath hoped in the Lord and hath been confounded." (Ecclus. ii. 11.)

From which it follows that we must make frequent use of humble and persevering prayer, for this is the only means of securing the assistance of Almighty God. We "can do all things in Him who strengtheneth us." (Philipp. iv. 13.) By prayer alone, then, can we obtain that strength, for it is the only means provided by God Himself, who urges us "always to pray and not to faint." (Luke xviii. 1.) But it is an infallible means. "I say to you," says Christ, "all things whatsoever you ask when you pray, believe that you shall receive, and they shall come unto you." (Mark xi. 24.)

Thus "they that hope in the Lord shall renew their strength, they shall take wings as eagles, they shall run and not be weary, they shall walk and not faint." (Isaias xi. 31.)

This confidence will help us to walk bravely forward in the way of God's commandments, our "feet shod with the preparation of the gospel of peace." What these commandments are in detail we learn from the Holy Word of God by reading spiritual books and by listening with attention and devotion to the instructions and sermons of the sacred ministers of the Gospel. "Take unto you the helmet of salvation and the sword of the Spirit, which is the word of God." Everywhere in Holy Scripture reference is made to the great value of this Holy Word in the work of our salvation. Looked at from a merely human point of view, it is "a grain of mustard-seed, which is the least indeed of all seeds, but when it is grown up, it is greater than all herbs." (Matt. xiii. 31.) It is the foundation of our faith, the teaching of truth, the cause of our salvation. "Faith cometh by hearing," says St. Paul, "and hearing by the word of Christ." (Rom. x. 17.) And again: "The word of God is living and effectual, and more piercing than any two edged sword." (Heb. iv. 12.) "When He, the Spirit of truth, is come, He will teach you all truth. For He shall not speak of Himself" (John xvi. 13.), said our divine Master, who also says: "Blessed are they who hear the word of God, and keep it." (Luke xi. 28.) Hence St. James advises: "With meekness receive the ingrafted word, which is able to save your souls." (James i. 21.) There is, therefore, a very special efficacy in the spoken Word. The priest is armed with the divine authority to preach and teach it, and so it comes from him "not according to man . . . but by the revelation of Jesus Christ." (Gal. i. 11, 12.)

It is in sermons and instructions that we hear about Almighty God and His precepts. The Holy Word teaches us to know Him and to know ourselves. It reminds us when we forget; reassures us when in doubt or uncertainty; warns us when in danger; threatens us when careless; helps us when in need; consoles us when afflicted by sin and its consequences. Above all, it helps us to think. And as want of thought is the great cause of the loss of souls, so the Holy Word of God is the cause of the salvation of those who hear it in the proper spirit and with the proper dispositions. "With desolation is all the land made desolate, because there is none that considereth in the heart" (Jer. xii. 11.), says Holy Scripture. And so St. John says: "This is eternal life: That they may know Thee, the only true God, and Jesus Christ, whom Thou hast sent." (John xvii. 3.)

It is in knowing Our Lord Jesus Christ that we know the infinite goodness and wisdom and power of God, for He is the mirror in which the divine attributes are reflected, "now through a glass in a dark manner" (1 Cor. xiii. 12.), as St. Paul says, but none the less faithfully, for He is "the brightness of His glory, and the figure of His substance" (Heb. i. 3.), as the same Apostle also asserts.

He is the perfect model of all sanctity upon which we must strive to form our lives and realize our duty to our Creator and Redeemer. "I am the way, and the truth, and the life" (John xiv. 6.), He says; and again: "I am the light of the world: he that followeth Me, walketh not in darkness, but shall have the light of life." (John viii. 12.)

We must, then, take Jesus for our model and look to Him for our example. His chief characteristic was love. So must our chief title to be considered His disciples and faithful imitators be our love for God and our neighbor. How often have we not been told by Him of this most necessary virtue of the true Christian! And how often have we not been told of the true test of its possession by us—the love of our neighbor. "By this shall all men know that you are My disciples, if you have love one for another." (John xiii. 35.) To-day our holy mother the Church again calls our attention to this great and most necessary qualification by the parable related in the Gospel. A servant of a great king owed his master an immense sum of money. Not being able to discharge the debt, he asked his lord for mercy, who in pity forgave him all. Immediately the servant went out and met a fellow-servant who owed him a small sum, and, as the Gospel graphically expresses, "laying hold of him, he throttled him, saying: Pay what thou owest." But the unfortunate man was unable to do so and was cast into prison. However, when the king heard of this harsh and unmerciful action he was very angry and told the wicked servant that he should have had compassion on his neighbor seeing that he himself had just been forgiven such a large sum by a merciful master. Our Lord points out the lesson for us in the words: "So also shall My Heavenly Father do to you, if you forgive not every one his brother from your hearts."

Whenever we say the Lord's Prayer we ask for mercy—"forgive us our trespasses." And we ask Almighty God to give it to us in the same measure and after the same manner in which we forgive our enemies—"as we forgive them that trespass against us." What a curse instead of a blessing we make of it then, if we forgive our enemies in words only, but not "from our hearts"! What if Almighty God should take us at our word and forgive us exactly in the same manner and measure. Alas, our Heavenly Father is constantly forgiving us an immensity of sin, and we think it hard to forgive a little offense or insult that we very often deserve at the hands of others! If we wish to obtain God's help in our war against Satan we must then be very forgiving, very meek, very humble, and very charitable in thought, word, and deed, for "charity covereth a multitude of sins" (1 Peter iv. 8.) and obtains for us many victories.

Seeing all our weakness and realizing all our wants, our divine Master instituted for our spiritual help and guidance those channels of grace by which the precious merits of His sacred passion and death are applied to our souls—the holy sacraments. Here all the wants of our souls are provided for. Here the power of Heaven itself ranges itself on our side in the conflict against the powers of sin, Satan, and hell. In the sacrament of Penance we learn to know our miserable weakness, to practise humility by our sincere confession, to make acts of contrition and of charity, to form good resolutions, and to realize the mercy and power of God when His sacred minister says, "I absolve thee from thy sins." In Holy Communion we receive as the food of our souls the Bread of Life that came down from heaven, Jesus Himself, who by His divine grace and presence strengthens us for the fight and accompanies us to final victory.

We should then frequently make use of these strong and sure means of defense against our infernal enemies. "If God be for us," says St. Paul, "who is against us?" (Rom. viii. 31.) With our divine Master and Leader on our side, and with our faithful allegiance to Him, victory is certain, and we can soon say with St. Paul: "I have fought a good fight, I have finished my course, I have kept the faith. As to the rest, there is laid up for me a crown of justice, which the Lord, the just judge, will render to me in that day." (2 Tim. iv. 7, 8.)

LVIII

TWENTY-SECOND SUNDAY AFTER PENTECOST

OF PERFECTION

"He who hath begun a good work in you, will perfect it." (EPISTLE: Philipp. i. 6–11.)
"Render therefore to Cæsar the things that are Cæsar's: and to God, the things that are God's." (GOSPEL: Matt. xxii. 15–21.)

OUR holy mother the Church places before us to-day for our consideration two most important truths, both of which are frequently lost sight of by many Christians. The first is that we are all bound to aim at the perfection of sanctity. And the second is that such perfection may be attained, as far as the weakness of human nature will allow, in all states of life, and even in our smallest and most ordinary actions. For our aim at the perfection of sanctity is not destroyed by venial faults of surprise, which are immediately repaired by true repentance and the love of God. "There is no just man upon the earth, that doth good, and sinneth not" (Eccles. vii. 21.), says Holy Scripture; but at the same time we are told that "a just man shall fall seven times and shall rise again." (Prov. xxiv. 16.) No one can serve God without such imperfections unless he has an extraordinary privilege of grace, such as was granted to our most holy mother Mary.

We are all bound to aim at perfection because it is the command of Almighty God, who, in announcing His precept, makes no exception of age, sex, condition, or class in life. "Thou shalt be perfect, and without spot before the Lord thy God" (Deut. xviii. 13.), says Holy Scripture. "Be you therefore perfect, as also your Heavenly Father is perfect" (Matt. v. 48.), says our divine Master Himself.

Whilst we can never attain the state of absolute perfection in this life, we must continually aim at becoming more and more perfect, more and more holy, "that our charity may more and more abound in knowledge and in all understanding." "Not as though I had already attained," says St. Paul, "or were already perfect; but I follow after, if I may by any means apprehend, wherein I am also apprehended by Christ Jesus. . . . Stretching forth myself to those that are before, I press toward the mark, to the prize of the supernal vocation of God in Christ Jesus." (Philipp. iii. 12–14.) Hence we can never say that we have attained a sufficient degree of sanctity, and thus rest satisfied, for the "supernal vocation of God in Christ Jesus" is that perfect love of God and union with Him, which we can hope for only in the life to come in the blessed company of those "who are written in the heavens . . . the spirits of the just made perfect." (Heb. xii. 23.) During our life upon earth, therefore "the path of the just, as a shining light, goeth forward and increaseth even to perfect day" (Prov. iv. 18.), for "they shall go from virtue unto virtue" (Ps. lxxxiii. 8.) "unto the day of Christ Jesus."

That such perfection is possible for all is quite clear in the first place from the words of St. Paul in the Epistle of to-day: "We are confident in the Lord Jesus, that He who hath begun a good work in you, will perfect it unto the day of Christ Jesus. As it is meet for me to think this for you all." Here the Apostle makes no exception, but hopes that *all* will aim at perfection of sanctity. In the next place it will be seen that this is not only possible but even easy for all, when we consider the nature of the perfection required of us. As Almighty God Himself says: "This commandment, that I command thee this day is not above thee, nor far off from thee: nor is it in heaven, that thou shouldst say: Which of us can go up to heaven to bring it unto us, and we may hear and fulfil it in work? Nor is it beyond the sea: that thou mayest excuse thyself and say: Which of us can cross the sea, and bring it unto us: that we may hear, and do that which is commanded? But the word is very nigh unto thee, in thy mouth and in thy heart, that thou mayest do it." (Deut. xxx. 11–14.) Some imagine that the pursuit of perfection can be attended to only in the religious state, and that it consists of constant prayers, mortifications, meditations, and vows of poverty, chastity, and obedience. But this is a grievous error, for God does not expect such. He has placed some in religion and some in the world, some in one state of life and some in another, and all that He expects is that each one discharge faithfully the duties of his particular state, no matter how humble or unspiritual-looking these duties may appear. If we do His will in this regard with fidelity and resignation, we can do no more. Hence He tells us that the commandment of which He speaks is near us and quite easy of fulfilment. It lies, according to St. Luke, in our own desire to do the holy will of God—

"Lo, the kingdom of God is within you." (Luke xvii. 21.) It simply means, then, according to Almighty God Himself: "Hear the voice of the Lord thy God, and keep His precepts and ceremonies, which are written in this law: and return to the Lord thy God with all thy heart and with all thy soul." (Deut. xxx. 10.)

Our divine Master Himself, who is our model in everything, spent thirty years of His sacred life discharging the humble duties of a poor carpenter's son. And He was perfect. Whatever He did was according to the holy will of His Eternal Father—"I always do the things that please Him" (John viii. 29.), He says. If we imitate Him, we, too, shall please God perfectly. And this is the state of sanctity for which we should aim.

Whilst it is true that Almighty God calls some to a more perfect state than others, and expects some to make use of certain means of perfection that He does not impose upon all, it by no means follows that perfection in itself consists either in the particular state in which it is to be sought, or in the means themselves of acquiring it. Just as the habit does not make the monk, it is not the religious state that of itself makes the saint, but rather the faithful discharge of the duties of that state. And as all have duties to perform with respect to their daily occupation, their business, their families, their social relations, so if one should neglect any of these for the purpose of prayer or some other religious work he would offend God rather than please Him. That this is true is quite evident from the strong language of Holy Scripture on the matter: "Doth the Lord desire holocausts and victims, and not rather that the voice of the Lord should be obeyed?" said Samuel, "for obedience is better than sacrifice." (1 Kings xv. 22.) "If any man hath not care of his own, and especially of those of his house, he hath denied the faith, and is worse than an infidel" (1 Tim. v. 8.), says St. Paul. How little they please God, then, who run about to churches to pray, to hospitals to visit the sick, to charity-meetings, bazaars, and concerts, and neglect their own families. They think that because the works are good in themselves that they are virtuous in doing them. Very often such labors are not blessed by God for this very reason and are thereby the cause of much uncharitableness in word and deed under the very cloak of charity, and so can not be called the Master's work, for "By their fruits you shall know them." (Matt. vii. 16.)

To assist in removing these false and erroneous ideas from the minds of her children, our holy mother the Church places before us to-day the teaching of our divine Master Himself with regard to the discharge of our twofold duties to God and to our neighbor. He was asked on one occasion whether it was lawful to pay tribute to Cæsar, or not. As His audience was composed of the two opposing classes of the Pharisees and the Herodians, He would have given offense to one or the other by answering either Yes or No. For the Pharisees held that it was not lawful for the Jews to subject themselves to any one but God. And the Herodians, who were the followers of King Herod, appointed over the Jews by the Romans, of course held that the taxes imposed by the Roman law should be paid by all. So Our Lord avoided the difficulty by pointing to the image and inscription of the emperor, whose power over them they implicitly acknowledged by the very use of his coinage, and saying: "Render therefore to Cæsar the things that are Cæsar's, and to God the things that are God's."

Here our divine Master clearly lays down that we have, besides our duty to God, a duty also included in it of lawful subjection to human authority, provided the latter does not interfere with the former. This is not a contradiction of that other principle, which says that "no man can serve two masters." (Matt. vi. 24.) For by obeying lawful authority we also obey God, who commands us to "Be subject to higher powers; for there is no power but from God: and those that are, are ordained of God. Therefore he that resisteth the power, resisteth the ordinance of God. And they that resist, purchase to themselves damnation. . . . Render, therefore, to all men their dues: Tribute, to whom tribute is due; custom, to whom custom; fear, to whom fear; honor, to whom honor." (Rom. xiii. 1–7.) Which means that by the conscientious and faithful discharge of our national, civic, social, and family duties we are doing the holy will of God and pleasing Him perfectly. Thus it is possible for all to aim at perfection with hope of success in every sphere and condition of life whether as rulers or subjects, as masters or as servants, as secular or as religious. "Be ye subject, therefore," says St. Peter, "to every human creature for God's sake; whether it be to the king, as excelling; or to governors as sent by him for the punishment of evil-doers, or for the praise of the good: for so is the will of God." (1 Peter ii. 13, 14.)

Let us, then, according to the holy will of God increase daily in perfection by the humble and faithful discharge of all the duties of our state of life. Some of these may not seem to be very noble or very spiritual in their nature, but a pure intention will sanctify them and make them rich and meritorious in the sight of God. Our ordinary actions may in themselves be like the dry bones seen in vision by the prophet Ezechiel, and may by their appearance lead us to think that we do not do much for God. The Lord set the prophet in the midst of a plain that was full of dry bones. And by the power of God "the bones came together, each one to its joint. And I saw, and behold the sinews, and the flesh came up upon them: and the skin was stretched out over them, but *there was no spirit in them.*" God, however, breathed on them and immediately "the spirit came into them, and they lived: and they stood up upon their feet, an exceeding great army." (Ezech. xxxvii.) So the multitude of our actions, looked at in themselves, may be only dry bones, or they may even be clothed with the flesh and blood, bone and sinews of what are apparently good and meritorious actions, but without the pure and right intention of doing them for God's sake they will have no spirit in them. But we have that intention. And so the Spirit of God will make all our actions live in His sight, "an exceeding great army" able to fight for us "unto the day of Christ, filled with the fruit of justice through Jesus Christ, unto the glory and praise of God."

LIX

TWENTY-THIRD SUNDAY AFTER PENTECOST

OF PERSEVERANCE

"Many walk . . . whose end is destruction."
(EPISTLE: Philipp. iii. 17—iv. 3.)
"Be of good heart, daughter, thy faith hath made thee whole."
(GOSPEL: Matt. ix. 18-26.)

ALL THE advice of our divine Master, all the preaching, teaching, and exhortation of our holy mother the Church with regard to our great affair of salvation, and all our good resolutions and meritorious works toward that end will be alike in vain if we do not at last secure our eternal happiness by dying in the grace and friendship of Almighty God. Hence to-day we are urgently exhorted to the great necessity for patience and perseverance in our efforts.

We are told in the Epistle the sad truth that many are now engaged in discharging the duties imposed upon them as Christians with apparent success, but who will, alas, not persevere. "Many walk," says St. Paul, "of whom I have told you often and now tell you weeping that they are enemies of the cross of Christ; whose end is destruction." And the chief cause of their ultimate damnation is set down to the fact that they become forgetful of their great destiny as heirs to the kingdom of heaven, and "mind earthly things." The result is that their spirit of faith becomes weakened, their charity cold, and their patience under the trials and temptations that surround them is unable of itself to bear up to the end.

No matter how well one may strive in any worldly contest of skill, strength, or endurance, it is only those who actually complete the allotted task that have any chance of winning the prize. All others are disqualified. So it is in the race for the kingdom of heaven. Here there is a prize for all. But only for those who finish. "The prize," says St. Bernard, "is promised to those who commence, but it is given only to those who persevere." Hence our divine Master Himself has said: "Because iniquity hath abounded, the charity of many shall grow cold. But he that shall persevere to the end, he shall be saved." (Matt. xxiv. 12, 13.)

We have seen on many previous occasions that our struggle for salvation is not an easy one: that "From the days of John the Baptist until now, the kingdom of heaven suffereth violence, and the violent bear it away" (Matt. xi. 12.) : that it demands a constant warfare against sin, resistance to temptation, and mortification of ourselves. "You have not yet resisted unto blood," says St. Paul, "striving against sin." (Heb. xii. 4.) We must, therefore, he adds, "persevere under the discipline of the Lord" so that when temptation comes we may be strong to resist it.

But why is it that so many who have begun well, and continued well, in the faithful service of God, at length fail and die in mortal sin? The causes are remote and proximate. The chief proximate causes are, of course, almost innumerable but may be generally included in the seductive influences of the three great sources of temptation mentioned by St. John —"the concupiscence of the flesh, and the concupiscence of the eyes, and the pride of life." (1 John ii. 16.) If we were allowed to continue our efforts to obtain salvation, without any such temptations or disturbing influences, the work might be considered comparatively easy; so easy, in fact, that we should deserve no reward for doing what in such circumstances would naturally please us. But such is not the will of Almighty God, who will only reward those whom He has tried and found faithful—"that could have transgressed, and have not transgressed: and could do evil things, and have not done them." (Ecclus. xxi. 10.) For God gave us the gift of free will to choose either good or evil—"I have set before thee this day life and good, and on the other hand death and evil." (Deut. xxx. 15.) Then He tries us in the fire of temptation—"Behold I will melt, and try them." (Jer. ix. 7.)

St. Paul compares the work of our salvation to the building of a spiritual edifice on the foundation of faith in Our Lord Jesus Christ which will be tested by the fire of temptation: "Now if any man build upon this foundation, gold, silver, precious stones, wood, hay, stubble; every man's work shall be manifest. For the day of the Lord shall declare it, because it shall be revealed in fire; and the fire shall try every man's work, of what sort it is. If any man's work abide, which he hath built thereupon, he shall receive a reward." (1 Cor. iii. 12–14.) We must build upon the foundation of faith in Our Lord Jesus Christ—"For other foundation no man can lay, but that which is laid; which is Christ Jesus." (1 Cor. iii. 11.) And this foundation must be tested. "You shall greatly rejoice," says St. Peter, "if now you must be for a little time made sorrowful in divers temptations: that the trial of your faith (much more precious than gold, which is tried by the fire) may be found unto praise and glory and honor." (1 Peter i. 4, 7.)

Here, then, we arrive at a definite conclusion: Firstly, we must have a lively faith, accompanied by the performance of good works. And secondly, we must be able to overcome temptation.

Although faith is in itself the free gift of Almighty God, the assent which we give to the truths it reveals, on account of God's authority, is a virtue for acts of which we obtain a reward through the merits of Our Lord Jesus Christ. Hence our divine Master frequently complimented and praised those who showed special proofs of a lively faith and rewarded them by the cure of their infirmities, or the granting of their other petitions, as the Gospel of to-day relates, for example. Thus He rewarded the faith of the ruler by raising his daughter to life, and the more simple though not less lively faith of the poor woman who secretly touched the hem of His garment by curing her of her long illness, saying: "Thy faith hath made thee whole"; whereas He sometimes rebuked even His own disciples for their want of lively faith, saying: "O ye of little faith" (Matt. vi. 30.); and again: "Why are you fearful? Have you no faith yet?" (Mark iv. 40.)

With regard to temptations, we have been warned to prepare to resist them. "Son," says Holy Scripture, "when thou comest to the service of God, stand in justice and in fear, and prepare thy soul for temptation." (Ecclus. ii. 1.) We must, then, in order to persevere to the end, be filled with the fear of God, knowing our own weakness and misery and the poverty of our faith. "The fear of the Lord is the beginning of wisdom" (Ps. cx. 9.), says Holy Scripture: and again: "The fear of the Lord is the lesson of wisdom: and humility goeth before glory." (Prov. xv. 33.) And this is so because we must realize how little we can do of ourselves and so must depend entirely on God alone. Self-confidence is hateful to God and is often punished by His abandoning us to our sins, or by allowing us to fall victims to temptations which we never experienced before, and the credit of freedom from the results of which we took to ourselves. "Wherefore he that thinketh himself to stand, let him take heed lest he fall." (1 Cor. x. 12.)

"Some suffer greater temptations in the beginning of their conversion," says the "Imitation of Christ," "and some in the end. And some there are who are much troubled, we may say all their life. Some are but lightly tempted, according to the wisdom and equity of the ordinance of God." (Book i. **13**.) So, some are never tempted in one matter, and some never in another. The danger is, then, of boasting, even to ourselves, of our untried virtue and taking the glory to ourselves as if we had by our own efforts made it "gold, firetried." (Apoc. iii. 18.) There is no credit due to the innocence which arises from mere ignorance. And there is no need to boast that there are some commandments which we have never transgressed, since no man has the temptation or the desire, even if he had the time or the opportunity, to break them all. "Blessed is the man that endureth temptation," says St. James, "for when he hath been proved, he shall receive the crown of life." (James i. **12**.)

As a lively faith and effective resistance to temptation are not to be got by our own unaided efforts, then, it is as clear as the existence of Almighty God Himself that we must obtain these favors from Him if we wish to persevere. And that can be accomplished by *prayer alone*—constant, persevering, and humble prayer, with every confidence in God's will and power to help us. Nothing else can save us. And this is why all the saints and spiritual writers insist upon the practice of prayer as an essential means to salvation. This is not a mere beautiful, poetical, or sentimental theory,

AFTER PENTECOST

but a matter of hard fact founded on the positive law of Almighty God. If we wish to persevere we must have a lively faith which will make us remember our last end, and make us desire to live as those whose "conversation is in heaven." We can obtain it by prayer alone. If we wish to carry out our desires we must get grace from God to resist temptation and engage in the constant practice of good works. We can obtain such by prayer, and by prayer alone. "Without Me," says Christ, "you can do nothing." (John xv. 5.) But by prayer and a lively faith we can do anything. When the poor man came to Jesus, complaining that he had brought his lunatic son to the disciples and they failed to cure him, Jesus Himself cured him immediately and complained of the want of a lively faith, not only on the part of the poor man himself, but even on the part of the disciples, for He explained their failure to them by saying in answer to their question "Why could not we cast him out?" "Because of your unbelief. For, amen I say to you, if you have faith as a grain of mustard seed, you shall say to this mountain; Remove from hence hither, and it shall remove: and nothing shall be impossible to you." (Matt. xvii.) Hence if we pray we shall persevere and be saved. If we do not pray we shall as surely be lost.

Let us, then, always pray. Whenever our divine Master praised people for their faith they were always asking Him for a favor. Not always in long words, but very briefly: "Lord, that I may see." "Jesus, master, have mercy on us." Sometimes not in words at all, like the poor woman in the Gospel of to-day, who merely "said within herself. If I shall touch only His garment, I shall be healed." But Jesus rewarded her prayer and her faith and granted her a perfect cure. Let us, then, often say: "Lord, increase our faith"; "Lord, teach us to pray"; "Lead us not into temptation." Let us often pray to our holy mother Mary to obtain for us the gift of faith and of prayer. She "will pour out upon the house of David, and upon the inhabitants of Jerusalem, the spirit of grace, and of prayers" (Zach. xii. 10.), and through her intercession we shall persevere unto the end, for, as she herself promises: "They that find me shall find life and shall have salvation from the Lord." (Prov. viii. 35.)

LX

TWENTY-FOURTH SUNDAY AFTER PENTECOST

OF JUDGMENT

"Who hath made us worthy to be partakers of the lot of the saints."
(EPISTLE: Col. i. 9–14.)
"Then shall all the tribes of the earth mourn." (GOSPEL: Matt. xxiv. 15–35.)

KNOWING the value of that salutary advice of Holy Scripture: "In all thy works remember thy last end, and thou shalt never sin" (Ecclus. vii. 40.), our holy mother the Church places before us on the last as well as on the first Sunday of her ecclesiastical year the great thought of the last judgment. She knows that the consideration of this important truth, upon which depend such terrible consequences, can not be too frequently before the minds of her children. "It is appointed unto men once to die, and after this the judgment" (Heb. ix. 27.), says St. Paul. Hence our eternal happiness in heaven or our everlasting misery in hell depends upon the moment of our death. No one can tell when that moment may arrive for him. It is altogether out of his hands. Men may by a certain amount of care avoid a certain amount of illness or accident. But when God calls them to "render an account of their stewardship" no human care, forethought, or precaution can delay even for a moment the answer to the summons. Sinners sometimes vainly imagine that by taking precautions they can guard against the approach of death, and so provide themselves with time for repentance. Because God does not immediately punish them for their crimes they are deluded by this false hope which they propose to themselves and which is so displeasing to Almighty God—"And their hope the abomination." (Job xi. 20.)

But God warns such, saying: "These things hast thou done and I was silent. Thou thoughtest unjustly that I should be like to thee; but I will reprove thee and set before thy face." (Ps. xlix. 21.) And this He will do when they least expect it, and they will fall into hell as suddenly as a man who falls to the ground when his foot slips: "Revenge is mine, and I will repay them in due time, that their foot may slide." (Deut. xxxii. 35.) Hence Holy Scripture tells us: "Say not: I have sinned, and what evil hath befallen me?" (Ecclus. v. 4.), but rather: "The mercies of the

Lord that we are not consumed." (Lam. iii. 32.) Let us prepare now to examine our affairs, according to the advice of St. Paul: "If we would judge ourselves, we should not be judged" (1 Cor. xi. 31.), for as the day of our death will come when we least expect it, so will the day of our judgment. "Of that day or hour no man knoweth" (Mark xiii. 32.), says St. Mark. "The day of the Lord shall so come as a thief in the night" (1 Thess. v. 2.), says St. Paul. Hence St. Luke advises us: "Be you ready: for at what hour you think not, the Son of man will come." (Luke xii. 40.)

On the first Sunday of Advent our holy mother the Church presented the thought of judgment to us in a different light and in a different spirit from that in which she invites us to the consideration of the same great truth to-day. Then she but briefly touched on the last great day, referring in a few short words to its preceding signs, whilst she hopefully and joyfully encouraged us to rise from sleep and begin the Master's Work. To-day, however, she not only describes in detail the general confusion, distress, and destruction which is to take place on the last day, but also refers to the sad and dismal scenes that were to precede and accompany the destruction of the city and temple of Jerusalem, and the ruin and dispersion of the Jews, who were to be thus punished for their obstinacy and hardness of heart in rejecting the Saviour and despising His divine character and sacred mission.

Such calamities actually happened a few years after our Saviour's death, when the Roman army under the emperor Titus besieged and conquered the Holy City, destroyed and utterly ruined everything in it, even the temple, and massacred all the miserable people that famine and disease had left. The famous Jewish historian Josephus relates that eleven hundred thousand Jews perished on that occasion in Jerusalem alone, but that *not even one of the followers of Christ was involved in the general destruction!* The reason was that they had been warned by the disciples of our Blessed Saviour, who had heard from their divine Master's lips the prophecy of the forthcoming destruction and the account of the signs that were to precede it. So they were all prepared for it when they saw the signs and they made it their business to leave in good time. They fled to a little town beyond the Jordan, called Pella, where they were quite safe.

The chief sign of the coming calamities was to be the appearance of the Roman standards. These carried figures of their false gods, which they brought with them into the very temple and thus profaned the holy place with their "abominations." (Dan. xi. 31; xii. 11.) When this happened, flight became an urgent and imperative necessity, as the Gospel of to-day so graphically describes: "Then they that are in Judea, let them flee to the mountains: and he that is on the house-top, let him not come down to take anything out of his house: and he that is in the field, let him not go back to take his coat." "Woe to them that are with child, and that give suck in those days," for such would be in an embarrassed and difficult state for hurried flight. "Pray that your flight be not in the winter, or on the Sabbath," because a difficult journey was impossible in winter in those days, and it was not lawful to travel more than about a mile on the Sabbath-day, as St. Luke indicates when he says: "The mount that is called Olivet, which is nigh Jerusalem, within a Sabbath-day's journey." (Acts i. 12.)

The few Jews who had embraced Christianity were thus enabled to escape the horrors which befell their brethren, and for their sake also God was pleased to shorten the time of calamity and thus preserve the remnants of the chosen race for their ultimate acceptance of the true Faith, for, as St. Paul says: "Isaias crieth out concerning Israel: If the number of the children of Israel be as the sand of the sea, a remnant shall be saved." (Rom. ix. 27.) And the chosen few were saved also from the destruction of their faith by the false prophets who at that time appeared in great numbers and tried to pervert the faithful, as Christ had also foretold.

In these days as then, "many are called but few are chosen." (Matt. xx. 16.) To us as to the chosen few our divine Master to-day offers a similar warning, a similar grace, and a similar chance of escaping the general destruction which will befall all sinners at the last judgment, of which the destruction of Jerusalem and its temple was but a figure and a prophecy. A prophecy which Christ proceeds to make clearer still by foretelling in detail the signs that will precede His coming to judge the living and the dead at the last great day—a judgment which will merely be a repetition and confirmation of the sentence He shall have already passed on us at the moment of our death, and which, as far as this short life is concerned, will literally be "immediately after the tribulation of those days," for, as St. Peter says, "One day with the Lord is as a thousand years, and a thousand years as one day." (2 Peter iii. 8.)

Then "the sun shall be darkened, and the moon shall not give her light, and the stars shall fall from heaven, and the powers of heaven shall be moved." These dismal disturbances in the physical order of the universe will be terrible enough for man to behold: but when there "shall appear the sign of the Son of man in heaven: and then shall all the tribes of the earth mourn; and they shall see the Son of man coming in the clouds of heaven with much power and majesty. And He shall send His angels with a trumpet and a great voice," saying: "Arise, ye dead and come to judgment."

What will the sinner be able to answer when this dreadful challenge will reach his ears in such awful circumstances: "Render an account of thy stewardship"? It is a dreadful thing for a guilty criminal to face the challenge of an angry judge who has over him the power of life and death. When Joseph mildly reproved his brothers for having sold him into slavery, they "could not answer him, being struck with exceeding great fear." (Gen. xlv. 3.) But when Christ as an angry judge will ask sinners, whom He treated as His own brothers, why they sold Him for the sake of a filthy pleasure or a little gain, and when they see hell open before them, and their deceiver the devil ready to plunge them into the yawning abyss, no wonder they will "begin to say to the mountains: Fall upon us; and to the hills: Cover us." (Luke xxiii. 30.)

Now is the time for us to prepare our answer to that awful summons which is "nigh even at the doors." Now is the time for us to act speedily and with decision, for now the springtime of hope is with us and summer is nigh—the summer of God's rich grace and love. "And from the fig-tree learn a parable: when the branch thereof is now tender, and the leaves come forth, you know that summer is nigh. So you also when you shall see all these things, know ye that it is nigh even at the doors. Amen I say to you, that this generation shall not pass, till all these things be done. Heaven and earth shall pass, but My words shall not pass."

Now is the time for us to examine our whole lives thoroughly and to correct at once and forever whatever is wrong in them, neglecting no detail, omitting no precaution, for even "every idle word that men shall speak, they shall render an account for it on the day of judgment." (Matt. xii. 36.), not to speak of positively sinful thoughts and actions. Christ Our Saviour now speaks to us as a dear friend, and our holy mother the Church prays for us to-day in the words of St. Paul in the Epistle that we may be made "worthy to be partakers of the lot of the saints in light" by learning His holy will and striving to accomplish it by imitating the example of His holy life. The time that remains is short indeed, but if we strive manfully we shall make up for the past—"Being made perfect in a short space, we shall fulfil a long time." (Wis. iv. 13.) God Himself will be with us. "And I will restore to you the ears which the locust, and the bruchus, and the mildew, and the palmerworm have eaten. . . . And you shall know that I am in the midst of Israel: and I am the Lord your God, and there is none besides: and My people shall not be confounded forever." (Joel ii. 25, 27.)

And our loving mother Mary will also help us, for next to Jesus Himself she loves us as her dearest children. May she as the Seat of Wisdom, as the Master's Mother "of fair love, and of fear, and of knowledge, and of holy hope" (Ecclus. xxiv. 24.) obtain for us those same precious gifts by obtaining for us the grace to listen with attention and devotion always to what was the source of her greatest happiness while she lived with her Divine Son, Jesus— THE MASTER'S WORD.

INDEX

The items set in heavy type are the titles of sermons.

A

Abandonment of sinner, I, 69; II, 166.
Abraham, I, 71, 113, 217; II, 146, 181.
  sons of, I, 72.
Abuse of grace, I, 69, 267; II, 166.
Acceptable time, the, I, 183.
Action, II, 17.
Actions, ordinary, I, 92, 118; II, 218.
  sanctification of, I, 92, 112, 175.
Activity, II, 207, 208.
Adam, earthly and heavenly, II, 141.
Advance in virtue, I, 193, 197; II, 265.
Advent, I, 15, 20, 31; II, 285.
  Sundays of, I, 15–51.
Advice, practical, I, 215.
All are sinners, I, 185.
Ambition, I, 133.
Anger, I, 122, 124; II, 111.
Application of Word, I, 293.
Apostles, commission of, I, 138, 151.
Arrangement of Epistles and Gospels, I, 18.
Armor of God, II, 255.

Arrogance, II, 213.
Ascension, II, 9.
  Sunday after the, II, 18.
Ash Wednesday, I, 17, 191.
Authority, I, 97, 132, 283.
  of Word of God, I, 283.
Avarice, I, 133.

B

Balthasar, I, 83.
Banquet, Christ's, II, 58.
Baptism, I, 73.
Barren fig-tree, I, 171.
Battle, spiritual, I, 112; II, 255.
Beatific vision, I, 277.
Beatitudes, I, 279.
Bethlehem, I, 53.
Bethsaida, I, 66, 231.
Birth of Christ, I, 52.
Blessed Eucharist, II, 58, 68.
Blessed Trinity, II, 38, 48.
Blessed Virgin, I, 101, 105.
Blind Man, healing of the, I, 180.
Blindness, spiritual, I, 66, 199, 211.
Blood, Precious, I, 73, 226.
Body, temple of Holy Ghost, I, 210.
Bond-woman, I, 217.
Burden, Our, I, 156.

Busybodies, II, 206.

C

Cæsar, tribute to, II, 270.
Calendars, I, 15.
Cana, I, 101.
Care, Christ's, II, 77.
Caspar, I, 83.
Catholics, our privileges as, II, 171.
Centurion's servant, healing of the, I, 127.
Certainty, A, I, 283.
Certainty of Christ's teaching, I, 286.
   of faith, I, 257.
Chance, Our, I, 183.
Change of heart, I, 125.
Character, II, 215.
Charity, II, 20, 219.
   definition of, I, 68, 175.
   fear not in, I, 236.
   fraternal, II, 22, 23, 56, 224.
   greatest, the, I, 139.
   God's and ours, II, 48.
   motive of, I, 174.
   opposed to scandal, I, 140.
   perfect, II, 22.
   precept of, II, 219.
   qualities of, I, 176; II, 223.
   results in peace, I, 180.
   reward of, I, 140.
   special reward of, I, 140.
   test of Christian, II, 20.
   virtue of, I, 175.
   want of, II, 72, 130.
Child Jesus, finding of, in the temple, I, 93.

Children and parents, I, 122, 125.
Children of the kingdom, I, 232.
   of light, I, 38, 158.
   scandal of, I, 144.
Christ,
   banquet of, II, 58.
   birth of, I, 52.
   care of, for us, II, 77.
   character of, I, 227; II, 19.
   circumcision of, I, 71.
   coming of, I, 52.
   compassion of, I, 27; II, 143.
   disposition of, I, 121, 143.
   divinity of, I, 247.
   glory of, I, 41.
   humility of, I, 54; II, 210.
   imitation of, I, 58.
   love of, for man, I, 229, 263; II, 48, 77.
   meekness of, I, 123, 234; II, 210.
   mercy of, I, 126, 127, 264; II, 77, 84.
   mind of, II, 216.
   miracles of (See *Miracles of Christ*).
   mission of, I, 71; II, 153.
   nativity of, I, 16, 52.
   object of His coming, I, 71.
   our advocate, II, 16.
   our foundation, II, 277.
   our high priest, I, 73, 226.
   our model, I, 91, 186; II, 260, 268.
   power of, II, 28.

parable of (See *Parables of Christ*).
passion, of, I, 189, 224, 232, 242.
prayer of, I, 296.
principles inculcated by, I, 56.
promise of, regarding prayer, I, 298.
prophecies concerning, I, 53, 83, 113, 287; II, 15.
rejection of, by Jews, I, 228; II, 148.
resurrection of, I, 244.
spirit of, I, 120.
sufferings of, I, 179, 195, 241.
sympathy of, II, 86, 143.
temporal glory of, expected by the disciples, II, 12, 29.
temptation of, I, 185.
test of, II, 18.
transfiguration of, I, 194.
word of, II, 95.
works of, I, 27, 287; II, 167.
Christianity, spread of, I, 150, 289.
Christians, true and false, II, 108.
Christmas, I, 16, 52.
Sunday after, I, 62.
Church, infallibility of the, I, 289.
precepts of the, I, 216.
the, and the Passion, I, 234.

Circumcision, I, 71.
of the heart, I, 74.
Cleansing of lepers, I, 126; II, 181.
Cleansing of the temple, I, 122; II, 151.
Cockle, parable of the, I, 141.
Coin of the tribute, II, 270.
Coming of Christ, I, 52.
preparation for, I, 24.
Coming of the Holy Ghost, II, 28.
Commission of Apostles, I, 138, 151.
Competitors, I, 157.
Concupiscences, II, 276.
Confession, I, 216, 219; II, 231, 260 (See also *Penance*).
matter of, II, 233.
shame of, II, 234.
Confidence in God, I, 129; II, 168.
Confirmation of St. Peter, I, 248.
Confraternities, I, 30; II, 93.
Conscience, I, 48.
Consideration, I, 36, 187, 294.
Consolation, II, 26.
Contrition, II, 232.
Conversion of St. Paul, II, 165.
Corozain, I, 65, 231.
Corporal needs, II, 191.
Corpus Christi, II, 58.
Council of Trent, I, 221.
Councils, Lateran, I, 217, 222.

Covenant, Abraham's, I, 71.
Covering of statues, I, 225.
Cowards, II, 209.
Criterion of true success, II, 152.
Cross, scandal of, I, 264.
   sign of, II, 46.
Crucifix, I, 182, 190.

D

Danger, the, I, 34.
Daughters of Sion, I, 213.
Day, Last, 1, 21; II, 283, 288.
Deaf and dumb man, healing of the, II, 163.
Death, certainty of, II, 284.
   spiritual, I, 205.
   uncertainty of, I, 22.
Defense, II, 255.
Descent of the Holy Ghost, II, 32.
Desire of God for man's love, I, 178.
   to save sinners, II, 150, 162.
Desires, fruitless, I, 178; II, 240.
Despair, II, 167.
Destruction of Jerusalem, II, 148, 285.
Destruction, spiritual, I, 70.
Devil, dumb, casting out of the, I, 206.
Difficulty of salvation, I, 156.
Distrust of self, II, 158.
Disciples, ignorance of, I, 180, II, 29.

   temporal glory of Christ, expected by, II, 12, 29.
Divinity of Christ, I, 247.
Doctor, tempts Christ, II, 219.
Doctrine, sound, I, 172.
Doubt of Thomas, I, 255.
Duties, the (Part VI), II, 199–291.
Duty, Easter, I, 216.
   of frequenting the Sacraments, I, 215.
Duty of spreading the Gospel, I, 155.

E

Easter, I, 16, 244.
   Sundays after, I, 253–302.
Easter Duty, I, 216.
Ecclesiastical year, I, 15.
Edifice, spiritual, II, 277.
Effects of the Holy Ghost, II, 34.
Efficacy of Prayer, I, 101, 179, 298; II, 257.
Efficacy of Word of God, I, 147, 165, 287; II, 34, 256.
Encouragement, I, 27.
End, last, I, 40.
   of man, II, 120.
Enemies, II, 107.
Enemies, love of, II, 24.
Energy, II, 201.
Epiphany, I, 16, 81.
   Sundays after, I, 91–155.
Epistles and Gospels, arrangement of, I, 18.

INDEX

Esdras, warning of, II, 134.
Eternal life, II, 124.
Eucharist, the, II, 58, 68.
  (See also *Holy Communion*.)
Example, Good, I, 238.
Expediency, II, 195.
Ezechiel, vision of, II, 272.

F

Failure, II, 143.
Failure of Word of God, causes of I, 166.
Faith, by hearing, I, 154.
  the centurion's, I, 127.
  certainty of, I, 257.
  gift of, I, 254.
  insufficiency of, I, 67.
  necessity of, I, 66.
  praised by Christ, I, 127.
  reward of, I, 52.
  trial of, I, 136.
  victory of, I, 253.
  want of, in the disciples, rebuked, I, 131.
  want of, punished, I, 65.
  virtue of, I, 254.
False independence, I, 59.
False piety, II, 269.
  prophets, II, 269.
  teachers, I, 166; II, 126.
Fast of Christ, I, 183.
Fasting, I, 187, 189.
Fear, not in charity, I, 236.
Fear of God, I, 25; II, 166.
Few chosen, II, 288.
Fig-tree, I, 171; II, 290.
Fishes, miraculous draught of, II, 97.
Fishes and loaves, multiplication of, I, 220; II, 118.
Flesh and spirit, II, 139, 189.
Fools, I, 169, 173, 211.
Fraternal charity, II, 22, 23, 56, 224.
Free-woman, I, 217.
Friends, II, 134.
Friends of God, I, 238.
Fruits, I, 125.

G

General Judgment, I, 21; II, 283.
Generosity in God's service, I, 198; II, 253.
Gentiles, manifestation of Christ to, I, 16, 81.
Gift, A, I, 253.
Gift of Faith, I, 254.
Gifts of the Holy Ghost, I, 285.
Gifts of the Wise Men, I, 86.
Gifts, various, I, 100; II, 156.
Glory, Christ's, I, 41.
God, armor of, II, 255.
  confidence in, I, 129; II, 168.
  fear of, I, 25; II, 166.
  friends of, I, 238.
  good will in the service of, II, 237.
  judgment of, I, 47; II, 155.
  justice of, I, 162.

kingdom of, within us, II, 268.
kindness of, II, 77, 121.
knowledge of, I, 137.
labor for II, 100.
love of, II, 219.
love of, for man, I, 129, 266; II, 48.
   proved by trials, I, 136; II, 77.
loyalty in the service of, II, 189.
mercy of, to all, I, 29.
mercy of, to sinners, l, 239; II, 52, 77, 84, 92, 121, 189, 241.
necessity for gratitude to, II, 180.
providence of, III, 77, 117, 192.
service of, I, 91.
stewards of, II, 138.
word of (See *Word of God*).
Gold, symbol of love, I, 88.
Good example, I, 138.
Good Samaritan, II, 177.
Good Shepherd, I, 263.
Good Will, II, 237.
Good intention, I, 50; II, 98, 242.
Good works, I, 67, 140; II, 264.
Gospel, I, 18.
   duty of spreading, I, 155.
   unchangeable, I, 151, 291.
Gospels and Epistles, arrangement of, I, 18.
Grace, II, 164.

abuse of, I, 69, 267; II, 166.
miracles of, I, 32; II, 163.
resistance to, I, 291.
special, of Lent, I, 183.
Groat, the lost, II, 82.
Gratitude, II, 180.
Guardians of youth, I, 209.
Guest, Christ's, II, 68.

H

Happiness, I, 51, 273; II, 132.
Hate, the world's, II, 24, 107.
Hearing, faith received by, I, 154.
Heart, change of, I, 125.
   circumcision of the, I, 74.
   symbol, II, 87.
Heaven, I, 157, 273; II, 238.
Hell, II, 112, 156, 239.
Helps, the (Part III), I, 203–302.
Herod, I, 85, 89.
Herodians, II, 270.
Hireling, I, 263.
Holy Communion, dispositions for, II, 66.
   institution of, II, 58.
   necessity of, I, 221.
   precept of, I, 221.
   promise of, I, 221; II, 119.
Holy Eucharist, II, 69, 70, 71 (See also *Eucharist*).
Holy Ghost, descent of, II, 28.
   effects of, II, 34.

INDEX

gifts of, I, 285.
love of, II, 54.
our body the temple of, I, 210.
promise of, I, 284.
Holy Name, the, I, 73, 111, 113.
feast of the, I, 111.
Honors, worldly, I, 58.
Hope, The, I, 24.
Human respect, I, 59; II, 195.
Humility, II, 210.
of Christ, I, 54; II, 210.

I

Idleness, II, 205.
Ignorance, of disciples, I, 180; II, 29.
Ignorance of God, man's, II, 221.
Imitation of Christ, I, 58.
Impurity, I, 205.
Incense of Prayer, I, 88.
Increase of sanctification, I, 193.
Independence, false, I, 59.
Infallibility of Church, I, 289.
Influence, Our, I, 138.
Ingratitude, of the Jews, I, 237; II, 147, 149.
of sinners, I, 27, 70, 237; II, 91, 182, 241.
Injury, sensitiveness to, I, 135.
Innocents, slaughter of the, I, 86.
Israelites, punishment of, II, 144.

Intention, good, II, 98, 242.

J

James and John rebuked, I, 124.
Jerusalem, I, 234; II, 145.
destruction of, II, 148, 285.
Jesus, name of, I, 73, 111, 113.
Jesus, presence of, II, 66.
Jews, rejection of Christ by, I, 228; II, 143.
Job, I, 134.
John the Baptist, I, 27, 31, 44.
Jonas, I, 184, 231.
Judas, I, 65.
Judgment, II, 283.
Jews, ingratitude of the, I, 237; II, 147, 149.
Judgment, Last, I, 21; II, 283.
God's, I, 47; II, 155.
man's, I, 44, 45; II, 155.
our, I, 46; II, 73, 285.
Just, tribulations of the, I, 134.
Justice of God, I, 162.

K

Kindness of God, II, 121.
King, A, I, 234.
Kingdom, children of the, I, 232.
Kingdom of God, within us, II, 268.
Kings, Three, I, 83, 86.

Knowledge of Christ, I, 137.

L

Labor for God, II, 100.
  in vain, II, 98, 193.
Laborers, parable of the, I, 159; II, 157.
Lamb, Paschal, The, I, 246.
Last Day, I, 21; II, 283, 288.
  end, I, 40.
  Judgment, I, 21; II, 283.
Last state of sinner, II, 186.
Lateran Councils, I, 217, 222.
Law, entire, to be kept, II, 129.
Law, old and new, II, 95, 172, 176, 177, 221.
Lawyer, tempts Christ, II, 177.
Lazarus, II, 202.
Leaven of sin, I, 251.
  parable of the, I, 148.
Length of life, II, 124.
Lent, season of, I, 17, 183.
  special grace of, I, 183.
  Sundays of, I, 183, 243.
Lepers, cleansing of, I, 126; II, 181.
Leprosy of sin, II, 187.
Letter and spirit, the, II, 177.
Life, II, 116.
  Eternal, II, 124.
  length of, II, 124.
  shortness of, I, 77, 280.
Life, state of, I, 76, 93; II, 194.

temporal and eternal, II, 116.
Light, children of, I, 38.
Loaves and fishes, multiplication of, I, 220; II, 118.
Lord's Prayer, II, 56, 261.
Loss of Child Jesus, I, 93.
Lost groat, II, 82.
  sheep, II, 82.
Lost years, I, 79; II, 291.
Love, Christ's, II, 48.
Love, for God, I, 175; II, 219.
Love, gold as symbol of, I, 88.
Love of God for man, I, 129, 266; II, 48.
  Jesus for man, I, 229, 263; II, 48.
  the Holy Ghost, II, 54.
  The Three Divine Persons, II, 48.
  enemies, II, 24.
Love of preference, I, 176.
Low Sunday, I, 253
Loyalty, II, 189.
Lukewarmness, I, 199; II, 249, 252.

M

Magi (See *Wise Men*).
Mammon, II, 190.
Man, end of, II, 120.
  judgment of, I, 44, 45, 46; II, 73, 155, 285.
Manner, The, I, 91.
Many called, II, 288.
Marriage at Cana, I, 101.

INDEX 301

Marriage feast, parable of the, II, 215, 240.
Martyrs, II, 278.
Mary Magdalen, I, 271; II, 83.
Master, the (Part IV), II, 7–103.
Matter of Confession, II, 233.
Means, The, I, 100.
Meditation, I, 179.
  of Rosary, I, 301.
  on the Passion, I, 179, 189, 190, 232, 242.
Meekness of Christ, I, 123, 234; II, 210.
Melchior, I, 295.
Mental prayer, I, 295.
Mercy of Christ, I, 126, 127, 264.
  of God to all, I, 29.
    to sinners, I, 239; II, 52, 84, 92, 14, 184, 241.
  want of, II, 83.
  works of, II, 226.
Message, Our, I, 147.
Messias, not accepted by Jews, II, 143.
Method, The, I, 81.
  of prayer, I, 104.
Mind, renewal of, II, 238.
Miracles, II, 162.
Miracles of Christ,
  Blind man, I, 180.
  Centurion's servant, I, 127.
  Deaf and dumb man, II, 163.
  Dumb devil, I, 206.
  Draught of fishes, II, 97.
  Lazarus, II, 202.
  Leper, I, 126.
  Loaves and fishes, I, 220; II, 118.
  Paralytic, II, 229.
  Ruler's daughter, II, 278.
    son II, 246.
  sick woman, II, 278.
  Tempest calmed, I, 131.
  Ten lepers, II, 181.
  Water changed into wine, I, 101.
  Widow's son, II, 203.
Miracles of Grace, I, 32; II, 163.
Mirror, A, I, 293.
Mirth, I, 51.
Misery of sinners, I, 35; II, 131.
Model, our, I, 91, 186; II, 260, 268.
Mortal sin, II, 71, 235.
Mortification, I, 31, 89, 158, 181; II, 140.
Moses, I, 67; II, 126, 146, 171.
Mother of Sorrows, I, 242.
Motive, Our, I, 174.
Motto, Our, I, 111.
Murder, spiritual, I, 142.
Mustard seed, parable of the, I, 148.

N

Naim, widow of, II, 203.
Name of Jesus, I, 73, 111, 113.
Nativity of Christ, I, 16, 52.
Nazareth, I, 95.
Necessity of Faith, I, 66.

Necessity of gratitude to God, II, 180.
  of prayer, I, 36, 101, 179; II, 280.
  of final perseverance, II, 274.
Neglect of prayer, I, 37, 294.
Neighbor, love of the, I, 129; II, 219.
New Law and Old, II, 95, 172, 176, 177, 221.
New Year, I, 15, 77.
Nineve, I, 188, 231.
Ninevites, I, 188, 231.

O

Obedience, II, 268, 270.
Obligation of striving for perfection, II, 264.
Object, The, I, 71.
Occasions of sin, I, 252.
Old Law and New, II, 95, 172, 176, 177, 221.
Ordinary actions, I, 92, 118; II, 218.
"Our Father," the, II, 56, 261.

P

Pain and pleasure, I, 35.
Palm Sunday, I, 234.
Parables of Christ:
  Cockles, I, 141.
  Fig-tree, II, 290.
  Good Samaritan, II, 177.
  Good Shepherd, I, 265.
  Laborers, I, 159; II, 157.
  Leaven, I, 148.
  Lost groat, II, 82.
  Lost sheep, II, 82.
  Marriage-feast, II, 215, 240.
  Mustard seed, I, 148.
  Pharisee and Publican, I, 106; II, 159.
  Sower, I, 166.
  Supper, II, 68.
  Talents, II, 157.
  Unjust steward, II, 136.
  Vineyard, I, 159; II, 157.
  Wedding garment, II, 239.
  Wicked servant, II, 261.
Paraclete promised, I, 284.
Paralytic, healing of the, II, 229.
Parents and children, I, 122, 125.
Paschal Lamb, I, 246.
Paschal Precept, I, 216.
Passion of Christ, I, 189, 224, 234, 242.
  meditation on, I, 179, 189, 190, 234, 242.
Passion Sunday, I, 224.
Passover, I, 246.
Patience, I, 60, 132.
Paul, Saint, I, 166, 207; II, 163–165, 210.
Peace,
  at Nativity, I, 52.
  of the wicked, II, 131.
  prince of, I, 120.
  result of charity, I, 180.
  spirit of, I, 123.
  why few possess, I, 130.

INDEX

Penance, errors about, I, 35.
 sacrament of, I, 271; II, 188, 229. (See also *Confession*.)
Penance, II, 228.
Pentecost, I, 17; II, 28.
 Sundays after, II, 38–291.
Perfection, II, 264.
Persecution, prophecy of, II, 26.
Perseverance, II, 274.
Peter, Saint, I, 113, 115, 248, 289; II, 33.
Petition, prayer of, I, 40, 101; II, 197.
Pharisee and Publican, parable of the, I, 106; II, 159.
Pharisees, I, 122, 172, 265, 283; II, 80, 109, 126, 214, 220, 270.
Picture-shows, II, 127.
Piety, false, II, 269.
Pilgrimage, our, I, 273.
Pilgrims, I, 274.
Pleasure and pain, I, 35.
Possibility of salvation, I, 75.
Poverty, I, 56, 60, 99.
Power, Christ's, II, 28.
Power of prayer, I, 36.
Prayer, causes of failure of, I, 36.
 conditions of, I, 298.
 dispositions for, I, 36.
 efficacy of, I, 101, 179, 298; II, 257.
 example of Christ's, I, 296.
 example of Blessed Virgin's, I, 101, 105.
 good with fasting, I, 189.
 incense of, I, 88.
 mental, I, 295.
 method of, I, 104.
 neglect of, I, 37, 294.
 necessity of, I, 36, 101, 179; II, 280.
 of petition, I, 40, 101; II, 197.
 power of, I, 36.
 promise of Christ regarding, I, 298.
 public, I, 30; II, 93.
Preaching, I, 139; II, 34, 93.
Precept, A, I, 215.
Precept, Paschal, I, 216.
Precepts of the Church, I, 216.
Precious Blood, I, 73, 226.
Preference, love of, I, 176.
Preparation for Christ's coming, I, 24.
Preparing the way of the Lord, I, 41.
Presence of Jesus, II, 66.
Presumption, I, 191; II, 169, 284.
Pride, II, 212.
Priesthood, spiritual, I, 138.
Prince of peace, I, 120.
Principles inculcated by Christ, I, 56.
Privileges, II, 173.
Privileges, our, I, 231, 238; II, 64, 171, 183.
Prize of heaven, I, 157.
Progress, Our, I, 193.

Progress in virtue, necessity of, I, 193.
Promise, The, I, 43.
  of the Holy Ghost, I, 284.
Proof, Christ's, II, 9.
P r o p h e c i e s concerning Christ, I, 53, 83, 113, 287; II, 15.
Prophecy of persecution, II, 26.
Prophets, false, II, 127.
Prospect, A, I, 273.
Prosperity, I, 136; II, 196.
Providence, divine, II, 77, 117, 192.
Public prayer, I, 30; II, 98.
Publican and Pharisee, parable of, I, 106; II, 159.
Punishment of Israelites, II, 144.
Purity of intention, II, 101, 238.

Q

Quinquagesima, I, 174.

R

Raca, II, 111.
Rejection of Christ by Jews, I, 228; II, 148.
Relapsing sinners, I, 240; II, 186.
Religion, true and false, II, 125.
Renewal of mind, II, 238.
Reputation, II, 215
Resignation, I, 76.

Resistance to grace, I, 291.
Respect, human, II, 195.
Resurrection, The, I, 244.
Results, the (Part V), II, 105–197.
Revenge, I, 123.
Reward, I, 157.
Reward, The, I, 52.
  of charity, I, 140.
  of faith, I, 52, 136.
Rosary, the, I, 301; II, 176.
Ruler's daughter, II, 278.

S

Sacraments, II, 69.
  duty of frequenting the, I, 215.
  dispositions for reception of, II, 70.
Sacred Heart, feast of the, II, 86.
Sadducees, II, 220.
Salvation, possibility of, I, 75.
  temporal aids to, II, 135.
  struggle for, I, 75, 157.
  task of, I, 161.
Samaritan, good, II, 177.
Sanctification of actions, I, 92, 112, 175.
  of our souls, I, 71.
  increase of, I, 193.
Scandal, I, 140.
  of children, I, 144.
  of the cross, I, 264.
Scapular, the, II, 176.
Scribes and Pharisees, I, 122; II, 109, 126.

INDEX

Scripture, value of, I, 20.
Seed, parable of the, I, 166.
Self, distrust of, II, 158.
  victory over, I, 251.
Senses, spiritual, I, 211.
Sensitiveness, our, to injury, I, 135.
Sensual man, II, 153.
Septuagesima, I, 17, 156.
Sermon, most useful, I, 173.
Servant, wicked, parable of the, II, 261.
Service of God, I, 91.
  generosity in, I, 198; II, 253.
Sexagesima, I, 165.
Shame of Confession, II, 234.
Sheep, lost, II, 82.
Shepherd, A, I, 263.
Shepherd, the good, parable of, I, 265.
Shortness of life, I, 77, 280.
Sick woman, II, 278.
Sidon, I, 66, 231.
Sign of the Cross, II, 46.
Simeon, I, 62, 63.
Sin, leaven of, I, 251.
  leprosy of, II, 187.
  mortal, II, 71, 235.
  occasions of, I, 252.
  venial, II, 251.
Sinner, abandoned, I, 69; II, 166.
  last state of, II, 186.
Sinners, all are, I, 185.
  desire of God to save, II, 150, 162.
  ingratitude of, I, 27, 70, 237; II, 91, 182, 241.
  misery of, I, 35; II, 131.
  relapsing, I, 240; II, 186.
  types of, II, 202.
Sins of others, I, 146.
Sins of the tongue, II, 113.
Sion, daughters of, I, 213.
Sloth, II, 203, 207.
Solicitude, II, 197.
Sons of Abraham, I, 72.
Sorrows, Mother of, I, 242.
Soul, value of, II, 155.
  vineyard of the, I, 69.
Sower, parable of the, I, 166.
Special grace of Lent, I, 183.
Spirit and flesh, II, 139, 189.
Spirit and letter, II, 177.
Spirit of charity, I, 120.
Spirit of Christ, I, 120.
Spirit of Peace, I, 123.
Spirit, Our, I, 120.
Spiritual battle, I, 112; II, 255.
  blindness, I, 66, 199, 211.
  death, I, 205.
  destruction, I, 70.
  edifice, II, 277.
  murder, I, 142.
  priesthood, I, 138.
  senses, I, 211.
  sloth, II, 203, 207.
  storms, I, 131.
  warfare, II, 255.
  weapons, II, 256.
Spread of Christianity, **I**, 150, 289.
Start, The, I, 15.

State of life, I, 76, 93; II, 194.
Statues, covering of, I, 225.
Steward, unjust, parable of the, II, 136.
Stewards of God, II, 138.
Storms, I, 131, 135.
Struggle for salvation, I, 75, 157.
Success, II, 152.
Success, true, the criterion of, II, 159.
Suffering, I, 135, 163, 186; II, 77.
Sufferings of Christ, I, 179, 195, 241.
Supper, parable of the, II, 68.
Symbol, the heart as, II, 87.
Sympathy, Christ's, II, 86.

T

Tale-bearers, II, 226.
Talents, parable of the, II, 157.
Tattlers, II, 206.
Task of salvation, I, 161.
Teachers, false, I, 166; II, 126.
Teaching of Christ, certainty of, I, 286.
Tempest calmed, I, 131.
Temple, cleansing of the, I, 122; II, 151.
  finding of child Jesus in the, I, 93.
Temporal aids to salvation, II, 135.

Temporal glory of Christ expected by disciples, II, 12, 29.
Temptation of Christ, I, 185.
Temptation proves us, I, 163, 186.
  St. Paul on, I, 135, 162, 186.
Ten lepers, II, 181.
Tepidity, I, 199; II, 249.
Terror of the wicked, II, 289.
Test, Christ's, II, 18.
Testaments, the two, I, 217.
Thessalonians praised, I, 147.
Thomas, St., doubt of, I, 255.
Threat, A, I, 205.
Time, the acceptable, I, 183.
  lost, I, 77, 78, 79; II, 291.
Tongue, sins of the, II, 113.
Transfiguration, the, I, 194.
Treasure of faith, the, I, 253.
Trent, Council of, I, 221.
Trial of faith, I, 136.
Trials, deserved, I, 162.
  proofs of God's love, I, 136; II, 77.
Tribulations of the just, I, 134.
Tribute to Cæsar, II, 270.
Trinity, Blessed, II, 38, 48.
Trinity Sunday, II, 38.
True and false doctrine, II, 125.
True and false virtue, II, 126.
Trust, Our, I, 129.

Two Testaments, I, 217.
Tyre, I, 66, 231.
Types of sinners, II, 202.

U

Unjust steward, II, 136.

V

Value of Scripture, I, 20.
  of the soul, II, 155.
  of word of God, I, 147; II, 258.
Venial sin, II, 251.
Victim, A, I, 224.
Victory, A, I, 244.
  over ourselves, I, 251.
Vineyard, of the soul, I, 69.
  parable of, I, 159; II, 157.
Virtue, advance in, I, 193, 197; II, 265.
Virtue, true and false, II, 126.
Vision, beatific, I, 277.

W

Want of charity, II, 72, 130.
  of faith, I, 65, 131.
Warfare, spiritual, II, 255.
Warning, The, I, 62.
Water changed into wine, I, 101.
Way of the Lord, preparation of, I, 41.
Weapons, spiritual, II, 256.
Wedding-garment, parable of the, II, 239.
Whitsunday (Pentecost), I, 17; II, 28.

Wicked, peace of the, II, 131.
  terror of the, II, 289.
  servant, parable of the, II, 261.
Widow's son, II, 203.
Wisdom, Our, I, 165.
Wise Men, the, I, 82, 86, 87.
Word, Christ's, II, 95.
Woman taken in adultery, mercy of Christ to, II, 84.
Word of God, the,
  application of, I, 293.
  authority of, I, 283.
  causes of failure of, I, 166.
  certainty of, I, 283, 286.
  effects of, in general, I, 147; II, 33.
    in individuals, I, 166, 293.
  efficacy of, I, 147, 165, 287; II, 34, 256.
  proper method of hearing, I, 168.
  value of, I, 147; II, 258.
Word, the Master's, II, 85.
Work, the (Part I), I, 13–108.
Workers, the (Part II), I, 109–201.
Works, good, I, 67, 140; II, 264.
  of Christ, I, 27, 287; II, 167.
  of mercy, II, 226.
World, this, children of, I, 38, 158.
  the, I, 273; II, 267.

World, hate of, II, 24, 107.
  honors of, I, 58.

Y

Year, new, I, 15, 77.

Youth, guardians of, I, 209.

Z

Zeal, II, 246.

STANDARD CATHOLIC BOOKS

PUBLISHED BY

BENZIGER BROTHERS

CINCINNATI: NEW YORK: CHICAGO:
343 MAIN ST.   36-38 BARCLAY ST.   214-216 W. MONROE ST.

Books not marked *net* will be sent postpaid on receipt of advertised price. Books marked *net* are such where ten per cent must be added for postage. Thus a book advertised as *net*, $1.00, will be sent postpaid on receipt of $1.10.

Complete descriptive catalogue sent free on application.

INSTRUCTION, DOCTRINE, APOLOGETICS, CONTROVERSY, DEVOTION, MEDITATION, THEOLOGY, LITURGY, HOLY SCRIPTURE, BIBLE, SERMONS, PHILOSOPHY, SCIENCE, HISTORY, BIOGRAPHY

ABANDONMENT; or, Absolute Surrender of Self to Divine Providence. CAUSSADE, S.J.	net, 0 50
ADORATION OF THE BLESSED SACRAMENT. TESNIÈRE.	0 50
ANECDOTES AND EXAMPLES ILLUSTRATING THE CATHOLIC CATECHISM. SPIRAGO.	net, 1 50
ANGELS OF THE SANCTUARY. For Altar Boys. MUSSER.	net, 0 15
AUTOBIOGRAPHY OF ST. IGNATIUS. O'CONOR, S.J.	net, 1 25
BEGINNINGS OF CHRISTIANITY, THE. A history of conditions of Christian life in the first three centuries of our era. SHAHAN.	net, 2 00
BENEDICENDA; or, Rites and Ceremonies to be Observed in some of the Principal Functions of the Roman Pontifical and Roman Ritual. SCHULTE.	net, 1 50
BIBLE, THE HOLY. Large type, handy size. Cloth, 1.00; finer bindings, 1.50—4.00; India paper edition,	3 00—5 00
BONOMELLI, RT. REV. J. HOMILIES ON THE EPISTLES AND GOSPELS. 4 vols.	net, 5 00
—HOMILIES ON THE COMMON OF SAINTS. 2 vols.	net, 2 50
—THE CHRISTIAN MYSTERIES; or, Discourses for all the Great Feasts except Those of the Blessed Virgin. 4 vols.	net, 5 00
BOOK OF THE PROFESSED. Vols. I, II, III. Each,	net, 0 75
BOY-SAVER'S GUIDE. Society Work for Lads in Their Teens. QUIN, S.J.	net, 1 35
CASES OF CONSCIENCE for English-speaking Countries. SLATER, S.J. 2 vols.	net, 3 50
CATECHISM EXPLAINED. SPIRAGO-CLARKE.	net, 2 50
CATHOLIC BELIEF. FAÀ DI BRUNO. Paper, net, 0.10; Cloth,	net, 0 35
CATHOLIC CEREMONIES. DURAND. Ill. Paper, 0.20; Cloth,	0 50
CATHOLIC HOME ANNUAL. Calendar, Stories, etc. Ill.	0 25
CATHOLIC PRACTICE AT CHURCH AND AT HOME. KLAUDER. Paper, 0.25; Cloth,	0 60
CATHOLIC WORSHIP. BRENNAN. Paper, *list price*, 0.15; Cloth, *list price*,	0 22
CATHOLIC'S READY ANSWER, THE. REV. M. P. HILL, S.J.	net, 2 00
CEREMONIAL FOR ALTAR BOYS. BRITT.	net, 0 35
CHILD PREPARED FOR FIRST COMMUNION, THE. ZULUETA, S.J.	0 05
CHRISTIAN APOLOGETICS. A Defense of the Catholic Faith. DEVIVIER-MESSMER.	net, 2 00
CHRISTIAN EDUCATION. O'CONNELL.	net, 0 60
CHRISTIAN FATHER, THE. Instructions. CRAMER. Paper, 0.15; Cloth,	0 35

CHRISTIAN MOTHER, THE. Instructions. CRAMER. Paper, 0.15; Cloth,	0 35
CHRIST IN TYPE AND PROPHECY. MAAS. Vols. I and II. Each,	net, 2 00
CHRIST'S TEACHING CONCERNING DIVORCE IN THE NEW TESTAMENT. GIGOT.	net, 1 50
CLERGYMAN'S HANDBOOK OF LAW. SCANLAN.	net, 1 35
COMMENTARY ON THE PSALMS (I-L). By REV. E. S. BERRY.	net, 2 00
COMPENDIUM JURIS CANONICI. SMITH.	net, 2 00
COMPENDIUM JURIS REGULARIUM. BACHOFEN.	net, 2 50
COMPENDIUM SACRAE LITURGIAE. WAPELHORST.	net, 2 50
CONSECRANDA; or, Rites and Ceremonies Observed at the Consecration of Churches, Altars, etc. SCHULTE.	net, 1 50
CONSTITUTION OF THE FRIENDS OF JESUS AND MARY, REV. P. GEIERMANN, C.SS.R.	0 15
CORRECT THING FOR CATHOLICS, THE. BUGG.	0 50
COUNSELS OF ST. ANGELA TO HER SISTERS IN RELIGION.	net, 0 25
DEVOTIONS AND PRAYERS FOR THE SICK-ROOM. KREBS.	0 50
DEVOTIONS TO THE SACRED HEART FOR THE FIRST FRIDAY OF EVERY MONTH. HUGUET.	0 25
DEVOTION TO THE SACRED HEART OF JESUS, THE. NOLDIN, S.J.	net, 1 25
DIVINE GRACE. Explains the doctrine of the Church on divine grace. WIRTH.	0 50
DIVINE OFFICE. Explanation of Psalms and Canticles. LIGUORI.	net, 1 50
DOGMATIC THEOLOGY, OUTLINES OF. HUNTER. Vols. I, II, III. Each,	net, 1 50
ECCLESIASTICAL DICTIONARY. THEIN.	net, 5 00
EDUCATION OF OUR GIRLS, THE. SHIELDS.	net, 1 00
ENCYCLICAL LETTERS OF POPE LEO XIII.	net, 2 25
EPISTLES AND GOSPELS. Large type.	net, 0 25
EUCHARISTIC CHRIST, THE. TESNIÈRE.	net, 1 25
EXPLANATION OF BIBLE HISTORY. NASH.	net, 1 60
EXPLANATION OF CATHOLIC MORALS. STAPLETON.	0 50
EXPLANATION OF THE BALTIMORE CATECHISM. KINKEAD.	net, 1 00
EXPLANATION OF THE COMMANDMENTS. ROLFUS.	0 50
EXPLANATION OF THE CREED. ROLFUS.	0 50
EXPLANATION OF THE GOSPELS AND CATHOLIC WORSHIP. LAMBERT. Paper, 0.20; Cloth,	0 50
EXPLANATION OF THE HOLY SACRAMENTS. ROLFUS.	0 50
EXPLANATION OF THE MASS. COCHEM.	0 50
EXPLANATION OF THE PRAYERS AND CEREMONIES OF THE MASS. LANSLOTS, O.S.B.	net, 1 25
EXPLANATION OF THE SALVE REGINA. LIGUORI.	net, 0 75
EXTREME UNCTION. Paper,	0 05
FLOWERS OF THE PASSION. Devout Thoughts.	0 50
FOR FREQUENT COMMUNICANTS.	0 05
FOUR LAST THINGS. Meditations. COCHEM.	net, 0 75
FUNDAMENTALS OF THE RELIGIOUS LIFE. Translated by REV. J. P. M. SCHLEUTER, S.J.	net, 0 60
GENERAL INTRODUCTION TO THE STUDY OF THE HOLY SCRIPTURES. GIGOT.	net, 2 50
GENERAL INTRODUCTION TO THE STUDY OF THE HOLY SCRIPTURES. Abridged. GIGOT.	net, 1 50
GENERAL PRINCIPLES OF THE RELIGIOUS LIFE. VERHEYEN.	net, 0 30
GENTLEMAN, A. Manners and Social Usages. EGAN.	0 50
GIFT OF THE KING, THE. An Explanation of the Mass for Children.	0 60
GLORIES OF MARY, THE. Vols. I and II. LIGUORI. Each,	net, 1 50
GLORIES OF MARY. Popular edition.	0 50
GLORIES OF THE SACRED HEART. HAUSHERR, S.J.	0 50
GOFFINE'S DEVOUT INSTRUCTIONS.	1 00
GREAT MEANS OF SALVATION, THE. LIGUORI.	net, 1 50
GREETINGS TO THE CHRIST-CHILD.	0 60

GROWTH AND DEVELOPMENT OF THE CATHOLIC SCHOOL SYSTEM IN THE UNITED STATES. BURNS.	net,	1 75
GUIDE FOR SACRISTANS.	net,	0 85
HANDBOOK OF THE CHRISTIAN RELIGION. WILMERS, S.J.	net,	1 50
HARMONY OF THE RELIGIOUS LIFE. HEUSER.	net,	1 25
HELPS TO A SPIRITUAL LIFE. SCHNEIDER.		0 50
HIDDEN TREASURE; or, The Value and Excellence of Holy Mass. BLESSED LEONARD. Paper, 0.15; Cloth,		0 35
HISTORY OF THE CATHOLIC CHURCH. ALZOG. 3 vols.	net,	8 00
HISTORY OF THE CATHOLIC CHURCH. BUSINGER-BRENNAN. 8vo.		2 00
HISTORY OF THE CATHOLIC CHURCH. BRUECK. 2 vols.	net,	3 00
HISTORY OF ECONOMICS. DEWE.	net,	1 50
HISTORY OF THE MASS. O'BRIEN.	net,	1 25
HISTORY OF THE PROTESTANT REFORMATION. COBBETT.		0 50
HOLY EUCHARIST, THE. LIGUORI.	net,	1 50
HOLY HOUR, THE. KEILEY.		0 05
HOLY MASS, THE. LIGUORI.	net,	1 50
HOLY VIATICUM OF LIFE AS OF DEATH, THE. A provision for the journey of life as well as of death. DEVER. Paper, 0.25; Cloth,		0.60
HOLY WEEK, COMPLETE OFFICE OF. Cheap Edition, flexible cloth, net, 0.20; Cloth,	net,	0 30
HOW TO COMFORT THE SICK. KREBS.		0 50
HOW TO MAKE THE MISSION.		0 10
INCARNATION, BIRTH, AND INFANCY OF CHRIST, LIGUORI.	net,	1 50
INDEX TO LIGUORI'S WORKS.	net,	0 10
IN HEAVEN WE KNOW OUR OWN. For those who have lost dear ones by death. BLOT, S.J.	net,	0 60
INSTRUCTIONS FOR FIRST COMMUNICANTS. SCHMITT.	net,	0 60
INSTRUCTIONS ON THE COMMANDMENTS AND SACRAMENTS. LIGUORI. Paper, 0.15; Cloth.		0 35
INSTRUCTIONS ON MARRIAGE, POPULAR. GIRARDEY. Paper, 0.15; Cloth,		0.35
INTERIOR OF JESUS AND MARY. GROU, S.J. 2 vols.	net,	2 00
JESUS LIVING IN THE PRIEST. MILLET-BYRNE.	net,	2 00
LADY, A. Manners and Social Usages. BUGG.		0 50
LAWS OF THE KING. Talks on the Commandments for Children.		0 60
LESSONS OF THE SAVIOUR. Christ's Miracles Described for Children.		0 60
LETTERS OF ST. ALPHONSUS LIGUORI. 5 vols. Each.	net,	1 50
LIFE OF BL. MARGARET MARY ALACOQUE. BOUGAUD.		0 50
LIFE OF POPE PIUS X.		2 00
LIFE OF ST. CATHERINE OF SIENNA. AYMÈ.		1 00
LIFE OF THE BLESSED VIRGIN. ROHNER-BRENNAN.		0 50
LIFE OF CHRIST AND OF HIS BLESSED MOTHER. BUSINGER-BRENNAN. Profusely illustrated.	net,	10 00
LIFE OF CHRIST. COCHEM-HAMMER.		0 50
LIFE OF SISTER ANNE KATHARINE EMMERICH. McGowan.	net,	1 75
LIFE OF ST. TERESA, POPULAR. REV. M. JOSEPH.		0 50
LIFE OF VEN. CRESCENTIA HOSS.	net,	1 25
LIGUORI. COMPLETE WORKS. Vols. I-XXII. Each,	net,	1 50
LITTLE COMMUNICANTS' PRAYER-BOOK. SLOAN.		0 20
LITTLE MANUAL OF ST. RITA. McGRATH.		0 50
LITTLE MASS BOOK. LYNCH.		0 05
LIVES OF THE SAINTS. Adapted from ALBAN BUTLER.		0 50
LIVES OF THE SAINTS FOR CHILDREN. BERTHOLD.		0 60
LIVES OF THE SAINTS, PICTORIAL. SHEA. Illustrated.		3 00
LIVES OF THE SAINTS, SHORT. DONNELLY.		0 60
LIVES OF THE SAINTS, LITTLE PICTORIAL. Illustrated.		1 25
LOURDES. Its Inhabitants, Its Pilgrims and Miracles. CLARKE, S.J.		0 50
MANUAL OF CATHOLIC HYMNS. DIERINGER-PIERRON. Edition with melody and words, list price, 0.42; Edition for the organist,	net,	3 00
MANUAL OF HOMILETICS AND CATECHETICS. SCHUECH.	net,	1 25
MANUAL OF MORAL THEOLOGY. SLATER, S.J. Vols. I and II. Each,	net,	2 75

3

MANUAL OF THEOLOGY FOR THE LAITY. GEIERMANN, C.SS.R. Paper, 0.25; Cloth,		0 60
MARIÆ COROLLA. FR. EDMUND, C.P.		1 25
MARY, HELP OF CHRISTIANS. Instructions, Legends, Novenas, and Prayers. HAMMER.		2 00
MARY THE QUEEN. A life of the Blessed Virgin for Children.		0 60
MEANS OF GRACE. Complete Explanation of the Sacraments. Fully illustrated. BRENNAN.		3 00
MEDITATIONS FOR EVERY DAY. BAXTER.	net,	1 50
MEDITATIONS FOR EVERY DAY. HAMON. 5 vols.	net,	5 00
MEDITATIONS FOR EVERY DAY. VERCRUYSSE, S.J. 2 vols.	net,	3 50
MEDITATIONS FOR EVERY DAY OF THE MONTH. NEPVEU-RYAN.		0 50
MEDITATIONS FOR MONTHLY RETREATS. For Religious.	net,	0 50
MEDITATIONS FOR THE USE OF THE SECULAR CLERGY. 2 vols. CHAIGNON, S.J.	net,	4 50
MEDITATIONS FOR THE USE OF SEMINARIANS AND PRIESTS. BRANCHEREAU. 5 vols.	net,	5 00
MEDITATIONS ON THE LAST WORDS FROM THE CROSS. PERRAUD.	net,	0 50
MEDITATIONS ON THE LIFE, THE TEACHING, AND THE PASSION OF JESUS CHRIST. ILG. 2 vols.	net,	3 50
MEDITATIONS ON THE MYSTERIES OF OUR HOLY FAITH. According to the Plan of Ven. L. de Ponte, S.J. By REV. C. W. BARRAUD, S.J. 2 vols.	net,	3 00
MEDITATIONS ON THE PASSION. By a Passionist.		0 50
MEDITATIONS ON THE SUFFERINGS OF JESUS CHRIST. PERINALDO.	net,	0 75
MESSAGE OF MOSES AND MODERN HIGHER CRITICISM. GIGOT.	net,	0 15
MIDDLE AGES, THE. Sketches covering the period from the fifth to the fifteenth century. SHAHAN.	net,	2 00
MIRACLES OF OUR LORD. RELIGIOUS OF THE SOCIETY OF THE HOLY CHILD JESUS.		0 60
MISCELLANY. LIGUORI.	net,	1 50
MISSAL EXPLAINED, THE.	net,	1 65
MISSAL FOR THE LAITY.	net,	1 85
MISSAL, THE NEW. In English. For Every Day in the Year. According to the Latest Decrees. With Introduction, Notes, and a Book of Prayer. By REV. F. X. LASANCE, author of "My Prayer-Book." Cloth,		1 50
MOMENTS BEFORE THE TABERNACLE. Prayers and Aspirations. RUSSELL, S.J.	net,	0 50
MONTH, LITTLE, OF THE SOULS IN PURGATORY.		0 35
MONTH OF MAY, LITTLE.		0 35
MONTH, NEW, OF THE HOLY ANGELS. ST. FRANCIS DE SALES.	net,	0 35
MORAL PRINCIPLES AND MEDICAL PRACTICE. COPPENS, S.J.	net,	1 00
MORE SHORT SPIRITUAL READINGS FOR MARY'S CHILDREN. MADAME CECILIA.		0 50
MY FIRST COMMUNION. The Happiest Day of My Life. BUCHMANN-BRENNAN.	net,	0 75
NARROW WAY, THE. REV. P. GEIERMANN, C.SS.R.		0 60
NEW TESTAMENT. 32mo, flexible cloth.	net,	0 18
NEW TESTAMENT. (India Paper.) Leather, gold edges.	net, 0 75—	1 60
NEW TESTAMENT. 12mo. Large, new type.		0 50
NEW TESTAMENT STUDIES. CONATY. List price,		0 54
OUTLINES OF NEW TESTAMENT HISTORY. GIGOT.	net,	1 50
OUTLINES OF SERMONS FOR YOUNG MEN AND YOUNG WOMEN. SCHUEN.	net,	2 00
PARADISE ON EARTH; or, A Religious Vocation the Surest Way in Life. NATALE, S.J.	net,	0 50
PARISH PRIEST ON DUTY, THE. HEUSER.	net,	0 60
PASSION AND DEATH OF JESUS CHRIST. LIGUORI.	net,	1 50
PASTORAL LETTERS, ADDRESSES, AND OTHER WRITINGS OF THE RT. REV. JAMES A. McFAUL, D.D., Bishop of Trenton. 8vo.	net,	1 50
PASTORAL THEOLOGY. STANG.	net,	1 50

PATRON SAINTS FOR CATHOLIC YOUTH. Illustrated.
Vols. I. II, III. MANNIX. Each. 0 60
PEARLS FROM FABER. Selections from His Works BRUNOWE. 0 35
POLITICAL AND MORAL ESSAYS. RICKABY, S.J. net, 1 75
PRAXIS SYNODALIS. net, 0 75
PREACHING. LIGUORI. net, 1 50
PREPARATION FOR DEATH. LIGUORI. net, 1 50
PRINCIPLES, ORIGIN, AND ESTABLISHMENT OF THE
CATHOLIC SCHOOL SYSTEM IN THE U. S. BURNS. net, 1 75
PRIVATE RETREAT FOR RELIGIOUS. GEIERMANN,
C.SS.R. net, 1 50
PULPIT SKETCHES. Outlines of Sermons. LAMBERT. net, 1 25
QUESTIONS OF MORAL THEOLOGY. REV. THOMAS
SLATER, S.J. net, 2 00
RAMBLES IN CATHOLIC LANDS. REV. MICHAEL BARRETT,
O.S.B. net, 2 00
REASONABLENESS OF CATHOLIC CEREMONIES AND
PRACTICES. BURKE. Paper, 0.15; Cloth, 0 35
RELIGIOUS STATE, THE. LIGUORI. net, 0 50
RETREATS FOR SISTERS, TWO. WIRTH. net, 1 00
RITUALE COMPENDIOSUM. Sacristy Ritual. net, 0 90
ROMA. Ancient, Subterranean, and Modern Rome in Word and
Picture. By REV. ALBERT KUHN, O.S.B., D.D. Preface by
CARDINAL GIBBONS. 18 bi-monthly parts, each 0.35 postpaid.
Subscription by the year, 6 parts, 2.00; complete work, 6.00.
938 text illustrations, 40 full-page illustrations, 3 plans of
Rome in colors. The best and most thorough production of
its kind.
ROMAN CURIA AS IT NOW EXISTS. MARTIN, S.J. net, 1 50
ROSARY, THE CROWN OF MARY, THE. 0 10
RULES OF LIFE FOR THE PASTOR OF SOULS. SLATER-
RAUCH. net, 0 75
SACRAMENTALS. The Sacramentals of the Church Explained.
LAMBING. Paper, 0.20; Cloth, 0 50
SACRED HEART STUDIED IN THE SACRED SCRIP-
TURES, THE. SAINTRAIN, C.SS.R. 0 50
SACRIFICE OF THE MASS WORTHILY CELEBRATED.
CHAIGNON, S.J. net, 1 50
SAINTS AND PLACES. AYSCOUGH. Description of Italy's
most historic spots. 22 full-page illustrations. net, 1 50
ST. ANTHONY. ANECDOTES AND EXAMPLES. KELLER. net, 0 75
ST. ANTHONY, THE SAINT OF THE WHOLE WORLD.
WARD. 0 50
SAINT FRANCIS OF ASSISI: SOCIAL REFORMER.
DUBOIS. 0 50
SCAPULAR MEDAL, THE. REV. P. GEIERMANN, C.SS.R. 0 05
SECRET OF SANCTITY. CRASSET. 0 50
SELF-KNOWLEDGE AND CHRISTIAN PERFECTION.
HENRY. Paper, 0.25; Cloth, 0 60
SERMONS FOR CHILDREN OF MARY. CALLERIO. net, 1 50
SERMONS FOR CHILDREN'S MASSES. FRASSINETTI. net, 1 50
SERMONS FOR SUNDAYS. LIGUORI. net, 1 50
SERMONS FOR THE SUNDAYS AND CHIEF FESTIVALS
OF THE ECCLESIASTICAL YEAR. 2 vols. POTTGEISSER. net, 3 00
SERMONS FROM THE LATINS. BAXTER. net, 2 00
SERMONS, FUNERAL. WIRTH. Vols. I and II. Each, net, 1 00
SERMONS, NEW AND OLD. WIRTH. 8 vols. Each, net, 2 00
SERMONS ON THE BLESSED SACRAMENT. SCHEURER-
LASANCE. net, 1 50
SERMONS ON THE CATECHISM, POPULAR. BAMBERG-
THURSTON, S.J. 3 vols. Each, net, 1 50
SERMONS ON THE DEVOTION TO THE SACRED HEART,
Six. BIERBAUM. net, 0 75
SERMONS, SHORT, FOR LOW MASSES. SCHOUPPE. net, 1 25
SERMONS, SHORT. HUNOLT. 5 vols. (WIRTH.) Each, net, 2 00
SHORT CONFERENCES ON THE SACRED HEART. BRINK-
MEYER, 0 50
SHORT COURSE IN CATHOLIC DOCTRINE. For Non-
Catholics Intending Marriage with Catholics. 0 10
SHORT HISTORY OF MORAL THEOLOGY. SLATER, S.J. net, 0 50
SHORT MEDITATIONS FOR EVERY DAY. LASAUSSE. 0 50

SOCIALISM AND CHRISTIANITY. STANG.	net, 1 00
SOCIALISM: ITS THEORETICAL BASIS AND PRACTICAL APPLICATION. CATHREIN, S.J.	net, 1 50
SOCIALISM, MORALITY OF MODERN. MING, S.J.	net, 1 50
SOCIALISM, CHARACTERISTICS AND RELIGION OF. MING, S.J.	net, 1 50
SPECIAL INTRODUCTION TO THE STUDY OF THE OLD TESTAMENT. Part I. GIGOT.	net, 1 50
SPECIAL INTRODUCTION TO THE STUDY OF THE OLD TESTAMENT. Part II. GIGOT.	net, 2 00
SPIRAGO'S METHOD OF CHRISTIAN DOCTRINE. MESSMER.	net, 1 50
SPIRITUAL CONSIDERATIONS. BUCKLER, O.P.	0 50
SPIRITUAL DESPONDENCY AND TEMPTATIONS. MICHEL, S.J.	net, 1 25
SPIRITUAL EXERCISES FOR A TEN DAYS' RETREAT. SMETANA, C.SS.R.	net, 0 75
SPIRITUAL PEPPER AND SALT. STANG. Paper, 0.25; Cloth,	0 60
SPIRIT OF SACRIFICE AND THE LIFE OF SACRIFICE IN THE RELIGIOUS STATE. GIRAUD-THURSTON.	net, 2 00
SPOILING THE DIVINE FEAST. ZULUETA.	0 05
STORIES FOR FIRST COMMUNICANTS. KELLER.	net, 0 50
STORY OF THE DIVINE CHILD. LINGS.	0 60
SUNDAY-SCHOOL DIRECTOR'S GUIDE. SLOAN.	net, 0 50
SUNDAY-SCHOOL TEACHER'S GUIDE. SLOAN.	0 50
SURE WAY TO A HAPPY MARRIAGE. Paper, 0.15; Cloth,	0 35
TALKS WITH THE LITTLE ONES ABOUT THE APOSTLES' CREED.	0 60
THEORY AND PRACTICE OF THE CONFESSIONAL. SCHIELER-HEUSER.	net, 3 50
THOUGHTS AND AFFECTIONS ON THE PASSION OF JESUS CHRIST FOR EVERY DAY IN THE YEAR. BERGAMO.	net, 2 00
THOUGHTS ON THE RELIGIOUS LIFE. LASANCE.	net, 1 50
TRAINING OF CHILDREN. MADAME CECILIA. Paper, 0.25; Cloth,	0 60
TRUE POLITENESS, LETTERS ON. DEMORE.	net, 0 75
TRUE SPOUSE OF CHRIST. LIGUORI.	0 50
TRUE SPOUSE OF CHRIST. Vols. I and II. LIGUORI. Each,	net, 1 50
VENERATION OF THE BLESSED VIRGIN. ROHNER-BRENNAN.	0 50
VICTORIES OF THE MARTYRS. LIGUORI.	net, 1 50
VIGIL HOUR. RYAN, S.J.	0 05
VISIT TO EUROPE AND THE HOLY LAND. FAIRBANKS.	1 50
VOCATION. VAN TRICHT-CONNIFF. Paper,	0 05
VOCATIONS EXPLAINED.	0 10
WAY OF THE CROSS. Paper,	0 05
WAY OF THE CROSS. Illustrated. Eucharistic Method.	0 10
WAY OF THE CROSS. Illustrated. Method of ST. FRANCIS ASSISI.	0 10
WAY OF THE CROSS. Illustrated. Method of JESUIT FATHER.	0 10
WAY OF THE CROSS. Illustrated. Method of ST. ALPHONSUS LIGUORI.	0 10
WAY OF SALVATION AND OF PERFECTION. Meditations. LIGUORI.	net, 1 50
WAY OF INTERIOR PEACE. DE LEHEN.	net, 1 50
WHAT CATHOLICS HAVE DONE FOR SCIENCE. BRENNAN.	net, 1 25
WHAT THE CHURCH TEACHES. DRURY. Paper, 0.25; Cloth,	0 60
WITH CHRIST, MY FRIEND. SLOAN.	net, 0 75

NOVELS, POETRY, ETC.

AGATHA'S HARD SAYING. ROSA MULHOLLAND.	0 50
BACK TO THE WORLD. CHAMPOL.	net, 1 35
BALLADS OF CHILDHOOD. By REV. MICHAEL EARLS, S.J.	net, 1 00
BLACK BROTHERHOOD, THE. GARROLD, S.J.	net, 1 35
BOND AND FREE. CONNOR.	0 50
"BUT THY LOVE AND THY GRACE." FINN, S.J.	1 00
BY THE BLUE RIVER. ISABEL C. CLARKE.	net, 1 35

Title	Price
CARROLL DARE. Waggaman.	1 25
CATHOLIC HOME ANNUAL.	0 25
CIRCUS RIDER'S DAUGHTER. Brackel.	0 50
CONNOR D'ARCY'S STRUGGLES. Bertholds.	0 50
CORINNE'S VOW. Waggaman.	1 25
DAUGHTER OF KINGS, A. Hinkson.	1 25
DION AND THE SIBYLS. M. Keon.	0 50
DOUBLE KNOT, A, AND OTHER STORIES.	0 60
ELDER MISS AINSBOROUGH. Marion A. Taggart.	1 25
FABIOLA. Wiseman. Illustrated.	0 50
FABIOLA'S SISTERS. Clarke.	0 50
FATAL BEACON. Brackel.	1 25
FAUSTULA. Ayscough.	net, 1 35
FINE CLAY. Isabel C. Clarke.	net, 1 35
FLOWERS OF THE CLOISTER. Poems. Sister La Motte.	1 25
FORGIVE AND FORGET. Lingen.	0 50
FRIENDLY LITTLE HOUSE, THE, AND OTHER STORIES. Taggart.	0 50
HEARTS OF GOLD. Edhor.	1 25
HEART OF A MAN, THE. Maher.	net, 1 35
HEIRESS OF CRONENSTEIN, THE. Hahn-Hahn.	0 50
HER BLIND FOLLY. Holt.	1 25
HER FATHER'S DAUGHTER. Hinkson.	1 25
HER FATHER'S SHARE Edith Power.	net, 1 25
HER JOURNEY'S END. Cooke.	0 50
IDOLS. Navery.	0 50
IN GOD'S GOOD TIME. Ross.	0 50
IN THE DAYS OF KING HAL. Taggart.	1 25
IVY HEDGE, THE. Maurice F. Egan.	net, 1 35
"KIND HEARTS AND CORONETS." Harrison.	1 25
LADY OF THE TOWER, THE, AND OTHER STORIES.	0 50
LIGHT OF HIS COUNTENANCE, THE. Harte.	0 50
"LIKE UNTO A MERCHANT." Mary A. Gray.	net, 1 35
LITTLE CARDINAL, THE. Parr.	1 25
LINKED LIVES. Douglas.	1 50
MARCELLA GRACE. Rosa Mulholland.	0 50
MARIE OF THE HOUSE D'ANTERS. Earls.	net, 1 35
MELCHIOR OF BOSTON. Earls.	1 00
MIGHTY FRIEND, THE. L'Ermite.	net, 1 50
MIRROR OF SHALOTT, THE. Benson.	1 50
MISS ERIN. Francis.	0 50
MONK'S PARDON, THE. Navery.	0 50
MR. BILLY BUTTONS. Lecky.	1 25
MY LADY BEATRICE. Cooke.	0 50
NOT A JUDGMENT. Keon.	1 25
ONLY ANNE. Isabel C. Clarke.	net, 1 35
OTHER MISS LISLE, THE. Martin.	0 50
OUT OF BONDAGE. Holt.	1 25
OUTLAW OF CAMARGUE, THE. De Lamothe.	0 50
PASSING SHADOWS. Yorke.	1 25
"PAT." Hinkson.	net, 1 35
PERE MONNIER'S WARD. Lecky.	1 25
PILKINGTON HEIR, THE. Sadlier.	1 25
PRISONERS' YEARS. Clarke.	net, 1 35
PRODIGAL'S DAUGHTER, THE, AND OTHER STORIES. Bugg.	1 00
PROPHET'S WIFE, THE. By Anna C. Browne.	1 25
RED INN AT ST. LYPHAR, THE. Sadlier.	1 25
ROAD BEYOND THE TOWN, THE, AND OTHER POEMS. Earls.	1 25
ROSE OF THE WORLD. Martin.	0 50
ROUND TABLE OF AMERICAN CATHOLIC NOVELISTS.	0 50
ROUND TABLE OF IRISH AND ENGLISH CATHOLIC NOVELISTS.	0 50
ROUND TABLE OF GERMAN CATHOLIC NOVELISTS.	0 50
ROUND TABLE OF FRENCH CATHOLIC NOVELISTS.	0 50

ROUND THE WORLD SERIES. Vol. I.		1 00
ROUND THE WORLD SERIES. Vol. II.		1 00
ROUND THE WORLD SERIES. Vol. III.	A series of inter-	1 00
ROUND THE WORLD SERIES. Vol. IV.	esting articles on a	1 00
ROUND THE WORLD SERIES. Vol. V.	great variety of sub-	1 00
ROUND THE WORLD SERIES. Vol. VI.	jects of much educa-	1 00
ROUND THE WORLD SERIES. Vol. VII.	tional value. Pro-	1 00
ROUND THE WORLD SERIES. Vol. VIII.	fusely illustrated.	1 00
ROUND THE WORLD SERIES. Vol. IX.		1 00
ROUND THE WORLD SERIES. Vol. X.		1 00
RULER OF THE KINGDOM, THE. Keon.		1 25
SECRET CITADEL, THE. Isabel C. Clarke.	net,	1 35
SECRET OF THE GREEN VASE, THE. Cooke.		0 50
SENIOR LIEUTENANT'S WAGER, THE, AND OTHER STORIES.		0 60
SHADOW OF EVERSLEIGH, THE. Lansdowne.		0 50
SHIELD OF SILENCE. M. E. Henry-Ruffin.	net,	1 35
SO AS BY FIRE. Connor.		0 50
SOGGARTH AROON. Guinan.		1 25
SON OF SIRO, THE. Copus.	net,	1 35
STORY OF CECILIA, THE. Hinkson.		1 25
STUORE. Earls.		1 00
TEMPEST OF THE HEART, THE. Gray.		0 50
TEST OF COURAGE, THE. Ross.		0 50
THAT MAN'S DAUGHTER. Ross.		1 25
THEIR CHOICE. Skinner.		0 50
THROUGH THE DESERT. Sienkiewicz.	net,	1 35
TRAIL OF THE DRAGON, THE, AND OTHER STORIES.		0 50
TRAINING OF SILAS. Devine, S.J.		1 25
TRUE STORY OF MASTER GERARD, THE. Sadlier.		1 25
TURN OF THE TIDE, THE. Gray.		0 50
UNBIDDEN GUEST, THE. Cooke.		0 50
UNRAVELING OF A TANGLE, THE. Taggart.		1 25
UP IN ARDMUIRLAND. Barrett.	net,	1 25
VOCATION OF EDWARD CONWAY, THE. Egan.		1 25
WARGRAVE TRUST, THE. Reid.		1 25
WAY THAT LED BEYOND, THE. Harrison.		1 25
WEDDING BELLS OF GLENDALOUGH, THE. Earls.	net,	1 35
WHEN LOVE IS STRONG. Keon.		1 25
WOMAN OF FORTUNE. Christian Reid.		1 25

JUVENILES

ALTHEA. Nirdlinger.	0 50
ADVENTURE WITH THE APACHES, AN. Ferry.	0 35
AS GOLD IN THE FURNACE. Copus, S.J.	0 85
AS TRUE AS GOLD. Mannix.	0 35
BELL FOUNDRY, THE. Schaching.	0 35
BERKLEYS, THE. Wight.	0 35
BEST FOOT FORWARD, THE. Finn, S.J.	0 85
BETWEEN FRIENDS. Aumerle.	0 50
BISTOURI. Melandri.	0 35
BLISSYLVANIA POST-OFFICE, THE. Taggart.	0 35
BOB O'LINK. Waggaman.	0 35
BROWNIE AND I. Aumerle.	0 50
BUNT AND BILL. C. Mulholland.	0 35
BY BRANSCOME RIVER. Taggart.	0 35
CAMP BY COPPER RIVER, THE. Spalding, S.J.	0 85
CAPTAIN TED. Waggaman.	0 50
CAVE BY THE BEECH FORK, THE. Spalding.	0 85
CHARLIE CHITTYWICK. Bearne.	0 85
CHILDREN OF CUPA. Mannix.	0 35
CHILDREN OF THE LOG CABIN. Delamare.	0 50
CLARE LORAINE. "Lee."	0 50
CLAUDE LIGHTFOOT. Finn, S.J.	0 85
COLLEGE BOY, A. Yorke.	0 85
CUPA REVISITED. Mannix.	0 35
DADDY DAN. Waggaman.	0 35
DEAR FRIENDS. Nirdlinger.	0 60
DIMPLING'S SUCCESS. C. Mulholland.	0 35

ETHELRED PRESTON. FINN, S.J.	0 85
EVERY-DAY GIRL, AN. CROWLEY.	0 35
FAIRY OF THE SNOWS, THE. FINN, S.J.	0 85
FIVE BIRDS IN A NEST. DELAMARE.	0 50
FIVE O'CLOCK STORIES.	0 50
FLOWER OF THE FLOCK. EGAN.	0 85
FOR THE WHITE ROSE. HINKSON.	0 35
FREDDY CARR'S ADVENTURES. GARROLD, S.J.	0 50
FREDDY CARR AND HIS FRIENDS. GARROLD, S.J.	0 50
FRED'S LITTLE DAUGHTER. S. T. SMITH.	0 35
GOLDEN LILY, THE. HINKSON.	0 35
GREAT CAPTAIN, THE. HINKSON.	0 35
GUILD BOYS' PLAY AT RIDINGDALE. BEARNE, S.J.	0 85
HALDEMAN CHILDREN, THE. MANNIX.	0 35
HARMONY FLATS. WHITMIRE.	0 50
HARRY DEE. FINN, S.J.	0 85
HARRY RUSSELL. COPUS, S.J.	0 85
HEIR OF DREAMS, AN. O'MALLEY.	0 35
HIS FIRST AND LAST APPEARANCE. FINN, S.J.	1 00
HOSTAGE OF WAR. BONESTEEL.	0 35
HOW THEY WORKED THEIR WAY. EGAN.	0 50
IN QUEST OF THE GOLDEN CHEST. BARTON.	0 50
IN QUEST OF ADVENTURE. MANNIX.	0 35
"JACK."	0 35
JACK HILDRETH ON THE NILE. TAGGART.	0 50
JACK O'LANTERN. WAGGAMAN.	0 35
JUNIORS OF ST. BEDE'S. BRYSON.	0 85
JUVENILE ROUND TABLE. First Series.	1 00
JUVENILE ROUND TABLE. Second Series.	1 00
JUVENILE ROUND TABLE. Third Series.	1 00
KLONDIKE PICNIC, A. DONNELLY.	0 50
LEGENDS AND STORIES OF THE CHILD JESUS FROM MANY LANDS. LUTZ.	0 75
LITTLE APOSTLE ON CRUTCHES, THE. DELAMARE.	0 35
LITTLE LADY OF THE HALL. NORA RYEMAN.	0 35
LITTLE GIRL FROM BACK EAST, THE. ROBERTS.	0 35
LITTLE MARSHALLS AT THE LAKE. NIXON-ROULET.	0 50
LITTLE MISSY. WAGGAMAN.	0 35
LOYAL BLUE AND ROYAL SCARLET. TAGGART.	0 85
MADCAP SET AT ST. ANNE'S, THE. BRUNOWE.	0 35
MAD KNIGHT, THE. O. v. SCHACHING.	0 35
MAKING OF MORTLAKE, THE. COPUS, S.J.	0 85
MARKS OF THE BEAR CLAWS, THE. SPALDING, S.J.	0 85
MARY TRACY'S FORTUNE. SADLIER.	0 35
MELOR OF THE SILVER HAND. BEARNE, S.J.	0 85
MILLY AVELING. S. T. SMITH.	0 50
MIRALDA. K. M. JOHNSTON.	0 35
MORE FIVE O'CLOCK STORIES.	0 75
MOSTLY BOYS. FINN, S.J.	0 85
MYSTERIOUS DOORWAY, THE. SADLIER.	0 35
MYSTERY OF CLEVERLY, THE. BARTON.	0 50
MYSTERY OF HORNBY HALL, THE. SADLIER.	0 50
NAN NOBODY. WAGGAMAN.	0 35
NED RIEDER. WEHS.	0 50
NEW BOYS AT RIDINGDALE, THE. BEARNE, S.J.	0 85
NEW SCHOLAR AT ST. ANNE'S, THE. BRUNOWE.	0 50
OLD CHARLMONT'S SEED BED. S. T. SMITH.	0 35
OLD MILL ON THE WITHROSE. SPALDING, S. J.	0 85
ON THE OLD CAMPING GROUND. MANNIX.	0 85
OUR LADY'S LUTENIST. BEARNE, S.J.	0 85
PANCHO AND PANCHITA. MANNIX.	0 35
PAULINE ARCHER. SADLIER.	0 35
PERCY WYNN. FINN, S.J.	0 85
PERIL OF DIONYSIO. MANNIX.	0 35
PETRONILLA, AND OTHER STORIES. DONNELLY.	0 50
PICKLE AND PEPPER. DORSEY.	0 85
PILGRIM FROM IRELAND, A. CARNOT.	0 35
PLAYWATER PLOT. WAGGAMAN.	0 50
POLLY DAY'S ISLAND. ROBERTS.	0 50
POVERINA. BUCKENHAM.	0 50
QUEEN'S PAGE, THE. HINKSON.	0 35

QUEEN'S PROMISE, THE. Waggaman.	0 50
RACE FOR COPPER ISLAND, THE. Spalding, S.J.	0 85
RECRUIT TOMMY COLLINS. Bonesteel.	0 35
RIDINGDALE FLOWER SHOW. Bearne, S.J.	0 85
ROMANCE OF THE SILVER SHOON. Bearne, S.J.	0 85
SANDY JOE. Waggaman.	0 85
SEA-GULL'S ROCK, THE. Sandeau.	0 35
SEVEN LITTLE MARSHALLS, THE. Nixon-Roulet.	0 35
SHADOWS LIFTED. Copus, S.J.	0 85
SHEER PLUCK. Bearne, S.J.	0 85
SHERIFF OF THE BEECH FORK, THE. Spalding, S.J.	0 85
SHIPMATES. Waggaman.	0 50
ST. CUTHBERT'S. Copus, S.J.	0 85
STRONG-ARM OF AVALON. Waggaman.	0 85
SUGAR-CAMP AND AFTER, THE. Spalding, S.J.	0 85
SUMMER AT WOODVILLE, A. Sadlier.	0 35
TALES AND LEGENDS OF THE MIDDLE AGES. Capella.	0 75
TALISMAN, THE. Sadlier.	0 50
TAMING OF POLLY, THE. Dorsey.	0 85
THAT FOOTBALL GAME. Finn, S.J.	0 85
THAT OFFICE BOY. Finn, S.J.	0 85
THREE GIRLS AND ESPECIALLY ONE. Taggart.	0 35
TOLD IN THE TWILIGHT. Mother Salome.	0 50
TOM LOSELY: BOY. Copus, S.J.	0 85
TOM'S LUCK-POT. Waggaman.	0 35
TOM PLAYFAIR. Finn, S.J.	0 85
TOORALLADDY. Walsh.	0 35
TRANSPLANTING OF TESSIE, THE. Waggaman.	0 50
TREASURE OF NUGGET MOUNTAIN, THE. Taggart.	0 50
TWO LITTLE GIRLS. Mack.	0 35
UPS AND DOWNS OF MARJORIE. Waggaman.	0 35
VIOLIN MAKER OF MITTENWALD, THE. Schaching.	0 35
WAYWARD WINIFRED. Sadlier.	0 85
WINNETOU, THE APACHE KNIGHT. Taggart.	0 50
WITCH OF RIDINGDALE, THE. Bearne, S.J.	0 85
YOUNG COLOR GUARD, THE. Bonesteel.	0 35

BENZIGER'S STANDARD FIFTY-CENT LIBRARY FOR EVERY-BODY

Novels, Juveniles and Religious Books by the best Catholic Authors. Copyright books. Substantially and attractively bound in cloth. Complete list of books in library sent on application. Each volume, $0.50.

BENZIGER'S THIRTY-FIVE-CENT JUVENILE LIBRARY

Books for young folks by the best authors. Copyright books. They are printed on good paper in large and readable type, and are neatly bound in cloth. Each book has an illustrated jacket. Complete list on request. Each volume, $0.35.

CATHOLIC LIBRARIES

Books of Religious Instruction, Novels, and Juveniles, put up in libraries of 10 volumes, at $5.00. Payable on the Easy Payment Plan of $1.00 a month. List of libraries sent on application.

SCHOOL-BOOKS

Catechisms, Readers (The Catholic National Readers, The New Century Readers), Charts, Spellers, Grammars, Bible History, United States Histories, Benziger's Advanced Geography, Benziger's Elementary Geography, Graded Arithmetics, Three-Book Series of Arithmetics, Hymnbooks, etc., etc. Complete list sent on application.

PRAYER-BOOKS

Complete illustrated catalogue will be sent on application.

Sizes of books in inches: 48mo, about 3¾ x 2¾; large 48mo, about 4 x 2⅞; small 32mo, about 4⅜ x 3; 32mo, about 4¾ x 3¼; oblong 32mo, about 5¼ x 3½; 24mo, about 5½ x 3¾; oblong 24mo, about 5½ x 3½; 16mo, about 6¼ x 4½; small 12mo, 7 x 5.

FATHER LASANCE'S PRAYER-BOOKS

	Imitation Leather, Red Edges.	Leather, Gilt Edges.
MISSAL, THE NEW. In English. For Every Day in the Year. With Introduction, Notes, and a Book of Prayer.	1 50	2 00—5 00
MY PRAYER-BOOK: HAPPINESS IN GOODNESS. Reflections, Counsels, Prayers and Devotions. 16mo.	1 25	1 75—2 50
MY PRAYER-BOOK. India Paper edition. 16mo.		2 00—4 25
MY PRAYER-BOOK. India Paper edition. With Epistles and Gospels. 16mo.		2 25—2 75
BLESSED SACRAMENT BOOK. Offers a larger and greater variety of prayers than any other book in English. Large 16mo.	1 50	2 00—4 50
WITH GOD. A Book of Prayers and Reflections. 16mo.	1 25	1 75—5 00
THE YOUNG MAN'S GUIDE. For manly boys and young men. Oblong 24mo.	0 75	1 25—2 50
THE CATHOLIC GIRL'S GUIDE. Counsels for Girls in the Ordinary Walks of Life and in Particular for the Children of Mary. Oblong 16mo.	1 25	1 75—2 50
PRAYER-BOOK FOR RELIGIOUS. A complete manual of prayers for members of all religious communities. Small 12mo. *net,*	1 50	2 50—3 50
THOUGHTS ON THE RELIGIOUS LIFE. Reflections on the General Principles of the Religious Life, on Perfect Charity. Small 12mo. *net,*	1 50	2 50
VISITS TO JESUS IN THE TABERNACLE. Hours and Half-Hours of Adoration before the Blessed Sacrament. 16mo.	1 25	1 75—2 75
MANUAL OF THE HOLY EUCHARIST. Conferences on the Blessed Sacrament and Eucharistic Devotions. Oblong 24mo.	0 75	1 25
SHORT VISITS TO THE BLESSED SACRAMENT. Oblong 32mo. Cloth.	0 15	
MASS DEVOTIONS AND READINGS ON THE MASS. Twelve methods of hearing Mass. Oblong 24mo.	0 75	1 25
THE SACRED HEART BOOK. Oblong 24mo.	0 75	1 25
LITTLE MANUAL OF ST. ANTHONY. Oblong 32mo. Cloth.	0 15	

PRAYER-BOOKS FOR GENERAL USE

	Cloth.	Leather, Gilt Edges.
ALL FOR JESUS. With Epistles and Gospels. Small 32mo.	0 30	0 60—1 90
BREAD OF LIFE, THE. A Complete Communion Book for Catholics. By Rev. F. Willam. Oblong 24mo.	0 75	1 25
COME, LET US ADORE. A Eucharistic Manual. By Rev. B. Hammer, O.F.M. Small 32mo.	0 75	1 25
DEVOTIONS AND PRAYERS BY ST. ALPHONSUS LIGUORI. A Complete Manual of Pious Exercises for Every Day, Every Week, and Every Month. Ward. 16mo.	1 25	1 75
DEVOTIONS AND PRAYERS FOR THE SICK-ROOM. A Book for Every Catholic Family. By Rev. J. A. Krebs, C.SS.R. 12mo.	0 50	
DOMINICAN MISSION BOOK. By a Dominican Father. 16mo.	0 75	1 50

	Cloth.	Leather, Gilt Edges.
FLOWERS OF PIETY. Approved Prayers for Catholics. 48mo.	0 25	0 50—3 25
FOLLOWING OF CHRIST, THE. By THOMAS À. KEMPIS. With Reflections, etc. 32mo.	0 35	0 65
FOLLOWING OF CHRIST, THE. By THOMAS À. KEMPIS. Illustrated. India Paper. Edition de LUXE. 32mo.		1 25—3 30
GARLAND OF PRAYER, THE. A dainty prayer-book. Contains Nuptial Mass. 32mo.		2 25—3 25
GOLDEN KEY TO HEAVEN. With Epistles and Gospels. Small 32mo.	0 35	0 70—1 10
HELP FOR THE POOR SOULS IN PURGATORY. By Jos. ACKERMANN. Small 32mo.	0 60	
HOLY HOUR OF ADORATION, THE. By RIGHT REV. W. STANG, D.D. Oblong 24mo.	0 60	
IMITATION OF THE SACRED HEART OF JESUS. By REV. FR. ARNOUDT, S.J. 16mo. *net*,	1 25	1 75
INTRODUCTION TO A DEVOUT LIFE. By ST. FRANCIS DE SALES. Small 32mo.	0 50	
KEY OF HEAVEN, THE. With Epistles and Gospels. 48mo.	0 25	0 60—1 50
LITTLE MANUAL OF ST. RITA. Prayers and Devotions. With the Story of Her Life. By REV. THOMAS S. MCGRATH.	0 50	0 75
LITTLE MASS BOOK. By RIGHT REV. MGR. J. S. M. LYNCH. Paper. 32mo.	0 10	
MANUAL OF THE HOLY NAME. 24mo.	0 50	1 10
MANUAL OF THE SACRED HEART, NEW. Oblong 24mo.	0 25	0 75—1 25
MANUAL OF ST. ANTHONY, NEW. 32mo.	0 50	
MANUAL OF ST. JOSEPH, LITTLE. By RIGHT REV. MGR. A. A. LINGS. Oblong 32mo.	0 15	
MISSION-BOOK FOR THE MARRIED. By REV. F. GIRARDEY, C.SS.R. 32mo.	0 50	1 00
MISSION-BOOK FOR THE SINGLE. By REV. F. GIRARDEY, C.SS.R. 32mo.	0 50	1 00
MISSION-BOOK OF THE REDEMPTORIST FATHERS, THE. 32mo.	0 50	1 00
MISSION REMEMBRANCE OF THE REDEMPTORIST FATHERS. By REV. P. GEIERMANN. 32mo.	0 50	1 00
OFFICE OF HOLY WEEK, THE, COMPLETE. 16mo. Flexible Cloth, *net*, 0.20; Cloth, *net*,	0 30	0 70
OUR FAVORITE DEVOTIONS. By RIGHT REV. MGR. A. A. LINGS. Oblong 24mo.	0 75	1 25
OUR FAVORITE NOVENAS. By RIGHT REV. MGR. A. A. LINGS. Oblong 24mo.	0 75	1 25
POCKET COMPANION. Approved Prayers. Oblong 48mo.	0 10	
SERAPHIC GUIDE, THE. 24mo.	0 60	0 75
VEST-POCKET GEMS OF DEVOTION. Ob. 32mo.	0 15	0 45—0 90
VEST-POCKET GEMS OF DEVOTION. India Paper Edition. With Epistles and Gospels. Oblong 32mo.	0 45	0 65—1 25
VISITS TO THE MOST HOLY SACRAMENT AND TO THE BLESSED VIRGIN MARY. By ST. ALPHONSUS LIGUORI. 32mo.	0 35	0 75

PRAYER-BOOKS WITH LARGE TYPE

	Cloth.	Leather, Gilt Edges.
KEY OF HEAVEN. With Epistles and Gospels. 24mo.	0 50	0 90—1 70
POCKET MANUAL. Epistles and Gospels. Ob. 32mo.	0 25	0 50—1 35
WAY TO HEAVEN. With Epistles and Gospels.	0 35	0 75

PRAYER-BOOKS FOR CHILDREN AND FIRST COMMUNICANTS

	Cloth.	Leather, Gilt Edges.
BREAD OF ANGELS. Instructions and Prayers Especially Suited for First Communicants. By REV. B. HAMMER, O.F.M. Large 48mo.	0 25	0 65—0 95
CHILD OF MARY, THE. Especially for the Use of First Communicants. 32mo.	0 45	0 95

	Cloth.	Leather, Gilt Edges.
CHILD'S PRAYER-BOOK, THE. 48mo.	0 15	0 50
DEVOUT CHILD, THE. With 18 full-page illustrations of the Mass. 48mo.	0 12	
LITTLE ALTAR BOY'S MANUAL. Instructions for Serving at Mass, Vespers, etc. With prayers.	0 20	0 60
LITTLE COMMUNICANTS' PRAYER-BOOK. By Rev. P. J. Sloan. 32mo. Imitation Cloth, 0 15.	0 20	
PIOUS CHILD, THE. With 18 full-page illustrations of the Mass. 48mo.	0 12	
SODALIST'S VADE MECUM, THE. Prayer-Book and Hymnal for the Children of Mary. 32mo	0 40	0 65

BENZIGER'S MAGAZINE

THE POPULAR CATHOLIC FAMILY MONTHLY

The best stories and articles—1,000 illustrations a year. Recommended by 70 Archbishops and Bishops of the United States. Subscription, $2.50 a year. Three years, $5.

WHAT BENZIGER'S MAGAZINE GIVES ITS READERS IN A YEAR: Several complete Novels. Fifty to sixty complete stories by the best writers. One thousand illustrations. Twelve double-page reproductions of celebrated paintings. Articles on travel and adventure; on the manners, customs, and home life of peoples; on the haunts and habits of animals. Articles on our country, historic events, times, places; important industries. Fashions, fads and fancies, gathered at home and abroad; helpful hints for home workers, household column, cooking recipes, etc. Current events. "Question Box." Science Notes, etc.

Read the heroic stories of the saintly men and women of our own times

THE HOLINESS OF THE CHURCH IN THE NINETEENTH CENTURY

SAINTLY MEN AND WOMEN OF OUR TIMES

By REV. CONSTANTINE KEMPF, S.J. From the German by REV. FRANCIS BREYMANN, S.J. 412 pages, 8vo, size 5¼ x 8 inches, net $1.75, postage 15 cents extra.

Holy Bishops—Holy Secular Priests—Holy Religious—Holy Laymen and Women—The Martyrs.

COMBINATION OFFER: "The Holiness of the Church in the Nineteenth Century" and a year's subscription to "Benziger's Magazine," $3.25 instead of $4.25.

THE CATHOLIC'S READY ANSWER

A Popular Vindication of Christian Beliefs and Practices Against the Attack of Modern Criticism. By REV. M. P. HILL, S.J. 490 pages, 8vo, size 5¼ x 8¼ inches, net, $2 (postage 15 cents extra).

Among the up-to-date questions treated are: Luther, Mixed Marriages, Divorce, Workingmen's Conditions, Labor Unions, Strikes, Socialism, Eugenics, Cremation, Evolution, Science and the Bible, Free Thought, Free Love, The Higher Criticism, Apes and Men, Eve and the Serpent, Celibacy of Priests, etc., etc.

COMBINATION OFFER: "The Catholic's Ready Answer" and a year's subscription to "Benziger's Magazine" for $3.50 instead of $4.50.

Father Lasance's Prayer-Books

A PRAYER-BOOK containing the best general prayers and devotions, reflections and counsels; a prayer-book teaching happiness in goodness; a prayer-book that is different; the most popular of all prayer-books: Father Lasance's

MY PRAYER-BOOK
HAPPINESS IN GOODNESS
BY REV. F. X. LASANCE
702 pages, 5⅝ x 4 inches

Imitation Leather, round corners, gold side and back, red edges....	$1.25
Imitation Leather, round corners, gold side and back, gold edges....	1.50
American Seal, limp, round corners, gold side and back, gold edges.	1.75
Embossed Calf, limp, round corners, gold edges......................	1.85
Morocco, limp, gold side and back, round corners, gold edges........	2.00

Finer Bindings up to $5.00

SPECIAL COMBINATION OFFER: A copy of "My Prayer-Book" and a year's subscription to "Benziger's Magazine" for $3.00 instead of $3.75. In leather binding, 50 cents additional.

A PRAYER-BOOK to enable you to follow the priest at Mass *every day of the year;* including a complete Book of Prayer, with all the usual devotions, and giving all the ceremonies to be observed: Father Lasance's

THE NEW MISSAL FOR EVERY DAY
BY REV. F. X. LASANCE
1254 pages, 3½ x 5⅝ inches
The most complete up-to-date Missal for every day.

Imitation Leather, round corners, gold side and back, red edges....	$1.50
Imitation Leather, round corners, gold side and back, gold edges....	1.75
American Seal, limp, round corners, gold side and back, gold edges.	2.25
Morocco, limp, gold side and back, round corners, gold edges.......	2.50

Finer Bindings up to $5.00

SPECIAL COMBINATION OFFER: A copy of "The New Missal for Every Day" and a year's subscription to "Benziger's Magazine" for $3.00 instead of $4.00. In leather binding, 50 cents additional.

A PRAYER-BOOK to enable you to follow the priest at Mass on *all the Sundays and the principal feasts of the year;* with all the ceremonies, and including a complete Book of Prayer, with all the usual devotions: Father Lasance's

THE SUNDAY MISSAL
BY REV. F. X. LASANCE
675 pages, 3⅛ x 5¼ inches

Imitation Leather, round corners, gold side and back, red edges....	$0.75
Imitation Leather, round corners, gold side and back, gold edges..	1.00
American Seal, limp, gold side and back, gold edges................	1.35
Morocco, limp, blind side, round corners, gold edges...............	1.50
Morocco, long grain, limp, gold side and back, gold edges...........	1.75
Morocco, limp, fine long grain, blind and gold side, gold edges.....	2.00

Finer Bindings up to $4.50

SPECIAL COMBINATION OFFER: A copy of "The Sunday Missal" and an eight-months' subscription to "Benziger's Magazine" for $2.00. In leather binding, 50 cents additional.

BENZIGER BROTHERS
NEW YORK
36-38 Barclay Street

CINCINNATI
343 Main St.

CHICAGO
214-216 W. Monroe St.

CATHOLIC THEOLOGICAL UNION
BX1756.F59   C001 V002
THE MASTER'S WORD IN THE EPISTLES AND GO

3 0311 00043 7314

53626

WITHDRAWN